Praise for *Against Apartheid*

"This book is a tour de force: a must read that belongs on the nightstand of every decent human being on this earth concerned with peace and justice. Superbly edited, it brings together the most powerful and cogent cases ever made for BDS: the now widely global, non-violent civil disobedience that Palestinians and their supporters have launched against the vicious monstrosity of Zionist theft of their homeland. BDS is the civilized people's response to the barbarity of Israeli colonial occupation of Palestine and *Against Apartheid* provides a relentlessly persuasive body of brilliant scholarship to prove the point. Do not miss it!"
–Hamid Dabashi, Hagop Kevorkian Professor of Iranian Studies and Comparative Literature at Columbia University in the City of New York

"A stunning collection by leading scholar-activists—offering rigorous, challenging, clearly argued and fiercely urgent examinations of the role of the academic boycott in the Palestinian struggle for freedom. It is crucial reading for anyone interested in the intellectual and moral underpinnings of the BDS movement in the academy."
–Rebecca Vilkomerson, Executive Director of Jewish Voice for Peace

"Voices resound through this book with the reasoned argument that Israeli apartheid must be ended—and the way for intellectuals and artists to participate in this struggle is to boycott Israeli institutions that participate in and benefit from the occupation of Palestinian lands. This is an intellectual guidebook for the Boycott-Divestment-Sanctions (BDS) movement."
–Vijay Prashad, editor of *Letters to Palestine: Writers Respond to War and Occupation*

"A specter is haunting Israel–the specter of a new anti-apartheid movement, working to end occupation, home demolitions, illegal settlements, detentions, relentless state violence, and the complicity of its most respected institutions in the brutal subjugation of the Palestinian people. Against Apartheid is its text, its manifesto. It is at once a powerful indictment of Israeli apartheid and the university's role in designing, maintaining, and protecting the system, and an inspiring history of how Palestinian activists, artists, and intellectuals turned a global appeal into a global movement."
–Robin D. G. Kelley, Gary B. Nash Professor of US History at UCLA

"The explosive growth of the BDS movement on US campuses has been one of the sparks that is firing the critical exit of business from Israel's illegal West Bank settlements, and it owes much of ' .... of the writers of this book. There is already a sea cha............................ world to Israel's decades long record of impu........................ sion of Palestinians, the assassinations of thei..................

T0125990

children, the theft of their land and water, the denial of dignity and hope in their shameful refugee camps across the region. Key to this book's intervention is its demonstration of the silent complicity between Israeli universities and the military establishment. This alone is enough to force a rethink for those who still think boycotting Israeli universities is an issue of freedom of speech."
–Victoria Brittain, author of *Shadow Lives: The Forgotten Women of the War on Terror*

AGAINST APARTHEID:

THE CASE FOR BOYCOTTING ISRAELI UNIVERSITIES

EDITED BY ASHLEY DAWSON
AND BILL V. MULLEN

FOREWORD BY ALI ABUNIMAH

Haymarket Books
Chicago, Illinois

Published by
Haymarket Books
P.O. Box 180165
Chicago, IL 60618
773-583-7884
info@haymarketbooks.org
www.haymarketbooks.org

ISBN: 978-1-60846-526-2

Trade distribution:
In the US through Consortium Book Sales and Distribution, www.cbsd.com
In the UK, Turnaround Publisher Services, www.turnaround-uk.com
In Canada, Publishers Group Canada, www.pgcbooks.ca
All other countries, Publishers Group Worldwide, www.pgw.com

This book was published with the generous support of the Wallace Action Fund
and Lannan Foundation.

Cover design by Josh MacPhee.

Printed in Canada by union labor.

Library of Congress CIP Data is available.

10 9 8 7 6 5 4 3 2 1

TABLE OF CONTENTS

III. The Academic Boycott of Israeli Universities in Historical Context

IV. Scholars and Students in the Struggle, under Attack

V. New Horizons for the Academic Boycott Movement

FOREWORD

ALI ABUNIMAH

The reelection victory in March 2015 of the far-right government led by Benjamin Netanyahu provided stark clarity for many who were still in denial about what Israel is and where it may be headed if its rogue power remains unchecked.

In the near term, more massacres of the kind Israel perpetrated in Gaza in 2008–2009, 2012, and the summer of 2014 may be inevitable—and that is true regardless of whether Netanyahu's Likud Party or the ostensibly more "dovish" Labor Party occupies the prime minister's office.

But Netanyahu's victory offers supporters of justice in Palestine an important opportunity. In the final days of the election campaign, Netanyahu bared to the world the racist face of Israel that Palestinians have always known. He railed against Arab voters—Palestinian citizens of Israel—"advancing on the ballot boxes in droves." He confessed openly that his participation in the US-sponsored "peace process" has always been a deception and that he would never permit the creation of any sort of Palestinian state, not even a Bantustan.

In so doing, he robbed the so-called international community of the opportunity to hide its complicity with Israel's crimes behind the peace process charade.

For two decades, fruitless negotiations—during which violent Israeli colonization continued relentlessly—provided the principal excuse for endlessly deferring any initiative to hold Israel even minimally accountable. The refrain from gutless officials is always some version of "yes, isn't it terrible what's going on, but there's a peace process and we support the peace process."

This fake peace process has no less been an important weapon in the arsenal of anti-Palestinian forces combatting the growth of the boycott, divestment, and sanctions (BDS) movement on campus.

"When the Israelis and Palestinians engage in negotiations for peace, their bilateral engagement makes the unilateralism of BDS seem heavy-handed at best and destructive at worst," wrote University of California student government president Avinoam Baral, days after Netanyahu's reelection.[1] Baral, who was elected with

ix

financing from off-campus Israel lobby groups,[2] continued: "When the conflict seems solvable and the Israeli government seems dedicated to doing so, even the worst aspects of the status quo—the military occupation, the errant missiles in Gaza—can be painted as what I truly believe they are: a dark, temporary chapter of our collective history before a momentous resolution."[3]

Palestinians know, however, that occupation, apartheid, land theft, mass imprisonment, constant killings, and attacks on Palestinian cultural and educational institutions are permanent, foundational features of Zionist settler-colonialism and have not varied with changes in government between "left" and "right."

"The situation has gotten so bad, so indefensible, that, over the past year, the pro-Israel community has given up on defending Netanyahu's policies," Baral admits. "Instead, on-campus activism consists of harmless events about Israel's startup scene or innovative water conservation research."[4]

It is no wonder then that Baral lamented Netanyahu's re-election as "a victory for BDS."

But pro-Israel activism consists of far more than "harmless" seminars, as many of the contributors to this book attest. In addition to repression of and retribution against scholars and Palestine supporters on campus, pro-Israel groups have formed toxic alliances with the Islamophobic, often white supremacist far right, as well as with Islamophobic liberals who falsely portray Israel as a progressive oasis amid a region of backwardness.

The campus battles over Palestine are certain only to intensify as an inexorable generational shift in Europe and North America takes place: the traditional liberal and progressive bases of support for Zionism continue to erode, while powerful institutions—chief among them the corporatized neoliberal university—mount a ferocious counterattack.

Israel's most aggressive proponents understand that the future of US support for the Zionist settler-colony—without which the apartheid regime cannot survive—will be won or lost at universities.

"It is common for pro-Israel activists in the United States to say that campus matters because that is where the thinking of America's future political leadership is molded," Israel lobby group the David Project observed in a 2012 strategic white paper. "However, campus matters also because it is where the worldview of a large swath of influential people outside of the political class as well as the population at large is largely formed."[5]

In line with this thinking, a host of Israel lobby groups has invested millions of dollars in recent years in efforts to stem the influence of movements like Students for Justice in Palestine (SJP) among an increasingly diverse population and to disrupt their alliances with a broader social justice movement rooted in antiracism and anticolonialism.

As many of the essays in this book reveal, students and faculty alike have been targeted by unrelenting campaigns to delegitimize their scholarship, democratic associations, and activism and to forcibly reimpose the crumbling taboos that have for too long restrained discussion of Israel's crimes and institutional complicity in them.

In this sense, the battle for freedom of conscience and action over Palestine has highlighted a bigger existential crisis at universities: can they remain sites for dissent, critical scholarship, and innovation, without which there can be no educational process? Or are they doomed to become—like so many other "democratic" institutions—unaccountable and hollowed out, beholden only to the power and influence of capital?

In everyday speech, if you say something is "academic," it can mean that it is irrelevant to the pressing needs of everyday life.

But in the urgent global movement supporting the Palestinian struggle for liberation from a brutal Israeli occupation and apartheid regime, the academy is on the frontlines. This book is a critical tool for all those, inside and outside universities, who feel called upon to join the good fight.

March 2015

INTRODUCTION

ASHLEY DAWSON AND BILL V. MULLEN

THE PURPOSE OF THIS BOOK

This book is a tool, a guidebook, and a living chronicle of the growing international campaign to boycott Israeli universities in protest of Israeli apartheid and the illegal Israeli occupation of Palestine. It is a book made directly by activists in the boycott, divestment, and sanctions (BDS) movement against Israel. It includes contributions by cofounders of the original BDS campaign against Israel, Palestinian scholars living under occupation, South African antiapartheid activists, and faculty and students across a range of universities who are dedicated to fighting Israeli apartheid—some of whom have been harassed, intimidated, and even fired from their jobs for their activism.

In this introduction, we seek to define Israeli apartheid and the occupation as an international crime in need of urgent protest, most especially boycott, divestment, and sanctions. We also seek to explain the role of Israeli universities in sustaining the violent and discriminatory occupation of Palestine, and why it is urgent that scholars and students around the world boycott Israeli universities. Finally, we demonstrate how both Israeli and Western universities have become complicit sites of neoliberal capitalist hegemony, Western imperialist discourse, pro-Zionist politics, and settler-colonial ideology. These conditions demand an immediate response from campus activists seeking to build a radical alternative that can challenge capitalist-colonialism and offer a broad, democratic resistance that bridges schools and workplaces, campuses and factories, the global north and the global south. The academic boycott of Israeli universities, we argue, is essential to a larger project of not just defeating Israeli apartheid but also to building a wider left resistance in our neoliberal times.

ISRAEL: COLONIALISM, OCCUPATION, AND APARTHEID

In 2002, South African Archbishop Desmond Tutu penned a remarkably frank

letter to the British newspaper *The Guardian* following a visit to Israel and the occupied Palestinian territories; the letter was entitled "Apartheid in the Holy Land."[1]
Lamenting the conditions he encountered during his visit, Tutu wrote:

> I've been very deeply distressed in my visit to the Holy Land; it reminded me
> so much of what happened to us black people in South Africa. I have seen the
> humiliation of the Palestinians at checkpoints and roadblocks, suffering like us
> when young white police officers prevented us from moving about. On one of my
> visits to the Holy Land I drove to a church with the Anglican bishop in Jerusalem.
> I could hear tears in his voice as he pointed to Jewish settlements. I thought of
> the desire of Israelis for security. But what of the Palestinians who have lost their
> land and home?[2]

While Tutu may have been one the first figures of international renown to
compare conditions in Israel and Palestine to those in apartheid South Africa, he
was not the last. Former US president Jimmy Carter's book *Palestine: Peace Not
Apartheid* (2006) mobilized the analogy to South Africa's racist regime in order
to make the case for moving forward with Israeli–Palestinian peace negotiations.
More recently, secretary of state John Kerry's frustrated assertion that Israel risks becoming an apartheid state should the peace process fail caused a major diplomatic
row, and elicited a subsequent retraction by Kerry.[3] Despite the fact that there have
been similar warnings from senior Israeli politicians, "apartheid," Kerry remorse-
fully said, "is a word best left out of the debate [in the United States]."[4] We believe
that Kerry is completely wrong: it is precisely in the US context, where a great deal
of intellectual energy and capital are expended on obscuring from the public the
conditions that prevail in Israel and the occupied Palestinian territories, that the
term *apartheid* needs to be applied openly to the Israeli occupation.[5]

The definition of apartheid we employ here is derived from two key international treaties: the International Convention on the Suppression and Punishment
of the Crime of Apartheid (1973), which criminalizes "inhuman acts committed
for the purpose of establishing and maintaining domination by one racial group
of persons over any other racial group of persons and systematically oppressing
them"[6]; and the Rome Statute of the International Criminal Court (1998), which
in turn criminalizes inhumane acts committed in the context of, and to maintain, "an institutionalized regime of systematic oppression and domination by one
racial group over any other racial group."[7] Both of these conventions are focused
on systematic and institutionalized racial discrimination, distinguishing apartheid
from other crimes condemned by the international community. The prohibition of
apartheid has assumed the status not simply of international customary law but of a

peremptory rule of international law (a *jus cogens* norm), a status that obliges states and other international organizations to cooperate in order to end serious breaches of such norms. Given these obligations to intervene in situations that constitute apartheid, the question as to whether Israel is an apartheid state is of critical importance. As Omar Barghouti puts it, "The significance to the Palestinian struggle for self-determination of the fact that international law considers apartheid a crime against humanity that therefore invites sanctions—similar in nature and breadth to those imposed on apartheid South Africa—-cannot be overemphasized."[8]

When we analogize the conditions in the occupied Palestinian territories and Israel to those in South Africa during the apartheid era, we do not mean that the situation is identical. Although there are important demographic and geographical differences between South African and Israeli apartheid, these differences should not obscure their fundamental similarities. Israel, for example, does not have direct equivalents to noxious laws such as the Separate Amenities Act, which enforced petty apartheid—racially segregated bathrooms, beaches, water fountains, and so forth—in South Africa. In apartheid South Africa, a white minority sought to maintain domination over a Black majority. In Israel, by contrast, a Jewish majority engages in discriminatory treatment of a minority of Palestinians in Israel itself, as well as discriminatory treatment of Palestinians under a military occupation. Palestinians within Israel are treated differently than Palestinians in the occupied Palestinian territories, although these greater rights are increasingly eroding in what has been termed "creeping apartheid."[9] But since the Israeli state ultimately controls both Israel and the occupied Palestinian territories, and has pursued settlement policies that have thoroughly integrated the occupation, we believe that it makes little sense when considering the dimensions of Israeli apartheid to attempt to distinguish between regimes in Israel, the West Bank, and Gaza. We insist that Israel's policies in relation to the Palestinians amount to an institutionalized system of racial discrimination and domination. It is a system of apartheid in effect if not in explicit word.

What are some of the key similarities and differences between South African and Israeli apartheid? In South Africa, the apartheid regime was sustained by three key sets of laws.[10] The first of these divided the country's population into distinct racial groups and granted superior rights, privileges, and services to whites. Among these racializing laws were the Population Registration Act (1950), the Bantu Education Act (1953), and the Separate Amenities Act (1953). These laws institutionalized the informal racial hierarchies that had prevailed during the pre-apartheid era, creating rigid legal divisions between racialized groups such as whites, "coloureds," Indians, and Blacks.

The second cornerstone of South African apartheid was a series of laws that segregated the population into distinct geographical areas, which were allocated to different racial groups. This segregation, imposed by the Group Areas Act (1950), was then enforced by a series of Pass Laws (for example, the Native Laws Amendment Act of 1952), which restricted passage of Blacks and other racialized groups into areas of cities and of the country that were allocated to whites. These segregating measures were developed into what its architects called "Grand Apartheid," a policy through which the South African government established a series of "homelands" or Bantustans, into which denationalized Black South Africans were transferred and forced to reside. The apartheid regime claimed that Blacks enjoyed complete sovereignty in the Bantustans, which were characterized as autonomous nation states. Therefore, the architects of Grand Apartheid argued, Blacks did not need political rights within South Africa proper. The Bantustans, in other words, allowed the apartheid regime to claim that it had granted Blacks full self-determination while preserving white minority rule within South Africa.

Dissent from this transparently unjust regime was silenced through the third cornerstone of the apartheid order: a matrix of draconian "security" laws that legalized unlimited administrative detention, torture, censorship, banning, and assassination. The apartheid regime exercised a reign of terror over the majority of South African society, allowing a privileged white minority to live in complete denial of the multiple forms of violence perpetrated in its name.

Israeli apartheid is founded on three cornerstones that closely resemble those of apartheid in South Africa. The first key element of Israeli apartheid is a series of laws and policies distinguishing between Jews and non-Jews, granting preferred legal status and material benefits to the former.[11] Israel's Law of Return (1950), for example, defines who is a Jew for legal purposes and allows every Jew throughout the global diaspora to immigrate to Israel. The 1952 Citizenship Law subsequently granted automatic citizenship to all who immigrate to Israel under the Law of Return, while simultaneously establishing insurmountable obstacles to citizenship for Palestinian refugees. These laws according special standing to Jewish identity were then applied extraterritorially in the occupied Palestinian territories, extending preferential legal status and material benefits to Jewish settlers. A recent analysis of the situation in the occupied Palestinian territories by South Africa's national Human Sciences Research Council (HSRC) concludes, "The review of Israel's practices under Article 2 of the Apartheid Convention provides abundant evidence of discrimination against Palestinians that flows from that inferior status, in realms such as the right to leave and return to one's country, freedom of movement and

residence, and access to land."[12] These infractions of Palestinian rights have continued despite decades of condemnations of Israel's ongoing illegal occupation of the
West Bank and siege of Gaza.

The second cornerstone of Israeli apartheid consists of policies designed to
fragment the occupied Palestinian territories in order to facilitate segregation and
domination. These policies are long-standing and have been pursued systematically during the more than four decades of Israel's occupation of the West Bank
and Gaza. The Sharon-Wachman Plan, for example, drafted in 1978 while Ariel
Sharon was head of the Ministerial Committee on Settlements in Menachem Begin's Likud government, called for the establishment of one hundred urban, indus-
trialized Israeli settlements on mountain ridges across the West Bank, organized
into concentrated blocs connected by a skein of east–west running highways.[13]
Israeli architect Eyal Weizman argues that, under the Sharon-Wachman Plan, these
highways were explicitly designed to fragment Palestinian territory in the occupied
Palestinian territories, allowing the Israeli Army to withdraw from Palestinian cities
while continuing to dominate them spatially.[14] Sharon's plans for carving up the occupied Palestinian territories have largely been realized: Palestinians in the occupied
Palestinian territories now live in an archipelago of besieged and noncontiguous
enclaves. The occupied Palestinian territories are essentially a series of micro-Ban-
tustans, functioning to obscure Israel's domination of the occupied territories just
as the white regime in South Africa hoped its policy of Grand Apartheid would
obscure its stripping of self-determination from the country's Black population.
With regard to Israel's policies of occupation, the South African HSRC report states,

> That these measures are intended to segregate the population along racial lines in
> violation of Article 2(d) of the Apartheid Convention is clear from the visible web
> of walls, separate roads, and checkpoints, and the invisible web of permit and ID
> systems, that combine to ensure that Palestinians remain confined to the reserves
> designated for them while Israeli Jews are prohibited from entering those reserves
> but enjoy freedom of movement throughout the rest of the Palestinian territory.[15]

The HSRC's use of the term *reserve,* with its colonial connotations, is particularly
telling in this indictment of Israeli policies.

The third and final key element of Israeli apartheid is the matrix of "security"
laws and policies that the state employs, policies that include extrajudicial killing,
torture, and cruel, inhuman, or degrading treatment and arbitrary arrest and imprisonment of Palestinians. These policies are sanctioned by the Israeli state and
also often by the Israeli judicial system, and are supported in the occupied Palestinian territories by oppressive military laws and a system of improperly constituted

and harshly punitive military courts. Although this system of military rule by an occupying power is sanctioned by international law, it should be noted that an occupation is not supposed to last four decades. Conditions in the occupied Palestinian territories, with their system of checkpoints, racially segregated roads, and permanent settlements, are in total breach of international law. Indeed, in 2010 the United Nations Special Rapporteur on the Independence of Judges and Lawyers found that the "legal foundations and practices of the military justice system [in the occupied Palestinian territories] do not comply with international standards" and that "the exercise of jurisdiction by a military court over civilians not performing military tasks is normally inconsistent with the fair, impartial and independent administration of justice."[16] The parallel between Israel's mobilization of notions of security and apartheid South Africa's use of fears of internal threats is striking. Invoking such concerns, Israel engages in a draconian rule over Palestinians in the occupied Palestinian territories that is designed to quell any and all displays of protest and dissent. As the HSRC report concludes, "This study finds that Israel's invocation of 'security' to validate sweeping restrictions on Palestinian freedom of opinion, expression, assembly, association and movement also often purports to mask a true underlying intent to suppress dissent to its system of domination, and thereby maintain control over Palestinians as a group."[17]

There is one glaring and fundamental difference between South African and Israeli apartheid. The system of apartheid in South Africa depended on Black labor in order to function. Israeli apartheid, by contrast, is grounded in efforts to expel Palestinians from "Greater Israel," efforts that according to many historians are predicated on systematic policies of ethnic cleansing.[18] After all, Israel was founded on a glaring contradiction: it was intended to be both Jewish and democratic. Zionism was predicated on the creation of a state for an ethnic group: the Jewish people. As a result, although in theory all Israeli citizens are equal members of a state that is in some ways admirably democratic, in practice only Israel's Jewish citizens are nationals. Palestinians residing in Israel may be Israeli citizens, but they nevertheless live in an ethnocratic state explicitly devoted to its Jewish citizens alone.[19] Although they are not targeted with the same kinds of overt apartheid policies as Palestinians living in the occupied Palestinian territories, Palestinians in Israel suffer many inequalities. For instance, the Israeli state has never established an Arab-language university in Israel; as a consequence, Palestinians living in Israel are forced to pursue studies in Hebrew, a situation not wholly dissimilar to the imposition of Afrikaans on all schoolchildren in apartheid South Africa, a form of cultural oppression that sparked the Soweto Uprising in 1976.

The result of this constitutive inequality in Israel is constant enmity on the part of the Israeli establishment toward all those who are perceived as threatening the Jewish nation, even if only by their continued existence. Since Palestinians comprise an increasing percentage of the population in Israel itself, and a majority in the combined area of Israel and the occupied Palestinian territories, their reproduction is a threat to the state's founding formula as Jewish and democratic. This has led to increasing repression of Palestinians within Israel. In 2003, for example, the Citizenship and Entry into Israel law banned Palestinian family unification, providing explicit evidence of the way Israel's apartheid system regards Palestinians as a "demographic threat" to a national polity framed in ethnocratic terms. This constitutive inequality is plagued by its own destabilizing contradictions. As Ali Abunimah puts it, "Like the Afrikaner insistence on self-determination, which meant power over South Africa's Blacks, Zionism's claims for 'Jewish self-determination' of a settler-colonial group amid an intermixed population is in effect a demand to preserve and legitimate a status quo in which Israeli Jews exercise power in perpetuity, a quest that generates constant insecurity since it requires the active and violent suppression of the rights of millions of non-Jews."[20]

The founders of the state of Israel were aware of this constitutive contradiction. They proffered a "solution" that ought today to be morally anathema. According to Israeli historian Benny Morris, there was an almost total consensus among early Zionists and Israeli leaders about the desirability of "transferring" Palestinians out of Israel.[21] Indeed, during the course of what Palestinians call the *Nakba*, or catastrophic defeat in the 1948 war, approximately 87 percent of the Palestinians who lived in what is now Israel were removed, often by force.[22] An estimated four of every five Palestinian villages and towns inside Israel were either destroyed or settled by Jews after their inhabitants fled or were expelled.[23] From 1948 to 1966, Palestinians in Israel lived under military rule, with what remained of their land systematically being stripped from them. Today, although Israeli Arabs undeniably enjoy greater civil and human rights than do Palestinians in the occupied Palestinian territories, these rights are being eroded quickly. Over the last decade, successive Israeli governments have promulgated a litany of new restrictions on personal freedoms, employment, land ownership, and the political rights of Palestinian citizens.[24] In addition, the discourse of ethnic cleansing that circulated among early Zionists is making an alarming return. Openly racist talk of "punishing the Arab enemy," of stripping Palestinians in Israel of their citizenship and of establishing an "Eretz Yisrael" or Greater Israel by annexing most of the West Bank is not simply increasingly common but is also at the heart of the policy goals of rising Israeli political leaders such as Naftali Bennett, head of the settler-dominated Jewish Home Party.[25] Such proposals for a new, aggressive round of Israeli colonialism promise only to deepen the constitutive contradictions of Israeli national identity by adding the population of the occupied Palestinian territories to Israel. Unless, that is, a fresh round of ethnic cleansing takes place.

As we have shown, Israel is a de facto ethnonationalist state, existing in conditions of flagrant apartheid. The question we face is how to achieve a political formation to transform Israeli apartheid; how, that is, to mobilize around the demand for a system of government based on principles of equality in civil, political, social, and cultural rights for all its citizens. Such a transition toward genuine democracy and equality seems improbable today. Israel is moving increasingly toward intolerance, its internal politics dominated by strident xenophobia and right-wing organizations such as Bennett's Jewish Home Party. Moreover, Israel enjoys absolute military domination over not simply the Palestinians but all its regional foes. Yet, as Ali Abunimah has argued, the transition to democracy in South Africa offers an important precedent.[26] Like Israel, South Africa's apartheid regime also enjoyed total military superiority over the liberation movement. Like Israeli Jews, white South Africans became increasingly reactionary as the contradictions of apartheid tore apart their country during the 1980s. Yet it was ultimately a complete loss of legitimacy that did in the apartheid regime. Faced with international pariah status, South African whites lost their determination to support a system of racist oppression and violence. Israeli elites, too, may decide, like white South Africans, that the cost of maintaining a regime based on colonialism, occupation, and apartheid is too high.[27]

By challenging Israeli apartheid using some of the same strategies as the movement against apartheid in South Africa, the BDS movement has a vital role to play in bringing about a democratic transition in occupied Palestine. BDS is based on a set of key principles that call for an end to Israeli colonialism, occupation, and apartheid: the demand that Israel recognize the Palestinian people's inalienable right to self-determination and uphold international law by ending its occupation and colonization of Palestinian lands; the demand that Israel recognize the rights of all Arab-Palestinian citizens of present-day Israel to full equality; and the demand that Israel promote the rights of Palestinians to return and restitution of property, as stipulated in UN Resolution 194. Taken together, these central demands of the BDS movement constitute a charter for Palestinian self-determination, and a call for decolonization, equality, and justice. BDS is a clarion call by hundreds of Palestinian civil society organizations for international solidarity in a principled campaign of nonviolent resistance. The BDS movement has also made clear the centrality of Israeli universities to the maintenance of Israeli apartheid and the consequent need for academic boycott. It is to that movement, its history, its successes and its growth, that we now turn.

The Palestinian Campaign for the Academic and Cultural Boycott of Israel (PACBI) was launched in Ramallah, West Bank, in July 2004 by more than 170 groups representing Palestinian civil society. As PACBI cofounders Lisa Taraki and Omar Barghouti argue in essays in this volume, PACBI was directly inspired by the successful South African antiapartheid BDS movement. The original PACBI call made this explicit, while targeting Israeli Zionism and settler-colonial Israeli rule. As conditions for boycott, divestment, and sanctions, it specified Israel's

- Denial of its responsibility for the Nakba—in particular, the waves of ethnic cleansing and dispossession that created the Palestinian refugee problem—and therefore refusal to accept the inalienable rights of the refugees and displaced stipulated in and protected by international law;
- Military occupation and colonization of the West Bank (including East Jerusalem) and Gaza since 1967, in violation of international law and UN resolutions;
- The entrenched system of racial discrimination and segregation against the Palestinian citizens of Israel, which resembles the defunct apartheid system in South Africa...[28]

As had the South African Congress of South African Universities in the 1960s, PACBI included a call for global boycott of Israeli universities. "Whereas," they wrote,

Israeli academic institutions (mostly state controlled) and the vast majority of Israeli intellectuals and academics have either contributed directly to maintaining, defending or otherwise justifying the above forms of oppression, or have been complicit in them through their silence....We, Palestinian academics and intellectuals, call upon our colleagues in the international community to:
- Refrain from participation in any form of academic and cultural cooperation, collaboration or joint projects with Israeli institutions;
- Advocate a comprehensive boycott of Israeli institutions at the national and international levels, including suspension of all forms of funding and subsidies to these institutions;
- Promote divestment and disinvestment from Israel by international academic institutions;
- Work toward the condemnation of Israeli policies by pressing for resolutions to be adopted by academic, professional and cultural associations and organizations;

- Support Palestinian academic and cultural institutions directly without requiring
them to partner with Israeli counterparts as an explicit or implicit condition for
such support.[29]

The 2004 PACBI campaign came with endorsements from the Palestinian Federation of Unions of University Professors and Employees, the Palestinian General Federation of Trade Unions, and a number of other unions. Yet it wasn't until Israel's Operation Cast Lead invasion of Gaza in December 2008–January 2009, and the deaths of more than 1,500 Palestinians, that world outrage—and academic outrage—began to catch up to PACBI's call. Immediately in the wake of Operation Cast Lead, a small group of academics, including several contributors to this volume, formed USACBI, or the United States Campaign for the Academic and Cultural Boycott of Israel. USACBI declared its solidarity with PACBI by building a boycott movement modeled on the latter's founding principles. USACBI also declared its support for the three larger guiding principles of the BDS movement of which PACBI was initially a part:

1. Ending [Israel's] occupation and colonization of all Arab lands and dismantling the Wall;
2. Recognizing the fundamental rights of the Arab-Palestinian citizens of Israel to full equality; and
3. Respecting, protecting and promoting the rights of Palestinian refugees to return to their homes and properties as stipulated in UN resolution 194.[30]

Since 2009, USACBI has gathered signatures from more than 1,400 US and international scholars and 400 cultural workers in support of academic and cultural boycott of Israel. In 2013—in retrospect a landmark year in the BDS movement— three North American academic associations passed separate resolutions calling for the academic boycott of Israeli universities: the Association of Asian American Studies (AAAS), the American Studies Association (ASA), and the Native American and Indigenous Studies Association (NAISA). In 2014, the African Literature Association and Peace and Justice Studies Association passed similar resolutions. In the same span of time, the National Union of Teachers (UK); graduate students at York University, Canada; the Irish Student Union in Dublin; the Kings College London Students Union; graduate student unions at Loyola University, Chicago; and six of ten University of California campuses all passed resolutions supporting academic boycott or divestment from Israel. The momentum culminated in December 2014, when University of California graduate students in United Auto Workers Local Union 2865 voted by a nearly 2 to 1 margin to divest from Israel, the first vote by a major US union to divest.[31]

As Omar Barghouti argues in this book, this wave of successful resolutions in support of academic boycott and divestment constitutes a possible "tipping point" in the global campaign against Israeli apartheid. On college campuses worldwide, the Israeli occupation has become a political flashpoint for the development of a new generation of activists, much in the way the Vietnam War galvanized student and faculty protests in the 1960s. How has this happened? Why has academic boycott and divestment become so successful? And what must be done to build and grow the movement? Several factors are critically important to consider.

POST-INTIFADA AND POST-9/11 RESISTANCE

The success of the BDS movement reflects the emergence of a new generation of activists inspired by the First and Second Palestinian Intifadas, on one hand, and the "endless wars" against contemporary Arab states conducted by the US state, on the other. Both these factors have radicalized Arab, Palestinian, and Muslim students and scholars in particular, who have increasingly seen themselves in political kinship and solidarity with Palestinians under occupation as they are ignored, dismissed, or designated by Western media and imperialist allies as "terrorists." These activists have used BDS as a platform to mainstream criticism of the Israeli occupation, Israeli apartheid, and the role of Israeli universities in perpetuating both. They have broadened a set of social movement principles of Palestinian self-determination once associated with individual scholars and activists such as Edward Said, Ali Mazrui, Noam Chomsky, and Norman Finkelstein. Indeed, this new generation, sometimes called Generation Palestine, has in many cases pushed past its mentors who have often, like Chomsky, been supportive of Palestinian rights in name but not always of the strategies of the BDS movement.[32]

Wael Elasady is a good example. Radicalized by 9/11, the Second Intifada, and the US occupation of Iraq, Elasady, in his own words, "like many young Arabs and Muslims in the U.S., was beginning to draw radical conclusions about the nature of U.S. empire, the roots of Islamophobia and its connections to a system of capitalist exploitation."[33] When Elasady became a student at Portland State University, the BDS movement's insistence on Palestinian self-determination and criticism of the US-backed occupation offered a vehicle for attacking all three problems. As Elasady wrote, "It is young Palestinians of the diaspora who have taken the reins and are leading the charge of the BDS movement on campuses across the U.S. They are the one who are unafraid of calling Israel what it is: an apartheid state. More to the point, we are demanding nothing less than the full rights and liberation of the Palestinian people."[34]

Elasady's emphatic insistence on the "apartheid" designation for the Israeli movement highlights that Israel is a settler-colonial state for which the analogy of South Africa is both historically apt and politically urgent. The endorsement of the Palestinian BDS campaign by the African National Congress (ANC) and key figures in the South African antiapartheid movement, like Archbishop Desmond Tutu, has been critical to shaping this consensus. So, too, has academic scholarship documenting the brutal dimensions of Israeli settler-colonial rule. These would include important early works such as Maxime Rodinson's *Israel: Settler-Colonial State?* (1973); Rashid Khalidi's *The Iron Cage: The Story of the Palestinian Struggle for Statehood* (2006); Israeli scholar, BDS supporter, and contributor to this volume Ilan Pappé's *The Ethnic Cleansing of Palestine (2006)*, a harrowing account of the Zionist movement and *haganah* (Zionist paramilitary) in executing the Nakba; Ali Abunimah's *One Country* (2006) and *The Battle for Justice in Palestine* (2014); contributor Magid Shihade's *Not Just a Game: Colonialism and Conflict Among Palestinians in Israel* (2011); Saree Makdisi's *Palestine Inside Out: An Everyday Occupation* (2010); and special issues of academic journals, such as the 2011 issue of *Settler Colonial Studies* "Past Is Present: Settler Colonialism in Palestine."[35]

Cumulatively, this scholarship has provided activists political ammunition for a narrative central to support of the academic boycott movement, namely that Israeli apartheid and the occupation represent a systematic de-territorialization of Palestinian land and people; an illegal abrogation of Palestinians' universal human rights; a racist, Zionist, two-tier system of unequal and exploitative social relations; and a roadblock to Palestinian self-determination, both for Palestinian Arabs within Israel and in the occupied Palestinian territories, as well as in the Palestinian diaspora.[36]

The global academic boycott movement has cleaved to this interpretation of Israeli apartheid an analysis of the role of the Israeli university in the occupation faithful to the original 2004 PACBI call for academic boycott. Successful boycott resolutions passed by academic associations since 2013 have foregrounded the effects of Israeli apartheid and systemic discrimination on Palestinian scholars and students. The AAAS resolution of 2013, for example, noted that "Israeli institutions of higher education have not condemned or taken measures to oppose the occupation and racial discrimination against Palestinians in Israel, but have, rather, been directly and indirectly complicit in the systematic maintenance of the occupation and of policies and practices that discriminate against Palestinian students and scholars throughout Palestine and in Israel."[37] Likewise, the ASA resolution observed that "there is no effective or substantive academic freedom for Palestinian students and scholars under conditions of Israeli occupation, and Israeli institutions of higher learning are a party to Israeli state policies that violate human rights and negatively impact the working conditions of Palestinian scholars and students."[38]

Both the AAAS and the ASA also signaled the role of the US government in supporting and sustaining an occupation that is toxic to the academic work and academic freedom of Palestinians. The ASA council resolution noted that the United States "plays a significant role in enabling the Israeli occupation of Palestine and the expansion of illegal settlements and the Wall in violation of international law, as well as in supporting the systematic discrimination against Palestinians, which has had documented devastating impact on the overall well-being, the exercise of political and human rights, the freedom of movement, and the educational opportunities of Palestinians."[39] During public discussion of the ASA resolution at the organization's November 2013 annual meeting in Washington, DC, scholar after scholar, student after student from US-based universities noted that registering dissent from US support for Israel was a part of their rationale for supporting the boycott.

This analysis of Israeli apartheid has also become a political platform for much of the insurgent political practice of student activists fighting Israeli apartheid. Students for Justice in Palestine (SJP) chapters have arguably become the leading edge of the BDS movement on university campuses, helping to deepen and advance Palestinian civil rights struggles in a role akin to that of the Student Nonviolent Coordinating Committee chapters of the 1960s. As Nora Barrows-Friedman has written in her recent book *In Our Power: U.S. Students Organize for Justice in Palestine*, the confluence of the 2005 call by Palestinian civil society for BDS followed by the widely publicized atrocities of Operation Cast Lead in 2008–2009 reenergized SJP activism in the United States and elsewhere.[40] In 2011, representatives of nearly sixty campus-based SJPs inaugurated the National Students for Justice in Palestine at Columbia University. Since that time, the number of SJP chapters has grown to more than one hundred fifty in the United States. Between 2009 and 2014, twenty-four US campuses launched divestment campaigns and presented resolutions before their student body associations, most of these forwarded by SJP activists. The growth of SJP has helped mainstream discussion of Palestinian rights and spur other important campus conversations about Palestine, such as the decision by students at Swarthmore and Vassar to form Open Hillel chapters no longer beholden to the national Hillel consensus to exclude discussion of BDS.[41] SJP activists have also formed critical alliances with other struggles on university campuses for racial and gender justice; for example, sponsoring discussions of Israeli "pinkwashing," a strategy used by Israel to extol LGBT rights as a way of masking the horrors of the occupation, and forging connections with the recent and ongoing Black Lives

Matter movement against police violence.[42] Indeed, Stanford student Kristian Davis Bailey's contribution to this volume describing collaboration between African American students in the United States and Palestinian students emblematizes the dynamic, intersectional nature of campus Palestinian activism these days.

SJP thus constitutes a vanguard political actor in what Ali Abunimah has aptly called the "war on campus" around BDS. BDS and academic boycott now constitute the most sustained globalized challenge by campus activists to years of Zionist influence on university administrations: monitoring and surveillance of pro-Palestinian students and faculty; donor efforts to promote pro-Israel curriculum and hiring; and, more broadly, US universities' complicity with the state in legitimizing Israel as the "only democracy in the Middle East," while it serves as an imperial watchdog for US interests.[43] BDS has also confronted head-on the efforts of pro-Israel groups such as the David Project and the AMCHA Initiative, discussed in this volume, which have created strong *hasbara* or propaganda campaigns meant to delegimitize BDS and attack scholars and students who support it.[44] Essays in this volume by Rabab Abdulhadi, Steven Salaita, Sunaina Maira, Magid Shihade, and Tithi Bhattacharya and Bill V. Mullen all speak in part to this issue. Abdulhadi, who was targeted by AMCHA for her travel research to Palestine, and Salaita, who was fired from his job at the University of Illinois for tweeting out criticisms of Israel's Operation Protective Edge war in Gaza in 2014, are also not coincidentally vocal advocates for the academic boycott of Israeli universities.

In this regard, the "war on campus" around academic boycott also indexes a growing consciousness among students and faculty of what Piya Chatterjee and Sunaina Maira have called the "imperial university." In a 2014 volume of essays published under that title, Chatterjee and Maira argue that, especially since September 11, 2011, the US academy has become a third front (after the military and cultural fronts) in sustaining US imperialism and racial statecraft. Four of the essays in the book include testimonials from scholars who have faced criticism or disciplining for their campus work or scholarship in support of Palestinian rights. The book also demonstrates the deepening ties between the militarization of US universities after 9/11 and their complicity with neoliberal practices (such as privatization) that mirror those of US imperial expansion overseas. Chatterjee and Maira also document the way that certain academic fields and scholars within them, for example, Middle Eastern studies, have been targeted for scholarship or teaching perceived to be pro-Palestinian or critical of Israel.[45]

The imperial university is then a metaphor for the institutional alliances between imperial powers, in this case the United States and Israel, at the academic level, and the discourses produced by those alliances. Both are targets of the academic boycott movement. Examples would include institutional research collaborations between Cornell University and the Technion (Israel Institute of Technology), Israel's primary weapons manufacturing university; partnerships between US and Israeli universities featuring study abroad and "birthright" programs to Israel; for-profit activity by campus leaders, such as University of Illinois at Urbana–Champaign chancellor Phyllis Wise, a member of the board of trustees for Nike, which does business with illegal textile manufacturers in the occupied West Bank; and direct political support for Israel by former and current university leaders, including Lawrence Summers and UC Davis chancellor Linda Katehi. Summers, former president of Harvard, has been a constant critic of the academic boycott movement, calling the movement "anti-Semitic," while Katehi—who once led a faculty delegation to Israel—was quick to condemn the recent UC Davis student government resolution calling for divestment, while remaining silent about years of Islamophobic harassment and intimidation of Palestinian and Arab students on campus.[46] Indeed, the fact that more than 250 university presidents and the US Congress simultaneously condemned the ASA for passing its academic boycott resolution is among the clearest evidence we have of the "imperial" ties between current university leadership and US empire.[47]

BDS generally then, and the academic boycott movement more specifically, endeavor to break the imperial chains that currently bind students and faculty together in an alliance forged from above, in the interests of states, not citizens; apartheid, not justice; empire, not education. It is the "links" in this chain that this book is organized both to demonstrate and undo. The book is divided into five sections. Part I, "From the Front Lines: Palestinian Scholars Make the Case for Academic Boycott," foregrounds BDS's origins as a call from Palestinian civil society to the world. It is a reminder that academic boycott began as a movement to stand with Palestinian scholars and students living under daily Israeli occupation and threat of death. Here BDS cofounder Lisa Taraki, Birzeit University, West Bank; Haidar Eid, Al-Aqsa University, Gaza; Rima Najjar Merriman, Al-Quds University, Abu Dis; and Magid Shihade, Birzeit, provide firsthand testimonial of the routine complicity of Israeli universities in constricting the rights and personal freedoms of Palestinian scholars while advancing the militarization and violence of the occupation. Their essays also indicate that Palestinian scholars who support BDS are, as a class of intellectual and cultural workers under occupation, intensely vulnerable to Israeli discrimination, professional retribution, and physical violence.

Part II, "Taking on the Settler-Colonial University: Academic Boycott and Academic Freedom," asserts the efficacy of boycott for resisting the complicity of

Israeli universities in repressing academic freedom for Palestinian and Arab scholars not only under occupation but also in the Palestinian diaspora. Several essays in this section were prompted by a special issue of the *Journal of Academic Freedom* published just before the ASA boycott resolution, responding to attacks from Zionists, American political legislatures, and the mainstream press that the boycott would violate the academic freedom of Israeli scholars.[48] Here BDS cofounder Omar Barghouti, USACBI activist scholars Malini Johar Schueller and David Lloyd, PACBI member Sami Hermez and international scholar and activist Mayssoun Sukarieh, and US-based postcolonial scholar and USACBI cofounder Sunaina Maira expose "academic freedom" as a manipulable political double standard and ideological cover for the complicity of Israeli universities in the occupation, and speak to the erasure of Palestinian and Arab scholars from discussions—at least in the West—about the daily effects of Israeli apartheid.

Part III, "The Academic Boycott of Israeli Universities in Historical Context," demonstrates how the BDS movement against Israel has become a global justice movement and direct threat to both the occupation and US support for it. Essays by South African scholar-activist Salim Vally, Palestinian-American law professor Noura Erakat, Israeli scholar Ilan Pappé, and groundbreaking US historian of gender Joan W. Scott elucidate ways in which the academic boycott against Israeli universities has come to symbolize a global erosion of support for Israel and the occupation, while forging a wide-ranging social movement against political and academic elites who support it.

Part IV, "Scholars and Students in the Struggle, under Attack," details ways the imperial university seeks to discipline and punish campus activists for working against Israeli apartheid and occupation and has helped sharpen the struggle against these same forces. The essays testify to the on-the-ground stakes of supporting academic boycott as most dramatically evidenced in the University of Illinois's firing of boycott supporter Steven Salaita, an event that galvanized more than seventeen thousand signatures in protest and a commitment by more than five thousand scholars to boycott speaking engagements at the university. Here, Salaita himself, USACBI member and Palestine solidarity activist Rabab Abdulhadi, University of Minnesota American Indian studies professor Vicente M. Diaz, legal scholar and civil rights attorney Rima Najjar Kapitan, and Palestine solidarity student-activists Kristian Davis Bailey and Nerdeen Mohsen testify to the critical political urgency of doing BDS work, the political repression it can elicit, and strategies for negotiating between.

Part V, "New Horizons for the Academic Boycott Movement," proposes strategies and ideas and identifies challenges to the boycott movement while testing its current political potential and political limits. The essays remind us that academic boycott can be a spur to other forms of Palestine solidarity activism and that it is a necessary but not sufficient part of the struggle for Palestinian freedom, and caution against its appropriation or abuse by liberal political elites seeking cover strategies for preserving the Israeli state and Western hegemony in the Middle East. Here, scholar-activists Sarah Schulman, Andrew Ross, Nadine Naber, David Palumbo-Liu, USACBI Organizing Collective member Bill V. Mullen and BDS activist Tithi Bhattacharya, and Joseph Massad offer critical strategic reflection for advancing and widening the "war of position" that the BDS movement more generally has become.

The book concludes with a toolbox for academic boycott work. An appendix includes links to the PACBI website, with the original call for academic boycott and supporting materials, and to similar documents at USACBI. It also includes links to boycott resolutions passed by academic organizations such as ASA, links to materials that can be used to build new boycott resolutions, a list of publications and journals that routinely cover and given support to the academic boycott, links to international organizations, and materials useful for defending scholars and students under attack for doing BDS work. This appendix can be shared in electronic form by going to the Haymarket Books webpage for this book (www.haymarketbooks.org). We encourage readers to go from here to there as a step in advancing the academic boycott and divestment movement.

In solidarity,
Ashley Dawson
Bill V. Mullen

I. FROM THE FRONT LINES:

PALESTINIAN SCHOLARS MAKE THE CASE FOR ACADEMIC BOYCOTT

1

THE COMPLICITY OF THE ISRAELI ACADEMY IN THE STRUCTURES OF DOMINATION AND STATE VIOLENCE*

LISA TARAKI

The main rationale for the academic boycott of Israel is the complicity of the Israeli academy in Israeli state policies against the Palestinian people. The academy is firmly planted within the structures of power and domination in Israel and has historically been an active partner in the oppression of the Palestinian people. This chapter will explore some aspects of the complicity of the Israeli academy in this oppression.

The social and political history of the Israeli academy has yet to be written in a systematic fashion. Once written, it is certain to reveal the deep entrenchment of Israeli academic institutions in the Zionist colonial enterprise, beginning with the establishment of the Hebrew University in 1925 as an important institution of pre-state settler society. Today, Israel's universities and other academic centers are key components of Israel's cultural—and, increasingly, economic—capital. With mounting censure of Israel and the rapid growth of the international movement to boycott it, efforts to highlight the scientific and cultural achievements of Israel have taken on added significance. Israel portrays itself as a world leader in knowledge production, and, increasingly, of high-tech expertise and products, particularly weapons.

The emphasis on scientific innovation and advances in technological know-how is part of Israel's decades-long quest for legitimacy and acceptance by the rest of the world; it is meant to secure a place for Israel in the ranks of the enlightened Western academy. Israeli universities are therefore depicted as autonomous spaces encouraging freedom of expression, diversity of opinion, and democratic values. However, it is clear that in very critical ways, and declarations by defenders notwithstanding, Israeli universities are neither autonomous nor protected spaces for the expression of critical or dissident thought or for real democratic debate about the role of the university in the polity and its relation to dominant state institutions.

I hope to show in this short chapter that Israeli academic institutions are first firmly planted in the military intelligence–industrial establishment, and, second, that they fall squarely within the national consensus and are by no means centers of critical thinking about basic issues having to do with the "national interest" or national priorities as defined by hegemonic institutions. By this I mean that the universities, embodied by their administrations, departmental governing bodies, senates, unions, staff associations, student governments, and tenure and promotion committees—in short the main representative and decision-making forums and bodies—are part and parcel of the prevailing orthodoxy that accepts and treats the political regime in all its aspects—the military, the intelligence agencies, the government—as a benign feature of the social-political landscape. They also do not question in any fundamental way the role of their institutions in upholding the oppression of the Palestinian people through myriad military, bureaucratic, and legal measures and policies. The regime and its organs—security and intelligence agencies, and the fighting army in particular—are accommodated, legitimized, and their presence as well as their unquestionable authority normalized.

The ease with which academics have weaved in and out of the military, the government—even the military government—and the academy is quite banal in a society with a persistently high level of military mobilization and a steady regimen of violence, repression, and racist discrimination carried out against Palestinians.

I would like to begin with the relationship of Israeli universities to Palestinians living under Israeli rule. Israel's "Arab problem," as reflected in both mainstream and academic discourse has, since before the *Nakba* in 1948, involved the imperative of how to understand "the Arabs" in order to control and contain them. I will focus on the field of Middle Eastern studies, which in Israel has long embodied a dynamic partnership among colonial administrators, army officers, intelligence operatives, and academics. While I will be mentioning names of some Israeli academics here, it should be understood that it is not individual culpability that is significant, rather the active complicity or silence of institutions that not only did not find anything objectionable in the extra-academic activities of their faculty but also promoted and appointed them to important posts.

I will take three examples from Israeli social sciences and humanities to illustrate this point. The first example is that of Major General Yehoshafat Harkabi, an Arabist "spy and advisor," in the words of the *New York Times*.[1] He was the chief of Israeli military intelligence from 1955 to 1959. His professional biography is revealing: Harkabi joined the Hebrew University in 1968. He became professor and head of the department of international relations and director of the Leonard Davis Institute of International Relations several years later. In 1975 he was seconded to serve as assistant for strategic policy to the minister of defense, and, in 1977, after the Likud's rise to power, he became intelligence advisor to the prime minister, Menachem Begin. He retired from the Hebrew University in 1989 but continued to teach in the National Defense College. In 1993 Harkabi was awarded the Israel Prize in Political Science.[2]

Two other examples are Menahem Milson and Shlomo Gazit, whose names are well-known in Middle East studies circles. Milson began his career as a professor of Arabic literature at the Hebrew University in the early 1960s. Between 1976 and 1978, then minister of defense Shimon Peres appointed Milson as an advisor on Arab affairs to the Israeli military. Later, he was drafted by Ariel Sharon to head the Israeli "civil administration" from 1981 to 1982. In this capacity, he presided over the campaign to crush the Palestinian national movement, famously dismissing several Palestinian mayors and closing down Palestinian universities as punishment for student resistance to the occupation. He also formed the notorious Village Leagues, composed of local Palestinian collaborators installed in order to mediate colonial rule. However, that experiment in colonial administration failed and was unable to stem the tide of support for the Palestine Liberation Organization (PLO) within the West Bank and Gaza. Milson was also the architect of infamous Military Order 845, which imposed sweeping controls over Palestinian institutions of higher education. After the end of his brief stint at the civil administration, Milson moved back seamlessly into academic life, becoming head of the Department of Arabic Language and Literature, then director of the Institute of Asian and African Studies, dean of the faculty of humanities, and finally, provost of the Rothberg International School at the university. Milson is now chair of the board of advisors at MEMRI, the right-wing Middle East media monitoring organization founded and headed by none other than Colonel Yigal Carmon, who succeeded him as civil administration head in 1982.

Shlomo Gazit was a major general in the army and has had a long career in several of its agencies. He served as the head of a department in army intelligence, followed by appointment as the first coordinator of government operations in the occupied territories (1967–74) and head of military intelligence (1974–79). Gazit was promoted to head of the military intelligence directorate, a position he held from 1974 to 1978. Upon his retirement from the army, Gazit served as president of Ben Gurion University for eight years. He later joined the Jaffee Center for

Strategic Studies at Tel Aviv University. He is now a senior research fellow at the Institute for National Security Studies affiliated with Tel Aviv University.[3]

The objective of highlighting the careers of these three individuals is not to single them out but to show how the Israeli university leadership did not and does not find anything morally amiss in appointing to top posts individuals known to have supervised and designed repressive measures and persistently committed violations of international humanitarian law against Palestinians in their other careers as military and intelligence functionaries. And this is precisely the point: the two seemingly different career paths are not perceived as distinct within the prevailing academic culture at Israeli universities.

More generally, Israeli academic Gil Eyal has argued that "the relations between Middle Eastern studies and military intelligence are made possible by the construction of a liminal institutional setting, between academia and officialdom, and on the basis of a common form of expertise shared by both academics and intelligence officers."[4]

It might be claimed that the unabashed colonial mindset of a Menahem Milson—who said once that "to serve an Arab population responsibly, one needs to know language and civilization. That is why so many professors have been called to do this"[5]—is a thing of the past. But this is not just an unfortunate and sordid episode in the history of the Israeli academy. In fact, the collaboration of the academy with the military and intelligence services moved to a new phase in the 1990s with the establishment of strategic studies institutions in the form of think tanks and security studies departments and institutes, many of which are located at or affiliated with universities. A quick review of the names of the founders, directors, or staff of these institutes shows that they have had careers with the Israeli military and intelligence establishment.

There is only space to mention one of these institutions, the Institute for National Security Studies (INSS), an external institute of Tel Aviv University. The institute was launched in October 2006, incorporating the Jaffee Center for Strategic Studies at Tel Aviv University, founded in 1977 at the initiative of Tel Aviv University by Major General (res.) Aharon Yariv, former head of military intelligence, government minister, and member of Knesset. The institute describes itself as "non-partisan, independent, and autonomous. As an external institute of Tel Aviv University, it maintains a strong association with the academic environment. In addition, it has a strong association with the political and military establishment."[6] It is no surprise, therefore, to find that top retired army officers-turned-military analysts at the INSS were instrumental in developing the doctrine of "disproportionate force" and the targeting of civilian infrastructure in 2008, based on lessons from the war on Lebanon, and later applied to deadly use in the assault on Gaza. Needless to say, this doctrine is a gross violation of international humanitarian law.[7]

I will move to another, more public and highly visible form of partnership between the military and the university, which is the integration of army personnel and institutions within the universities. Reference is made to two reports for further details, one published by the Alternative Information Center in Jerusalem[8] and the other prepared by the SOAS Palestine Society.[9] An example of the partnership between the academy and the military was expressed thus, before it was removed from the website of the National Security Studies Center at Haifa University:

> For over a decade, the University of Haifa has maintained a special program of graduate studies in national security and strategic studies. This interdisciplinary program, based in the Department of Political Science, has by now trained hundreds of senior officers in the Israeli Defense Forces in modern social science and the various branches of strategic thinking. This program has created a warm and active relationship between the University, on the one hand, and the command of the IDF on the other. The Center builds on this relationship, and institutionalizes the links between the two, performing research tasks that are critical to planning the future needs of security in Israel.[10]

Tel Aviv University has not been hesitant to advertise its close partnership with the defense establishment. An issue of the *Tel Aviv University Review* expresses it well:

> In the rough and tumble reality of the Middle East, Tel Aviv University is at the front line of the critical work to maintain Israel's military and technological edge. While much of that research remains classified, several facts illuminate the role of the university. MAFAT, a Hebrew acronym meaning the R&D Directorate of the Israel Ministry of Defense, is currently funding 55 projects at TAU.... Seven highly-coveted Israel National Security Prizes have been awarded in recent years to members of TAU's Blavatnik School of Computer Science—more than any other institution in the country.[11]

One aspect of the close cooperation with the military is what has been called the academic reserve program, established by the Ministry of Defense and the army, academically administered by universities, and supervised by the Defense Ministry's Directorate for Research and Development (*Maf'at* in Hebrew). The competencies provided by these programs are in high-tech fields needed by industry and the army. About a thousand cadets are recruited by the Israeli Army annually to the academic reserve; students are allowed to postpone their mandatory military service, with the proviso that after graduation they will serve in the military as officers, their service prolonged by three to five years.[12]

One of the programs under this schema is the elite Talpiot program at the Hebrew University, where students excelling in the sciences, physics, and mathematics are recruited for a three-year funded program of study, after which they commit themselves to work for six years with the army's research and development programs. While at the university, the students study in uniform and live at a military base on campus, undergoing military training alongside their academic program. Another well-known program is the Psagot schema at Tel Aviv University and the Technion, the Israel Institute of Technology. Students in all of the academic reserve programs are screened by the military before admission.[13]

A further example is the elite military medical school that was established at the Hebrew University in 2009 after a successful bidding process. It is described by the university as a program based on cooperation between the university, the Ministry of Defense, and the Medical Corps.[14]

In reference to this unique medical school, one only wonders what type of medical ethics are taught there: are students warned against participating in the torture and mistreatment of Palestinian prisoners or of sick Palestinians finding themselves at checkpoints and other Israeli barriers and borders? The Israeli medical establishment has long remained silent in the face of well-documented charges concerning the role of medical personnel in torture and mistreatment of Palestinian prisoners and ill people, despite a vigorous international campaign to hold it accountable to medical ethics if not human rights principles.[15]

On a related issue, four years ago, Haifa University proudly announced its successful bid for an army tender to train graduate students in national security studies. The announcement was made in a routine press release by the rector: "Haifa University is proud to continue being the academic home for the security forces and to teach the IDF leadership a large number of different and diverse perspectives. This is the sole way to be better people and better commanders." It goes on to say that the "winning bid was made possible thanks to close cooperation between the School of Political Studies, Office of the President of the University, Office of the Rector and the Faculty of Social Sciences. The program was designed in collaboration with the IDF's National Security College."[16]

It should be added that major Israeli universities, as with other research universities around the world, are increasingly dependent on industry for support for research activities. In the case of Israel, cuts in government spending have encouraged more cooperation with arms manufacturers in high-tech fields. This partnership puts the earlier orientalist colonial advisors in a somewhat more favorable light, since their work perhaps had less lethal consequences for Palestinian and Arab lives.

The major institutions working with the arms industry are Tel Aviv University, Technion, the Weizman Institute, the Hebrew University, and Ben Gurion University.

As one example, it was announced in 2008 that Elbit Systems, a major Israeli arms developer, had signed a joint research agreement in vision systems with the Technion. Elbit provides electronic detection devices used in the Israeli Separation Wall in the West Bank and has also supplied UAVs (unmanned aerial vehicles) to the Israeli Army for use in combat in the West Bank and Gaza.[17]

According to Who Profits from the Occupation, an Israeli BDS group,

> In the month of July 2014 alone, during the peak of the assault on the Gaza Strip, Elbit's profits increased by 6.1%. This is the highest level of increase since 2010 for the company and its valuation on a price-to-earnings basis is near the most expensive in five years. According to economic analysts, Elbit's Haifa-based company is expected to see increasing demand for its products from both the Israeli and foreign governments *who were impressed by its lethal performance in Gaza.*[18]

It should be noted, however, that in the past several years, the international campaign against Elbit Systems has achieved several successes in Norway, Sweden, Denmark, Germany, and, more recently, Brazil.[19] An ongoing campaign in the United States by New Yorkers against the Cornell–Technion Partnership also targets Elbit.[20]

Finally, I would like to touch very briefly on the autonomy of the university. While Israeli academics' associations have been active in recent years protesting the commodification of knowledge and proposed and actual reforms in university governance that would compromise the universities' autonomy, there has been no equivalent protest against the deep involvement of the academy in military and related institutions, particularly after the lethal assault on the Gaza Strip in the winter of 2008–2009 and, more recently, in the summer of 2014. Generally, there have never been any protests by professional and academic associations of physicists, physicians, geographers, mathematicians, political scientists, architects, and others in Israel regarding the moral and professional implications of collaboration with the army, not to mention the danger to the autonomy of the university inherent in such a close partnership with the military. In the meantime, within Israel, universities took a public stance in support of the war in the summer of 2014, and no significant challenge was forthcoming from within the universities.[21]

In this regard, and even though the academic boycott of Israel is resolutely institutional and does not target individual Israeli academics, it is necessary to comment briefly on a frequently made claim that the boycott punishes one of the most antiestablishment communities in Israel, namely Israel's academics. This depiction of Israeli academics is seriously flawed. If we look for public statements initiated by

Israeli academics, we will find that on those occasions when they did take a stand by signing petitions or statements, they focused on the narrow issues of freedom of movement for Palestinian academics and students, ignoring the colonial context within which Israeli measures restricting movement were put in place.

In 2006, the Council of the Israel Academy of Sciences and Humanities decided to protest "a practice recently instituted by the Israeli military authorities, to deny or restrict the passage of Palestinian students and scientists to their venues of academic study or research." However, the resolution itself is so general as to dilute the message:

> The Israel Academy of Sciences and Humanities shall be on record in vigorous and unrelenting opposition to any measures, by any government, restricting or impairing the ability of scientists and students to carry out their scientific work and to discharge their scientific or academic responsibilities. In particular, the Council of the Academy calls on the government of the State of Israel to refrain from instituting any policy that hinders any group of scientists or academics, whether Palestinian or otherwise, from properly discharging their academic responsibilities. Cases where security considerations are deemed to require placing restrictions on a person's movements should be adjudicated as such, on an individual basis and with all due consideration for a person's human rights.[22]

Another example from which the colonial context is glaringly absent is the statement signed by the largest group of Israeli individual petitioners to date, the 2008 statement, "Academic Freedom for Whom?"

> We, past and present members of academic staff of Israeli universities, express great concern regarding the ongoing deterioration of the system of higher education in the West Bank and the Gaza Strip. We protest against the policy of our government which is causing restrictions of freedom of movement, study and instruction, and we call upon the government to allow students and lecturers free access to all the campuses in the Territories, and to allow lecturers and students who hold foreign passports to teach and study without being threatened with withdrawal of residence visas. To leave the situation as it is will cause serious harm to freedom of movement, study and instruction—harm to the foundation of academic freedom, to which we are committed.[23]

The comment from the Palestinian Campaign for the Academic and Cultural Boycott (PACBI) is apt:

> The initiators of the petition reported that out of about 9000 emails sent to Israeli academics… they received email endorsements from only 407 individuals.
> PACBI is neither surprised by the dismal results of this initiative nor indeed by the content of the petition. We note that the petition ignores the basic political context within which the academic freedom of Palestinian academics and students

is being violated. That context is no other than the illegal, four-decades-old military occupation of Palestinian land, an occupation that has striven consistently to destroy Palestinian society and its institutions, including universities and other educational institutions. Forty years of occupation—with whose brutal policies many Israeli academics are personally familiar, if not complicit, through reserve duty—do not figure in the activism of these Israeli academics, do not deserve a note as the only context within which the trampling of Palestinian academic freedom is taking place.[24]

This does not mean that there are no dissident academics in Israel. Many do voice opposition to their government's colonial policies as individuals, and some have initiated Boycott from Within, a BDS support group. But the fact remains that the Israeli academy as an institution is still complicit in violations of international law, grave violations of international humanitarian law, and outright war crimes. We have hope that the resounding calls from around the world to boycott Israel and its institutions will contribute to the struggle for justice and liberation for the Palestinian people.

2

GAZA AND BDS!

HAIDAR EID

On August 9, 2014, hundreds of thousands of people worldwide took to the streets in response to a call from Palestinian civil society in the occupied and besieged Gaza Strip and the Boycott, Divestment, Sanctions National Committee (BNC) for a Day of Rage. This mobilization came as grassroots pressure mounted on complicit Western governments to impose a military embargo on Israel. In its call for a Day of Rage, Palestinian civil society made it absolutely clear that

> As we face the full might of Israel's military arsenal, funded and supplied by the United States and the European Union, we call on civil society and people of conscience throughout the world to pressure governments to sanction Israel and implement a comprehensive arms embargo immediately. Take to the streets…with a united demand for sanctions on Israel.[1]

In response to an earlier call issued by the same civil society organizations in Gaza and endorsed by the BNC, Spain had announced "provisional" suspension of military exports to Israel on July 31. On August 7, Evo Morales, president of Bolivia, became the first head of state to declare his support for boycott, divestment, and sanctions (BDS). These actions were a precursor to the global support for Gaza and Palestine shown on August 9.

The Israeli wrath inflicted on the Palestinians of Gaza, two-thirds of whom are refugees entitled to the right of return, comes within an ideological context of tribal bigotry, racism, and exclusivism. In 2004, Israeli professor Arnon Soffer, head of the Israeli Occupation Force's National Defense College and advisor to Ariel Sharon, spelled out Israel's macabre expectations for the unilateral Israeli disengagement from Gaza (2005) in an interview with the *Jerusalem Post*:

> When 1.5 million people live in a closed-off Gaza, it's going to be a human catastrophe. Those people will become even bigger animals than they are today….

The pressure at the border will be awful. It's going to be a terrible war. So, if we
want to remain alive, we will have to kill and kill and kill. All day, every day....
If we don't kill, we will cease to exist.... Unilateral separation doesn't guarantee
"peace"—it guarantees a Zionist-Jewish state with an overwhelming majority of
Jews...[2]

The resemblance of Israel's campaign of tribal racist hate both to that of apartheid South Africa and to Hitler's murderous regime has recently been articulated
by African National Congress (ANC) freedom fighter and former South African
cabinet minister, Ronnie Kasrils, himself a Jew:

Certainly we South Africans can identify the pathological cause, fuelling the hate,
of Israel's political-military elite and public in general. Neither is this difficult for
anyone acquainted with colonial history to understand the way in which deliberately cultivated race hate inculcates a justification for the most atrocious and
inhumane actions against even defenseless civilians—women, children, the elderly
amongst them. In fact was this not the pathological racist ideology that fuelled
Hitler's war lust and implementation of the Holocaust?[3]

The Israeli establishment's stated goal of annihilating Palestinians to manage
the "demographic threat" and to maintain "calm" by "mowing the lawn" (Israeli-
speak for flattening Gaza every two years) is exactly why we in Palestine have concluded that the Palestinian struggle for self-determination must work to isolate
apartheid Israel in the same way that apartheid South Africa was isolated through
a BDS campaign.

Today, there is a growing, mass-based, nonviolent struggle inside Palestine,
alongside other forms of struggle, exactly as there was inside apartheid South Africa. It is also evident today that the Palestinian BDS campaign, modeled on the
South African antiapartheid global campaign, is gaining momentum as a democratic movement based on the universality of human rights and the implementation
of international law. These values are the antithesis of Zionism, Israel's hegemonic
ideology, which is about religious, ethnic, and racial superiority. Our struggle, like
that of Blacks in South Africa and African Americans in the United States, is inclu-
sive and pluralistic: one that maintains our humanity and dignity in the face of a
racist, genocidal state.

This is exactly what Steve Biko, a hero of the South African antiapartheid
struggle—who paid with his life for the freedom of all South Africans—meant
when he said:

Not only have the whites been guilty of being on the offensive, but by some skilful
manoeuvres, they have managed to control the responses of the blacks to the prov-

ocation. Not only have they kicked the black, but they have also told him how to react to the kick. For a long time the black has been listening with patience to the advice he has been receiving on how best to respond to the kick. With painful slowness he is now beginning to show signs that it is his right and duty to respond to the kick in the way he sees fit.[4]

And we Palestinians have decided to respond to the Zionist kick in the way we see fit! And for that, we need the support of the freedom-loving "every man and every woman," as opposed to the complicit, official world leaders who have chosen to support oppression and blame the victim. Now is the time for global civil society to help us end Israeli racism and genocide. The only way to ensure a just peace and redress for Palestinian dispossession is for global civil society to intensify the boycott of the apartheid Israeli state and to advocate for divestment from Israel and sanctions against it.

Veteran Australian journalist John Pilger wrote in the *New Statesman* on the 2009 assault on Gaza, "What happens in Gaza is the defining moment of our time, which either grants the impunity of war criminals the immunity of our silence, while we contort our own intellect and morality, or gives us the power to speak out."[5]

The global masses that demonstrated their support for Palestinian rights on the Day of Rage remind us of the demonstrations in the 1980s against apartheid South Africa. These global protests since 2009 have shown us in Palestine that this is our "South Africa moment." Just as the South African internal, mass-based, antiapartheid struggle and the international antiapartheid boycott and solidarity movement brought an end to the apartheid regime, Palestinians, with the support of people of conscience worldwide, will bring an end to Israel's multitiered system of oppression. Figures of the public profile and influence of Desmond Tutu, Stephen Hawking, Ahmed Kathrada, Roger Waters, Naomi Klein, Alice Walker, Judith Butler, John Berger, and Aijaz Ahmed—to mention but a few—have reached the conclusion that Israel's system of occupation, colonization, and apartheid cannot be brought to an end without ending international complicity and intensifying global solidarity, particularly in the form of BDS.

Governments across the world must be forced to act in accordance with the will of their people, to hold apartheid Israel accountable for war crimes and impose sanctions and an arms embargo. People of conscience globally have spoken and their voices have reached us here in Gaza. We know that their voices have been heard in the capitals of the world and that their voices signal an end to Israeli apartheid. The clock is ticking.

BDS AND ACCOUNTABILITY

As BDS activists, we are no longer interested in the sterile opposition to normalization generated by the Oslo Accords, but rather in formulating the kind of response that could actually defeat multiple forms of Zionist oppression, such as occupation, ethnic cleansing, and apartheid. The moment the entire international community—civil society and governments—decides to act the same way it did against the apartheid system of white South Africa, Israel would succumb to the voice of reason represented by the 2005 BDS call, which was issued by more than 170 civil society organizations and endorsed by almost all influential political forces across the political spectrum in historic Palestine and the diaspora.

Since the world is showing a growing disapproval of Israel's occupation of the West Bank and its settlement policies there, the urgent question now is: How long will the world tolerate Israel's blatant constitutional racism? The latest BDS success, the American Studies Association (ASA) resolution to endorse a boycott of Israeli academic institutions is, in fact, what we have been calling for since the 2004 launch of the Palestinian Campaign for the Academic and Cultural Boycott of Israel (PACBI). It is a strong indicator that the tide is changing in the Western mainstream against Israel's occupation, colonization, and apartheid, and that BDS is fast reaching its South Africa moment.

I, as a resident of Gaza and an academic, have been unable to fathom how it is that some reputable universities sign agreements with Israeli universities despite the policy of ethnic cleansing and the war crimes committed by Israel against the people of Gaza. Israeli academic institutions are known to be complicit in Israel's policy of colonization and apartheid. Is it not crystal clear, after all these years and thousands of reports by mainstream human rights organizations, that millions of Palestinians are denied the full right to education in the occupied Palestinian territories and in the refugee camps? Think about it—our education is denied because of more than six hundred Israeli checkpoints, the medieval siege of Gaza, and the apartheid-like discrimination faced by Palestinian students in Israel. We are discriminated against for the simple fact that we were not born to Jewish mothers. Thousands of Palestinian students and lecturers are in Israeli dungeons, often without trial or having been sentenced by military courts.[6] All credible international human rights and humanitarian organizations have detailed how the Israeli military deliberately targets Palestinian students and schools, including UN schools. Shouldn't academics and researchers be familiar with those reports?

We believe that it is our right to expect people of conscience, especially academics and students, to join us in our struggle against Israeli apartheid by boycotting this intransigent, racist, and militarized Israeli regime and the institutions that keep it thriving.

ASA members must have found it unconscionable that their association remained complicit in Palestinian oppression by pretending to do "business as usual" with apartheid. We Palestinians are an oppressed people without a state. We increasingly rely on international law and solidarity for our very survival. What we want is the implementation of international law: putting an end to the Israeli military occupation of Arab lands occupied in 1967, fighting against the policy of colonization and apartheid as practiced by Israel against the indigenous population of Palestine of 1948, and granting the right of return to Palestinian refugees who were ethnically cleaned in 1948. Now, is that a call for the end of the state of Israel? Was the boycott of apartheid meant to end South Africa as a country—or to end racism in its ugliest form?

Israel is a settler-colonialist, apartheid state, and the methods—or tools of struggle—used against apartheid South Africa can be used as a model in our struggle against apartheid Israel. Transforming Israel from an ethno-religious apartheid state into a democracy should be the objective of every single person believing in liberal democracy in general.

With pressure imposed by the international community through a BDS campaign similar to the antiapartheid campaign that brought apartheid South Africa to an end, we believe that Israel itself can be pressured to end its multitiered system of oppression. The BDS campaign is intended to lead to satisfying the democratic rights of the Palestinian people in its three components—including, of course, the Palestinian citizens of the state of Israel, who experience Israel's institutional racism firsthand. That is why one of the major demands of the BDS campaign, defended by all those who have endorsed the abovementioned BDS call in 2005, is the call for the end of the policy of apartheid practiced against the Palestinians of 1948. We strongly believe that the struggles of the Palestinian people, whether in 1948 or in 1967—that is to say, in the West Bank and Gaza Strip, and even in the diaspora—are inseparable. That is why we think that our rights-based alternative to Oslo's façade of "peace" based on normalization can provide *all* Palestinians with a solution that guarantees the right of return and equality for the 1948 inhabitants. We therefore strongly believe that the only available mechanism of accountability at the moment is BDS!

To echo a quote often attributed to Mahatma Gandhi: in 2005 they ignored the BDS call, then they laughed at us, now they are fighting us, then we will certainly win!

3

IT STARTS WITH KNOWING WHERE YOU WANT TO GO

RIMA NAJJAR MERRIMAN

For the past couple of years, the impending death of the two-state proposition in Israel/Palestine has been repeatedly announced in the media, but often only in the context of a warning. These alarms ignore the reality that the concept was dead on arrival, because it never guaranteed the minimum national and political rights of the Palestinian people in all their components—those living in the diaspora, in Israel, and in the West Bank and Gaza. Without a two-state arrangement, the warning goes, we are left with one state and a demographic threat to Israel's Jewishness. But, in fact, the status quo right now reflects Israeli-Jewish control that extends over most of historic Palestine.[1]

Throughout the Oslo years, the mainstream discourse on Israel/Palestine was hostage to the "peace process," which advocated for a Palestinian state alongside a racist Jewish state at the same time as it turned a blind eye to Israel's illegal settlements and annexation of East Jerusalem and the Palestinian Ghor (Jordan Valley).[2] The dominant narrative is Israel-centered with Israel's "security" and Israel's "right" to exist as a racist, apartheid Jewish state taking precedent over Palestinian rights. But thanks to high-profile boycott, divestment, and sanctions (BDS) successes in 2014,[3] among other developments—such as Israel's latest inhumane bombardment of the Gaza Strip as well as a strong backlash resulting from the Steven Salaita[4] case and the zealous counter-campaign against BDS academics by overreaching Zionist groups such as the AMCHA Initiative[5]—the balance of power in controlling the discourse on Israel/Palestine is shifting, and Palestinian voices as well as voices in the solidarity movement are being raised, boldly reclaiming the right to claim *all* Palestinian rights.

The vigor of the counterattack against these raised voices is a measure of the threat that BDS successes pose for Israel's "national security."[6] But these voices are still finding their way into the mainstream through cautious formulations.[7] In December 2013, American Studies Association (ASA) members voted to endorse a resolution that referred, first and foremost, to the significant role that the United States plays in "enabling the Israeli occupation of Palestine and the expansion of illegal settlements and the Wall in violation of international law," and also pointed out the constraints on "effective or substantive academic freedom for Palestinian students and scholars under conditions of Israeli occupation."[8] The document ends with the resolve to "honor the call of Palestinian civil society for a boycott of Israeli academic institutions" without specifying the ultimate demand or goal that the academic boycott is meant to achieve—ethical decolonization[9] in all of historic Palestine, equality, and justice for all Palestinians, including those in the diaspora. According to the BDS movement, the call for the "non-violent punitive" measures of boycott and sanctions are to be maintained until "Israel meets its obligation to recognize the Palestinian people's inalienable right to self-determination and fully complies with the precepts of international law by: 1) Ending its occupation and colonization of all Arab lands and dismantling the Wall; 2) Recognizing the fundamental rights of the Arab-Palestinian citizens of Israel to full equality; and 3) Respecting, protecting and promoting the rights of Palestinian refugees to return to their homes and properties as stipulated in UN resolution 194."[10]

At the time of the ASA resolution, there was a lack of clarity among BDS solidarity activists as to what "Israel's obligation to recognize the Palestinian people's inalienable right to self determination, etc." actually meant in practice. Mahmoud Abbas, whose elected term in office has long expired,[11] his Palestinian Authority (PA), and the defunct Palestinian Liberation Organization (PLO)[12] contributed to this confusion in no small measure. In November 2012 their bid to upgrade the PA United Nations status from "non-member observer entity" to "non-member observer state" was successful. But what did this development mean? Solidarity groups took various positions on the question of statehood and others wondered what position to adopt.[13]

The Palestinian BDS National Committee (BNC) explicitly defined, in August 2011, the goal behind recognition of statehood at the international level:

> Diplomatic recognition must result in protection of the inalienable right to self-determination of the entire Palestinian people represented by a democratized and inclusive PLO that represents not just Palestinians under occupation, but also the exiled refugees, the majority of the Palestinian people, as well as the discriminated citizens of Israel …. The most fundamental, inalienable right of the people of Palestine is the right to self determination. Ending the occupation is

one pillar in exercising that right. The right to self-determination, which in the case of Palestinians is represented by the Palestine Liberation Organization (PLO), is commonly defined as the right of "all peoples … freely to determine, without external interference, their political status and to pursue their economic, social and cultural development." It is a right held by all Palestinians, irrespective of their current location, by virtue of international law and the principles of popular sovereignty and democracy. All Palestinians, including the refugees in the *shatat* (diaspora) and Palestinian citizens of Israel, have a right to participate in and be represented by—in the UN and elsewhere—a democratic PLO that determines the political status and pursues the economic, social and cultural development of the entire Palestinian people.[14]

Although many, most notably Edward Said,[15] recognized the Oslo Accords as a sham early on, the illusion of a viable independent Palestinian state alongside Israel was fostered by Fatah, along with other major Palestinian political factions, who are all complicit in the Palestinian political failure to date.[16] This illusion took root in a whole generation of Palestinians in the occupied territories, largely through an exploitative economic system that is now deeply entrenched.[17] With every setback to the US-backed "peace process," with every flagrant violation of international and humanitarian law on the part of the Israeli government,[18] Israel chipped away at the option of a two-state negotiated settlement that it never really desired in the first place.[19]

Efforts to achieve a "two-state solution" have finally collapsed. As the most recent US-led negotiations were meandering toward their inevitable end,[20] many in the BDS movement were wondering where the struggle was headed. The discussion at first appeared to revolve around the dichotomy of one state or two states. Omar Barghouti had this to say on the subject: "The BDS movement is neutral on the issue of one state vs. two states, because we are not a political movement. We are a human rights movement. The predominant majority in the coalition of Palestinian civil society are for two states, in fact. But we say, regardless of the political outcome, Israel must accommodate the three basic Palestinian human rights—ending the occupation, ending the apartheid system, and allowing Palestinian refugees to return."[21] Ali Abunimah reiterated the same idea, adding that these rights can be more easily met through one democratic state. The PA's response to the collapse of the negotiations (this time without the PLO) was to submit a UN resolution draft in December 2014 setting a deadline (2017) for Israel to withdraw from the occupied West Bank and Gaza. This draft was blasted by Fatah's Marwan Barghouti[22] and other Palestinian political factions, who still believed in the possibility of two states (except for Hamas[23]), quibbling only

over "wording."[24] The PA revisions of the draft as reported in *Haaretz* defined East
Jerusalem as the capital of the Palestinian state and included a demand for full
sovereignty over all areas captured after June 4, 1967, emphasizing the idea that
all the Jewish settlements violate international law and that any demographic and
geographic changes made by Israel are illegal. But these were not shared with other
factions before being submitted.

The only option under consideration in this resolution is the two-state option,
which will inevitably entail "a Jewish state for a Jewish people" in Israel.[25] In response to the draft resolution, Ali Abunimah invoked the BDS call: "I evaluate any
steps related to Palestine through a simple and consistent lens: does this measure
take us closer to the fulfillment of Palestinian rights, all Palestinian rights? These
rights are set out most succinctly in the Palestinian call for boycott, divestment and
sanctions (BDS).... Those 'recognition' initiatives are an effort to undo the death
of the 'two-state solution' and rescue Israel as a racist Jewish state."[26] When Marwan
Barghouti wrote from prison, objecting to the wording of the UN resolution draft
of statehood that the PA submitted, he stated: "I have always urged the Palestinian
leadership to take the question of Palestine to the UN to obtain a Security Council
resolution, but any proposal must be in line with inalienable national principles."[27]
The predominant majority in the coalition of Palestinian civil society in favor of
two states also takes the same position.

In reaching out to the UN Security Council, the PA had to water down its proposal in order to garner political support.[28] It tabled "final status issues" and proposed a return to the "peace process," which has unequivocally proven, throughout
the Oslo years, to be aimed at consolidating a Zionist Jewish state based on colonial
and racial privileges alongside a fake Palestinian state.[29]

In an important article in the *Electronic Intifada* titled "Recognizing Palestine,
BDS and the Survival of Israel," Joseph Massad points out that the parliaments
of some EU countries and the EU Parliament itself are using BDS as a goal to
"strengthen the Jewish settler-colony and the Israeli liberal project that backs it" and
to guarantee the survival of Israel as a racist state. He also criticizes the recent resolutions of academic associations, describing their efforts thus far in many cases as
"the result of long and fierce battles waged by members deeply committed to all Palestinian rights, [but] they mostly fail to articulate positions that accord with all the
explicit goals of BDS. Indeed, not one of these organizations mentioned the third
goal of BDS, namely the right of the Palestinian refugees to return, which Israel
continues to deny in defiance of UN resolutions and international law in order to
safeguard a Jewish majority in the country." Massad concludes: "Palestinians must

insist that those in solidarity with them adopt BDS as a strategy and not as a goal, in order to bring about an end to Israel's racism and colonialism in all its forms inside and outside the 1948 boundaries."[30]

Articulating positions that accord with all the explicit goals of BDS, especially the third goal referring to the return of refugees, is considered by Israel and its supporters to be a threat not only to the "national security" of Israel but also to that of the United States.[31] In moves that echo the backlash by funders against Steven Salaita, who was fired from a tenured position at University of Illinois at Urbana–Champaign, even people such as Chris Hedges and Ari Roth, who by their own admission support Zionism and "Israel's right to exist within the (1949–67) borders," have been attacked and penalized for criticizing Israel—journalist Hedges was disinvited from speaking at the University of Pennsylvania[32] and Roth was fired as artistic director of Theater J in Washington, DC.[33]

The BDS message that is now slowly becoming more dominant is expressed clearly in Ali Abunimah's book *The Battle for Justice in Palestine*, and it is simply this:

> We don't need to allow our vision of justice to be constrained only by what seems realistic from the perspective of today, and especially not by what powerful and privileged groups deem acceptable or pragmatic. Frederick Douglass's observation that "power concedes nothing without a demand" remains as true today as it did during the struggle to abolish slavery. Things change because people change them—and as situations change, so do the boundaries of what is considered achievable. But it starts with knowing where you want to go.[34]

The BDS movement defines what is happening in Israel/Palestine as a struggle for justice, not as a "conflict" in which the oppressor and the oppressed have equal claims. In the past couple of years, we have seen an Israel that has come out in the open with its racism and strategic goals, without shame or conscience, confident in its impunity from censure.[35] The failure of the Security Council to pass even the undesirable PA draft resolution demonstrates a lack of political will among the strongest UN member states to bring justice to the Palestinian people in their struggle for self-determination against a settler-colonial regime. It is time for the peace process charade to end. Also, importantly, it is time for Palestinian activists to "push the PLO to reconfigure national priorities, with refugees and the right of return at the center of the cause and not its margins."[36] Considering economic sovereignty and the refugees' right of return in combination with Israel's insistence on being recognized as a Jewish state, and so on, it becomes clear how unbridgeable the two positions are.

The news about Palestinians, as 2014 comes to a close, is incredibly daunting and grim, most of which goes unreported in the mainstream media. In breach of the August truce, Gazans are fired upon by Israel almost on a daily basis,[37] and they remain encaged, as the Rafah crossing is closed "until further notice."[38] Legalized discrimination against Arab Palestinian citizens of Israel and racial harassment in daily life are on the rise,[39] as are administrative detention orders—orders for imprisonment without charge or trial[40]—and the killing of Palestinians by Israeli forces with no justification for using deadly weapons in the West Bank.[41] About 85 percent of Palestinian refugees living in Yarmouk Camp near Damascus have fled the fighting in Syria and subsist in dire poverty, with little hope of relief.[42]

And yet, as Ramzy Baroud writes, 2014 is also a year "in which the collective resistance of the Palestinian people, and their supporters, proved too strong to bend or break." Baroud discusses five developments that he believes are game changers:

> 1) The long-orchestrated plot to divide Palestinians is breaking apart and a new collective narrative of a common struggle against occupation is finally forming.
> 2) The debate regarding what form of resistance Palestinians should or should not adopt is being sidelined and settled, not by international do-gooders, but by Palestinians themselves. They are opting to use whatever effective form of resistance they can that could deter Israeli military advances, as resistance groups have actively done in Gaza.
> 3) BDS successes have normalized the debate on Israel in many circles around the world. While any criticism of Israel was considered a taboo in yesteryears, it has been forever broken.
> 4) The debauched EU policy toward Palestinians is being challenged by citizens of various European countries. The Israeli summer 2014 war on Gaza exposed Israel's human rights violations and war crimes like never before, revealing along the way EU hypocrisy.
> 5) The Jewish and democratic paradigm is dying for good, exposing Israel's reality the way it is.[43]

The changing political landscape in Israel/Palestine today gives rise to a "crucially needed dose of educated hope," as Omar Barghouti describes Abunimah's *The Battle for Justice in Palestine*, a book whose first sentence is "Palestinians are winning."[44] Abunimah draws important lessons from solidarity struggles waged by Palestinian rights activists on campuses and communities in the United States and elsewhere. Forget about bogus diplomatic efforts, he says. Focus on global grassroots organizing for justice and demand decolonization in order to establish one secular and democratic state for all those living in historic Palestine. Make economic justice a central part of the discussion, and deepen the solidarity between various struggles for equality. As Omar Barghouti puts it, the BDS movement "has dragged

Israel and its well-financed, bullying lobby groups into a confrontation on a bat-tlefield where the moral superiority of the Palestinian quest for self-determination, justice, freedom, and equality neutralizes and outweighs Israel's military power and financial prowess."[45] This quest is where Palestinians want to go.

4

THE ACADEMIC BOYCOTT
OF ISRAEL AND ITS CRITICS

MAGID SHIHADE

"Besiege your siege, there is no alternative."
—Mahmoud Darwish

INTRODUCTION

In this short chapter, I will address several points that are often raised for and against the academic boycott of Israeli institutions. The perspectives here are those of a Palestinian with Israeli citizenship, who after high school attended the Hebrew University for one year and then decided to leave the country to study abroad, first in Germany, then in the United States, where I completed my graduate studies and taught as adjunct faculty at various colleges and universities in the field of Middle East studies. I was never offered a full-time position in the United States and thus have taught in many different places, the most recent among them Birzeit University in Palestine. Mine is also the perspective of a cofounder of the US Campaign for the Academic and Cultural Boycott of Israel (USACBI). This chapter, while weaving between the personal and the collective, argues for boycott and offers some ideas and insights on how to proceed in the context of current debates around this issue. The first part will address points raised by detractors; the second part of the chapter will engage with important issues often raised by those who are interested in the boycott but still have reservations.

I.

While engaging with several points raised by detractors of the academic boycott of Israeli institutions, one could relate a personal story—supported and corroborated by many sources and thus not exceptional, and hence reflective of a collective experience—that might shed light on the limited academic freedom and access Palestinians with Israeli citizenship have in the Israeli education system; on how the Israeli education system designed for Arabs (Palestinian citizens of Israel) aims at degrading Arab and Muslim history, while idealizing Zionism and "Jewish" history in order to push Palestinians to identify with it and reject their own culture; and on the aim of Israeli education to create a new identity for Palestinian citizens as "Israeli-Arab" or as sects (Muslims, Christians, Druze) as a means to suppress Palestinian national identity and demobilize the Palestinian community.

One could also tell a personal story about making a trip to the university because the office of admissions wouldn't return a call or respond to a letter about the status of one's application, and on the way to the university being dragged out of the bus by Israeli soldiers who told the bus driver to continue the trip, being humiliated and belittled as an Arab going to the university, left in the open air afterward, not knowing where one is. One could also describe how after receiving the best grades in the region where one grew up, and scoring high grades on the national Israeli exam, not being allowed to pursue certain subjects at the university. One was allowed to study only "Arabic and Middle Eastern history," and as an introductory course all students had to take a class on Arab nationalism. In that class, we were told by the Israeli professor that we were not Arabs, and that we would pass the class only if we wrote accordingly on the final exam. One could write about how on campus Arabs are monitored and surveilled upon entry and exit to and from campus and housing, or about repression of political dissent on campus.

One could also talk about the way Israeli authorities since 1948 have been using schooling and education in general as a form of surveillance, of repression, and of punishment and reward in order to increase internal frictions and suspicion within the Palestinian community.

Or, finally, one could talk about a Palestinian academic with Israeli citizenship who cannot get a long-term visa for his partner in Israel so that they could live together, and, as a result, both continue to live like nomads, moving from one place to another with months of separation each year.

Moving the narrative from the personal to the collective, one can start by talking about the destruction of archives and institutions of learning since the massive book robbery of 1948 by the Zionist forces. In the intervening years, education, writing, and archives continue to be targeted by Israeli policies, as exemplified by the attacks on academic institutions, research centers, laboratories, and archives as occurred during the most recent Israeli invasion in the West Bank and Gaza. Restrictions on access and mobility for Palestinians to study at Palestinian institutions continue to be the norm, especially following the so-called peace process, whereby students from Gaza can no longer study in the West Bank and vice versa, which contributes to separation and further isolation of the student body in each location. Due to Israeli control of travel permits, Palestinian scholars in areas colonized in 1967 continue to face restrictions on travel for conferences. Also continuing unabated are the restrictions on the import of lab supplies to universities that have been in place since the beginning of Israeli occupation in 1967.

Take Birzeit University as an example. Especially since the start of the Oslo period, the university has become more localized in the makeup of its student body, compared to the past. The university has become more neoliberal in its finances, relying highly on grants from USAID, Open Society, and the like for philanthropic funding, as well as on grants from the EU, various European countries, and Canada. This funding is accompanied by the dumping of mainstream books on the university by these donors, while free and easy book imports are denied. Thus, the student body and faculty are ghettoized and their scope of thinking and research provincialized.

Speaking of the real boycott!

International scholars and students who wish to engage with Palestinian education, again taking Birzeit as an example, cannot say openly at the time of entry through Israeli-controlled borders that they are going to Birzeit University. Rather, they have to lie about their visit and say that they are entering as tourists. Thus, their length of stay is limited to a three-month tourist visa, and, if they wish to stay longer, they have to keep exiting and reentering the country every three months, often risking lengthy interrogations and possible denial of visa renewal.

Both international scholars and Palestinians with Israeli citizenship who wish to work at a Palestinian educational institution in the West Bank must do so in secret. International students can only study at Palestinian universities for short periods due to visa restrictions by Israeli authorities, and thus their ability to engage with the Palestinian community is severely restricted. All of this contributes to the undermining of education and educational exchange for Palestinians and international scholars.

Speaking of the real boycott!!

Some might argue that the issues above may be similar to those of other states, and thus the question is often raised: Why focus on Israel? I think this is an important topic because it is based on denial of the repression and silencing in the US academy around Israel, which is unlike the case with any other state. From repression of Palestinian activism on campuses to interference in courses by outside Zionist groups, warnings to graduate students to avoid an academic specialization on Israel if one is critical, blacklisting of scholars who are not supportive of Israel, blocking of employment, and even loss of tenured jobs because of critique of Israel—all of these make the case that Israel is an exception in the United States.

In my case, for example, despite my record of honors, grants, and fellowships, along with my list of publications, I did not receive one job offer in the United States. In interviews for academic positions I have been asked about terms used in the titles of my papers and book: "colonialism" and "settler-colonialism," which seemed strange to an interviewing faculty member, a participant in the systematic normalizing of an abnormal state, a systematic denial of the Israeli state's accurate description and structure—a settler-colonial state. In other interviews I have been asked my opinion on political figures and groups: Hamas, Fatah, Yasser Arafat, and so forth. I was astonished to read the letter that came in response to one application. Rather than the usual verbiage of "thanks for applying for this position, etc., it was a difficult choice, but the committee chose the candidate who was the best fit," I received an additional informal apology, imbued with a sense of guilt in that the letter specified, "The department chose a progressive Jewish Israeli for the position." I looked up the academic record of the person mentioned in the letter and found only one co-edited article in an obscure local journal, a rehash of the much-discussed "two state solution" in a summary of pieces previously written on the subject; nothing new or original.

In many discussions around who might be harmed by the boycott, the concern is always with Israeli scholars. This discourse is accompanied by a denial and erasure of Palestinian and Palestinian American voices and concerns, as well as their academic freedom. Furthermore, the boycott targets institutions, not individuals, and thus individual Israeli academics can cooperate with international scholars and have been doing so.

In sum, there is already a boycott against Palestinians taking place both in Israel and in the United States. Thus, I argue that the boycott against Israeli institutions is a means to open space by normalizing critical views of Israel and the study of Israel in academic institutions and associations to treat it as any other case, without repression and silencing. Boycott may also allow more access to Palestinian voices and can lead to an honest dialogue.

II.

When, in December 2008, a discussion began on an academic listserv in California about how to respond to the Israeli invasion of Gaza, Palestine, some of us thought that keeping silent in the academy amounted to complicity, and at least in part contributed to the dominance of the Zionist narrative both in the academy and among the public at large. For me, at least, the continued silence amounted also to aiding the Israeli and Zionist siege and boycott of Palestinian and Palestinian Americans in body and voice.

Arguments at the time and continuing today, often raised by non-Zionists questioning the usefulness of the boycott as a tool, are not convincing. For example, the argument that boycott focuses on being against Israeli policies rather than helping Palestinians is not convincing; one can do both, and there is no contradiction in doing so. One can boycott Israeli institutions and at the same time, which is very important, work to collaborate with Palestinian academics and open space for them.

Often one hears that boycott resolutions must be pursued if success is to be guaranteed. To follow such an approach to its logical end would mean that no resolution at any association could be pursued, since success is never guaranteed. Furthermore, pursuing a boycott resolution, while the aim is to be adopted, is more concerned with fostering debate, awareness, discussion, and knowledge about Israel and its harmful policies against Palestinians and their education.

Related to the previous argument is the stance that boycott resolutions are to be pursued only when members and officials in the association are ready to adopt them. Here again, such a line of reasoning would effectively block us from pursuing boycott resolution at all, since one can never know when associations' officials are ready. We can only gain that knowledge by pursuing boycott resolutions. These arguments have even been made regarding associations' members whose focus of study is the Middle East. Such arguments assume that we know more, but they can only be tested if resolutions are proposed and debated.

Some argue that junior academics and graduate students are afraid of openly supporting boycott resolutions against Israel because they fear the ramifications for job opportunities and tenure. Thus, they conclude, they should not take a public position on this issue. This argument assumes that sympathy for Zionism is strong at academic institutions in the United States, but it does not reflect reality. For example, at the American Studies Association (ASA), many junior academics and graduate students openly argued for the boycott. Furthermore, such an argument basically calls for the majority of the academic world to remain silent, since junior faculty and graduate students comprise the largest sector in the academy. How can change occur if this is the case? I believe that the more graduate students and junior faculty, as well as senior faculty, who speak up against censorship about Israel in the academy, the safer it will be for everyone, and the harder it will be for outside groups to target academics.

Each association has its own sense of exceptionalism. Some associations profess that they have no connection to the study of Israel/Palestine. But, as stated earlier in the article, Americans are already implicated in Israeli settler-colonialism, and this claim of innocence is a form of denial and evasion of responsibility. Even when an association has a connection to the region, officials invariably cite other forms of exceptionalism, as in the case of Middle East studies; for example, that the association is partially funded by the US government and thus risks losing revenues. But the question should be why such an association does not follow the example of others that are funded by membership dues and private donations?

Some argue that pursuing boycott resolutions is a political act and that academic associations should focus only on academic issues. This is not only contrary to the history of political stands that many associations have taken over decades, but is also, in my view, anti-intellectual and represents a political argument in its own right, for not taking a political stand is in itself a political position.

Boycotting Israeli institutions does not target individual Israeli academics. Academics in the United States can continue to collaborate with them. Furthermore, many progressive Israeli academics have themselves called for boycott as the only alternative that can push for change. Finally, these arguments never take into consideration Palestinian academics and the harmful Israeli policies against them individually and against Palestinian academic institutions in general. Why do Palestinian academics matter less, if at all, in these debates?

CONCLUSION

As Israeli academia is implicated in repression and racism against Palestinians, and Israeli policies harm and target Palestinian education, students, academics, and institutions, the arguments against the boycott are flawed. Given the sense of impunity that the Israeli government enjoys, as reflected in its policies, and owing to the heavy implication of the United States in the Israeli settler-colonial project, denial, evasion, and silence can no longer be accepted: a boycott movement in the United States must respond to the Palestinian civil society call for boycott. This should acknowledge the fact discussed briefly above, that a boycott against Palestinians in Palestine and the diaspora is already in place.

Since the launch of USACBI in 2008–2009, and after much hard work by many of its participants, the boycott movement has grown with very positive results, as is reflected in the boycott resolutions of many academic associations over the past couple of years and the discussions taking place at many other associations. In addition, more Palestinian voices are being heard in all these associations, and the silence surrounding Israel and the boycott of Palestinian voices is breaking apart. The only way forward is to continue with these efforts while paying attention to the potential pitfalls that can happen with any movement.

The boycott against Palestinians in Palestine and elsewhere and against pro-Palestinian voices on US campuses is already in place, and the only way to counter the surveillance, repression, and silencing is by going further with more boycott resolutions against Israel in all academic associations, opening the space for more honest discussion, and increasing the numbers in the boycott movement to make it safe to stand for justice in Palestine.

In the loosely translated words of Mahmoud Darwish, the internally displaced Palestinian poet who graduated from the same high school as I did in Kafr Yassif, Galilee: "In times of siege, we have no alternative but to besiege the state of siege in the hope to open new horizons for us and others."

II. Taking On the Settler-Colonial University:

Academic Boycott and Academic Freedom

5

THE ACADEMIC BOYCOTT OF ISRAEL: REACHING A TIPPING POINT?

OMAR BARGHOUTI

Shabtai Shavit, longtime former chief of the Israeli Mossad, recently wrote: "For the first time since I began forming my own opinion, I am truly concerned about the future of the Zionist project," citing "the critical mass of the threats" compiled against Israel.[1] The strained relations with the United States came first in his list of perceived threats, followed immediately by the potential of Europe "imposing sanctions" and the growth of the Palestinian-led global boycott, divestment, and sanctions (BDS) movement.

Shavit specified: "University campuses in the West, particularly in the U.S., are hothouses for the future leadership of their countries. We are losing the fight for support for Israel in the academic world. An increasing number of Jewish students are turning away from Israel. The global BDS movement...against Israel, which works for Israel's delegitimization, has grown, and quite a few Jews are members."[2]

The most decorated Israeli general, Ehud Barak—who in 2012, as defense minister, upgraded the settler-colonial Ariel College, built on occupied Palestinian land, to a university[3]—concurred with Shavit's fears:

> Gradual processes of Israel's delegitimization are occurring below the surface. The BDS movement is developing.... Look at Israel's standing in the community of labor organizations worldwide—it's a very grim situation. That will continue with consumer organizations, pension funds, the universities.... These groups are quantitatively negligible, but in terms of their essence, they are the future leadership of the United States and of the world. It's a gradual trend, but it's sliding toward a tipping point, and at the end of that tipping point awaits a slope or, heaven forbid, an abyss.[4]

Putting aside the peculiar use of the term "delegitimization,"[5] intentionally used by Israeli officials in attacking BDS, the expansion into the mainstream of the Palestinian-led, global BDS movement in the last two years—especially on US campuses, among some of the largest European pension funds and banks, as well as in cultural spheres—has sent a rare wake-up call to the Israeli regime[6] of occupation, settler-colonialism, and apartheid.[7]

The principled and very valuable role played by anticolonial Israeli academics, cultural figures, and activists, especially those in the group Boycott from Within,[8] in the BDS movement has helped aggravate the Israeli establishment, considerably undermining the arguments of "us versus them" and "anti-Semitism" often lobbed at any critics of Israel's regime.

If current trends escalate and a new, more principled, democratic, and intelligent Palestinian leadership emerges, Israel may soon be facing its South Africa moment.[9]

BDS Mainstreaming

It is instructive before examining the academic boycott dimension of BDS to look into the overall BDS movement's palpable impact on Israel's world standing and increased isolation. It is worth noting that, according to the BBC's authoritative international public opinion poll, Globescan, Israel is neck and neck with North Korea in its global popularity ranking,[10] despite spending billions on propaganda.

The BDS movement was already perceived by Israel as a "strategic threat"[11] well before the recent Israeli massacre[12] in Gaza. In light of Israel's assault on Gaza, its unprecedented colonization[13] of the occupied West Bank, especially in East Jerusalem, and its overt shift to the far right over the last few years, BDS has witnessed an exceptional streak of qualitative successes.[14]

Begun in 2005 by the largest coalition[15] of Palestinian political parties, trade union federations, refugee advocacy networks, and mass organizations, BDS calls for an end to Israel's 1967 occupation, including the removal of all settlements and the Separation Wall, an end to its institutionalized racial discrimination,[16] which fits the UN definition of apartheid,[17] and the right of Palestinian refugees to return to the homes and lands from which they were uprooted and dispossessed in 1948.[18]

While Israel remains a major nuclear military power and still has a strong economy, thanks mainly to heavy support from and preferential treatment by the West, Israel's international isolation[19] is predicted to escalate.[20] A White House official warns that Israel's isolation may become a "tsunami" if it fails to end its "occupations."[21]

When the crimes against humanity committed by Israel in Gaza were revealed to the world, not only was the grassroots outrage unprecedented but even some Western politicians, whose countries are deeply complicit in enabling Israel's occupation and apartheid, were indignant. A former British deputy prime minister[22] and a former French prime minister[23] called for sanctions. The deputy chairman of Germany's second-largest party called for an arms embargo on Israel, Saudi Arabia, and Qatar.[24] Five Latin American governments[25] imposed diplomatic and trade sanctions,[26] while the Bolivian president, Evo Morales,[27] joined dozens of leading Latin intellectuals and public figures in endorsing the boycott of Israel. The ruling Alliance of South Africa[28] also explicitly adopted BDS.

Oil-rich Kuwait became the first state to implement the August 14 decision of the Organization of Islamic Cooperation to "impose political and economic sanctions on Israel, and boycott the corporations that operate in the colonial settlements built on occupied Palestinian territory."[29] The Kuwaiti Ministry of Trade and Industry[30] said it will no longer deal with fifty international companies and institutions that operate in settlements.

Particularly alarming to Israel is the fact that the boycott has reached India, Turkey, South Africa, and even the captive economy[31] of the occupied Palestinian territory. For the first time in decades, Palestinian consumers, businesses, and a number of municipalities precipitated a flood[32] of popular boycotts[33] against Israeli goods.

Gaza brought the issue of Palestine back to the fore, reviving its status as "the litmus test for human rights," as South African jurist John Dugard describes it.[34] This is most evident in the steady growth of international support, including at the grassroots level in the United States,[35] for pressuring Israel economically,[36] academically,[37] and otherwise until it abides by international law and ends its subjugation of the Palestinian people.

WHY *ACADEMIC* BOYCOTT?

Few forms of pressure have triggered as much alarm in Israel's establishment as the growing divestment movement on US college campuses and the mushrooming support for a comprehensive academic boycott of Israel among US academic associations. In parallel, many individual academics around the world have joined the widespread *silent* academic boycott of Israel—that is, the unannounced, yet very effective, shunning of academic visits to and relations with Israeli academic institutions.

Israel realizes as much as Palestinians and their supporters do that an effective, comprehensive academic boycott of Israel would irreversibly hurt the "Brand Israel"[38] and feed the growing economic boycotts and, eventually, sanctions. Israel's academic institutions, after all, have been one of the pillars of Israel's regime of oppression, playing a major role in planning, implementing, justifying, and whitewashing Israel's crimes against the Palestinian people. Isolating those institutions would deprive Israel of a weapon arguably more potent and effective on a day-to-day basis than its entire nuclear arsenal.

This is why the Palestinian Campaign for the Academic and Cultural Boycott of Israel (PACBI)[39] was established in 2004, a year before the historic call for BDS by Palestinian civil society, which PACBI played a key role in drafting. PACBI consistently advocates a broad boycott of Israeli academic—and cultural—institutions, not individuals. These institutions are partners in denying or hampering the exercise of basic Palestinian rights[40] that are guaranteed by international law, including academic freedom and the right to education.

The complicity of Israeli universities in human rights violations takes many forms, from developing weapon systems and military doctrines used in the commission of Israeli war crimes and crimes against humanity to systematically providing the military-intelligence establishment with indispensable research—on archaeology, demography, geography, hydrology, and psychology, among other disciplines—to tolerating and often rewarding racist speech, theories and "scientific" research. It also includes institutionalizing discrimination[41] against Palestinian Arab citizens, among them scholars and students[42]; suppressing Israeli academic research on Zionism and the *Nakba* (the forced dispossession and eviction of the indigenous Palestinian Arabs during the creation of the State of Israel); and the construction of campus facilities and dormitories in the occupied Palestinian territories, as the Hebrew University has done in East Jerusalem, for instance.[43]

The institutional academic boycott that PACBI has called for is in line with the authoritative call for the academic boycott of Israel issued by the Palestinian Council for Higher Education (CHE) and is endorsed by a wide spectrum of Palestinian civil society, including the Palestinian Federation of Unions of University Professors and Employees (PFUUPE).

By isolating Israeli universities, the cost of their entrenched collusion in human rights violations rises sharply, pressuring them to end it. The academic boycott of Israel remains controversial in some countries, especially in the West, but after Israel's massacre in Gaza it is no longer taboo.

ENTRENCHED COMPLICITY

During the Israeli assault on Gaza in the summer of 2014, Israeli academic institutions issued official statements declaring support[44] for the massacre, promising faculty and student reserve soldiers actively involved in war crimes in Gaza various perks and privileges[45] to show appreciation for their contribution to the state's "security." Israeli academics failed to distinguish themselves from the rest of Jewish-Israeli society, of whom 95 percent found the bloody assault on the Palestinian people in Gaza to be justified, according to a July 2014 poll.[46]

The deep collusion of Israel's academic institutions with the occupation army's crimes against the Palestinian and Lebanese peoples is well documented. Technion (the Israel Institute of Technology), for instance, prides itself on having developed many of the weapon systems, in particular drone technologies, that were employed by the Israeli forces in their bloodbath in Gaza.[47] Not only has Tel Aviv University (TAU) designed dozens of weapons used by the Israeli occupation forces, but its Institute for National Security Studies (INSS) also takes credit for the development of the so-called Dahiya Doctrine[48]—a doctrine of disproportionate force, adopted by the Israeli Army—which calls for "the destruction of the national [civilian] infrastructure, and intense suffering among the [civilian] population," as means of defeating an otherwise "impossible" to defeat nonstatal resistance.[49] As a PACBI statement asserts,[50] "This means that TAU is directly responsible for the deliberate[51] and premeditated commission of war crimes and crimes against humanity[52] in Gaza. Moreover, TAU's leading philosopher, Asa Kasher, has coauthored with an army general an 'ethical' code of conduct for the Israeli Army that justified[53] killing a large number of civilians in the process of targeting resistance fighters."

But universities in many countries in the West are also involved with their respective military establishments, so what makes the complicity of Israeli academic institutions more worthy of censure and boycott? Israeli experts themselves provide a decisive answer to this. Prominent TAU professor Avraham Katzir observed[54] that the relationship between academic institutions and the army in Israel is far more organic and solid than in the West. He argues that "each one of us is both an Israeli citizen and working in these [military] fields." Academia and the army, writes Katzir, are "helping one another–something which doesn't happen [elsewhere]; I've been in the US and Europe, and there there is a disconnect between the [academic] workshops and the army; they hate the army! [With us], I think that we succeed by virtue of the fact that we help one another so much." Haim Russo, CEO of Israeli drone manufacturer Elbit, went further, crediting academia with "standing behind this whole vast [military] industry."[55]

In what PACBI describes[56] as "a new low, even by the already dismal Israeli academic institutions' ethical standards," renowned Israeli academic Mordechai Kedar of Bar-Ilan University urged raping the wives, sisters, and mothers of Palestinian militants as a deterrence tactic.[57]

Organically connected to cheering the murder of Palestinian civilians in Gaza is the atmosphere of militarization, repression, and intimidation that has prevailed in Israeli universities, where administrations joined the Israeli police and internal intelligence services, Shin Bet, in clamping down on dissent by students and faculty peacefully protesting the war of aggression on Gaza.[58]

What about Academic Freedom?

The BDS movement, including PACBI, upholds the universal right to academic freedom and therefore calls for an *institutional*, not an *individual*, boycott. PACBI subscribes to the UN-set definition of academic freedom which prohibits the infringement on the academic freedom of others as well as discrimination and repression.[59] Anchored in precepts of international law and universal human rights, PACBI rejects, on principle, any McCarthyist-type political tests or boycotts of individuals based on their opinion or identity (such as citizenship, race, gender, or religion). If, however, an individual is representing the state of Israel or a complicit Israeli institution (such as a dean, rector, or president), or is commissioned/recruited to participate in Israel's efforts to "rebrand" itself, then her/his activities are subject to the institutional boycott the BDS movement is calling for.[60]

Some opponents of the academic boycott may argue, still, that it contravenes academic freedom because it cannot but hurt individual academics if it is to be effective at all. This argument is problematic on many levels. By ignoring the real, systematic Israeli suppression of Palestinian academic freedom and focusing solely on the hypothetical infringement on Israeli academic freedom that the boycott allegedly would entail, this argument is racist.

Israel's relentless and deliberate attack on Palestinian education, which some have recently termed scholasticide,[61] goes back to the 1948 *Nakba*, the wave of systematic ethnic cleansing of a majority of the indigenous Palestinians to establish a Jewish-majority state in Palestine. An Israeli researcher's dissertation reveals that during that period tens of thousands of Palestinian books were stolen from homes, schools, and libraries in Jerusalem, Jaffa, Haifa, Safad, and elsewhere by Zionist— later, Israeli—militias, and destroyed.[62]

In the first few weeks of the First Palestinian Intifada (1987–1993), Israel shut down all Palestinian universities—some, like Birzeit,[63] for several consecutive years—and then it closed all 1,194 Palestinian schools[64] in the occupied West Bank (including East Jerusalem) and Gaza. Next came the kindergartens, until every educational institution in the occupied Palestinian territories had been forcibly closed. This prompted Palestinians to build an illegal network of underground schools.

Palestinian scholars and students are methodically denied their basic rights, including academic freedom,[65] and are often subjected to imprisonment, denial of freedom of movement, even violent attacks on their persons or their institutions.[66] If exercising the right to academic freedom is conditioned upon respecting other human rights and securing what Judith Butler calls the "material conditions for exercising those rights,"[67] then clearly it is the academic freedom of Palestinian academics and students that is severely hindered, as a result of the occupation and policies of racial discrimination, and must be defended.

Palestinian citizens of Israel have also suffered for decades from the structural racism that pervades the Israeli educational system. According to Human Rights Watch:

> Discrimination at every level of the [Israeli] education system winnows out a progressively larger proportion of Palestinian Arab children as they progress through the school system—or channels those who persevere away from the opportunities of higher education. The hurdles Palestinian Arab students face from kindergarten to university function like a series of sieves with sequentially finer holes.[68]

Moreover, the "boycott conflicts with academic freedom" argument also confuses academic privileges with academic freedom and fails, accordingly, to grasp how an institutional academic boycott can work.[69]

An effective international isolation of Israeli academic institutions will undoubtedly curtail some privileges that Israeli scholars take for granted, from generous travel subsidies to various perks and services that have no bearing on their academic freedom. These privileges are only made possible, these scholars forget, by their universities' lucrative, business-as-usual relations with Western academia.

Even though the academic boycott of Israel does not undercut academic freedom, PACBI founders, in harmony with the BDS movement's profound commitment to universal human rights, have consistently argued that this freedom should not be privileged as above other human rights.[70] The 1993 World Conference on Human Rights proclaims, "All human rights are universal, indivisible . . . interdependent and interrelated. The international community must treat human rights globally in a fair and equal manner, on the same footing, and with the same emphasis."[71]

Those who are still reluctant, on principle, to support a boycott that expressly targets Israel's academic institutions while having in the past endorsed, or even struggled to implement, a much more sweeping academic boycott against apartheid South Africa's academics and universities are hard-pressed to explain this peculiar inconsistency. Unlike the institutional boycott that PACBI has called for, the South African boycott targeted individual academics as well as academic institutions.

SINGLING OUT ISRAEL?

Much has been written to respond to the disingenuous argument that BDS "singles out" Israel. Here are some additional thoughts on this:

- When Rosa Parks triggered the civil rights boycott campaign against the Montgomery Bus Company over its racial discrimination policies, was the US civil rights movement's singling out of that company hypocritical, given the presence of far more atrocious companies operating in Africa or in neighboring Mexico?
- As Desmond Tutu once said, South African apartheid was not the most egregious form of human rights violations if compared to widescale genocide elsewhere around the world. But should South Africans have struggled against all worse forms of abuse before fighting apartheid?
- If you suffer from the flu and seek medication for it, is it misguided to do so when there are worse diseases out there? Well, the flu is the disease that is afflicting you!

Our direct oppressor is Israel's regime and its complicit institutions. If we were to call for boycotting all the partners in Israel's regime of occupation and apartheid, the United States being the most important, we would end up doing nothing but empty gesturing, which in situations of dire and intensifying oppression is unethical. As human rights defenders and activists, we have limited resources that we cannot but invest strategically to achieve maximum impact to achieve our basic rights under international law.

BDS, after all, is not an academic exercise; it is a deeply ethical praxis aimed at realizing our freedom, justice, and equality. Morality aside, and as Naomi Klein once argued,[72] a boycott of the United States is patently fantastical, as it cannot possibly work, given US hegemony and superpower status, including in academia. Conditioning support for the academic boycott of Israel on first boycotting US academic institutions is therefore unethical and, in effect if not by intention, would serve to protect Israel's regime of oppression from international accountability.

RIGHT TO HOPE

In his poem "Message to the Living," Henk van Randwijk, a Dutch poet of resistance against the Nazi Germany occupation of the Netherlands during WWII, wrote[73]:

A people giving in to tyrants
will lose more than body and goods
the light will be extinguished

On Sunday, September 14, 2014, shortly after the end of the Israeli attack on the besieged and occupied Gaza Strip, and despite all the death, destruction, and trauma, hundreds of thousands of Gaza's children almost literally rose from under the rubble to which much of Gaza was reduced and went with enthusiasm to their damaged schools, carrying their dusty books, injured souls, and hope for freedom and dignity. Whether it is reaching a tipping point or will require a few more years to do so, BDS, including the academic boycott, empowers Palestinians and world-wide supporters of a just peace to keep this hope alight.

6

THE ISRAELI STATE OF EXCEPTION AND THE CASE FOR ACADEMIC BOYCOTT

DAVID LLOYD AND MALINI JOHAR SCHUELLER

Since the initial call for an academic and cultural boycott of Israel was issued by Palestinian intellectuals in October 2002 and reaffirmed by the launching of the Palestinian Campaign for the Academic and Cultural Boycott of Israel (PACBI) in April 2004, it has been a significant—perhaps the most significant—element in an international and growing movement for boycott, divestment, and sanctions against Israel (BDS). Endorsed by more than 170 Palestinian organizations, including the Palestinian Federation of Unions of University Professors and Employees (PFUUPE), BDS and PACBI are widely popular, nonviolent means to pursue the end of a regime of occupation, siege, dispossession, and discrimination that Israel has imposed with almost complete impunity for decades. This is a rights-based campaign that calls on civil society internationally to seek redress for gross violations of international law and human rights while governments refuse to act. PACBI has called specifically for an institutional academic boycott; that is, a boycott not of individual academics or artists but of educational and cultural institutions whose complicity in the maintenance and furtherance of occupation is indubitable and continuing.[1] It also calls for the boycott of institutions or cultural organizations that operate explicitly under the auspices of the Israeli state as ambassadors who seek to normalize the occupation and to promote a benevolent image of Israel as part of its campaign of propaganda (*hasbara*).

Despite the American Association of University Professors' (AAUP) history of censuring governments and institutions for violations of academic and intellectual freedoms, and despite the principled stand that it took against South African apartheid in supporting the divestment campaign, it has to date refused to endorse PACBI's call for academic boycott. The grounds that it has given publicly for this refusal are so confused and inconsistent with past policy and practice that we must again clarify the rationale for boycott and question the exceptional exoneration that AAUP grants to Israel alone among states.

A boycott is a nonviolent instrument that both expresses disapproval of the prolonged conduct of a person or institution that injures others and withdraws material support from that person or institution so long as they persist in such conduct. It is generally called for and applied by those to whom other means of action are denied. That said, a boycott is a specific tactic, deployed in relation to a wider campaign against injustice and under quite determinate circumstances. It should not be exercised indiscriminately in ways that would inevitably be ineffective. The optimal conditions for applying boycott as a tactic include the following:

a) The entity aimed at must be vulnerable to a boycott as a result of its connections with, or dependence on, the nations whose publics boycott it. An economic boycott of the European Union, United States, or China, for example, would probably be politically futile because it would be economically ineffectual, much as we might desire it in principle.

b) There must be a relatively open public sphere in the nation boycotted in order for their public to influence their leaders, and the boycotted nation's public must care about the opinion of those boycotting them. This is the case with Israel, as it was with South Africa, since their populations largely wish to be counted among "civilized" or "democratic" Western nations. In both cases the campaign for cultural and academic boycott exerts more rather than less impact than economic sanctions: it goes directly to citizens' sense of integration in the global cultural community. This is not to say that either South Africa was, or that Israel is, a democracy in any meaningful sense of the word: apartheid systems function precisely by claiming democratic and civil rights for only a part of their population and systematically denying those rights to the subordinated remainder.

c) The boycott should be explicitly supported by the occupied or oppressed people concerned, who often stand to suffer most from the consequences of its application. This was the case with the divestment campaign against South Africa, called for by the African National Congress, and is the case with BDS against Israel.

d) The boycott must make demands that are realizable by the nation boycotted, such as conforming to international law, ending an occupation or blockade, dismantling a racist or apartheid system, negotiating in good faith, and so forth. BDS invokes three summary principles, in conformity with the norms of human rights conventions and international law. Israel must:

1. End its occupation and colonization of all Arab lands, end the siege of Gaza, and dismantle the Segregation Wall; 2. Recognize the fundamental rights of the Arab-Palestinian citizens of Israel to full equality; 3. Respect, protect, and promote

the rights of Palestinian refugees to return to their homes and properties as stipulated in UN Resolution 194.

e) Finally, a boycott should be based on nonviolent principles and is implicitly a
rejection of the resort to violence by those engaging in it. The Palestinian BDS
campaign is expressly opposed to all forms of racial, religious, gender, or other
discrimination universally, which accords with its insistence on Israel's coming
into conformity to international law and human rights conventions.

To what extent, then, does Israel meet these criteria? To the usual charge that
BDS singles Israel out for exceptional sanctions when many nations—including
the United States—are guilty of some egregious injustice or aggression, an initial
response is simply that the fact that many states infringe international law does not
in any way exonerate Israel from its obligations to end an illegal occupation or to
apply universal standards of human rights. Indeed, it is because Israel is constantly
distinguished or singled out from other nations, particularly in the United States,
that a BDS campaign is justified. As is by now well known, Israel is the largest recipient of US aid, receiving currently about $3 billion per year. US aid underwrites
Israel's commission of war crimes and crimes against humanity, including not only
the use of weapons like white phosphorous against civilians, but also such offenses
as collective punishment, systematic torture, and the extended occupation of Palestinian territory in violation of the Geneva Conventions. In fact, Israel has violated
more UN resolutions than any other state in the world, including twenty-eight
Security Council resolutions that are legally binding on member states, largely because it has been consistently protected by the Security Council veto power of the
United States from any attempt to enforce those resolutions.[2]

Nonetheless, public officials and academics who have critiqued Israel have
faced campaigns of distortion, intimidation, threats of termination, and/or denial
or loss of tenure. While Steven Salaita's may currently be the best-known academic
case, campaigns have also targeted scholars such as Joseph Massad, Nadia Abu El
Haj, Sami Al-Arian, William Robertson, David Shorter, and David Klein in direct attempts to restrict their freedom of speech and even to have them denied or
removed from academic positions. Well-orchestrated efforts to define criticism of
Israel as anti-Semitism or to intimidate members of Students for Justice in Palestine
(SJP) have resulted in the extraordinary prosecution of the Irvine 11, University of California–Irvine students who peacefully protested a speech by the Israeli
ambassador, or California Assembly Resolution, HR 35, which effectively defines
peaceful protests against Israeli policies as hateful, hence prohibited, and is clearly
an attempt to model legislation for that and other states. Israel is singled out most
clearly by being the only country that cannot be criticized openly in the United

States and on its university campuses without serious repercussions. This climate of orchestrated harassment of critics of Zionism, designed to intimidate and silence, bears no comparison with the no less orchestrated complaints that Jewish students on campuses feel that criticism of Israel is tantamount to anti-Semitism. To concede that point would be to undermine the very foundations of the university, which must allow any belief and any system, political or religious—however deeply held—to be subjected to reasonable criticism.

The censorship that US academics and citizens face regarding criticism of Israel is negligible compared to the daily regime of occupation and siege that denies Palestinian scholars the right to free movement and prevents them from attending classes, taking exams, or studying abroad on fellowship; that subjects universities to frequent and arbitrary closures that constitute collective punishment; or that willfully destroys academic institutions, such as the American International School and the Islamic University of Gaza, which were destroyed in 2009 along with some twenty other schools and colleges. If there has been anywhere a systematic denial of academic freedom to a whole population, rather than to specific individuals or to institutions, it is surely in Palestine under Israeli occupation.[3]

Yet it is putatively on the grounds of academic freedom that the AAUP has rejected the academic boycott of Israel. Because the AAUP is an old and respected body whose opinions are taken seriously by universities and academics in the United States and worldwide, it is important to trace its position in relation to boycott and explain why it is untenable. In 2005, responding to the UK Association of University Teachers' call for a boycott of two Israeli universities, Haifa and Bar-Ilan (a resolution overturned the resolution a few months later), the AAUP roundly condemned the boycott on the basis of academic freedom and stated:

> Since its founding in 1915, the AAUP has been committed to preserving and advancing the free exchange of ideas among academics irrespective of governmental policies and however unpalatable those policies may be viewed. We reject proposals that curtail the freedom of teachers and researchers to engage in work with academic colleagues, and we reaffirm the paramount importance of the freest possible international movement of scholars and ideas.[4]

A year later, the AAUP released a statement, published as "On Academic Boycotts," in order to support its position about boycotts as "prima facie violations of academic freedom."[5] This condemnation of the academic boycott on the grounds of academic freedom has been thoroughly critiqued by scholars such as Mohamed Abed, Marcy Newman, Lisa Taraki, Omar Barghouti, and Judith Butler who contend that the academic freedom extolled by the AAUP is a geopolitically based privilege rather than a transhistorical right.[6] Judith Butler has called for a "more robust conception of academic freedom, one that considers the material and institutional foreclosures that make it impossible for certain historical subjects to lay claim to the discourse of rights itself."[7] Notably, the AAUP allowed critics of its statement to voice their opinions in *Academe*; ironically, in so doing they appeared to the many academics expressing outrage at these critics to be condemnatory of Israel.

Nothing could be farther from the truth. The AAUP's deliberations on the academic and cultural boycott of Israeli universities effectively promoted the idea of Israel as a state of exception. While the state of Israel governs through an order "that allows for the physical elimination not only of political adversaries but of entire categories of citizens who for some reason cannot be integrated into the political system,"[8] the AAUP has proceeded to eliminate the rights of Palestinians from its arguments by making Israel a state of exception.

The "On Academic Boycotts" statement referred to academic freedom as defined in the 1940 Statement of Principles on Academic Freedom and Tenure: "institutions of higher education are conducted for the common good . . . [which] depends upon the free search for truth and its free exposition."[9] But if universities are conducted for a universal idea of the common good, the grounds for the academic boycott of Israeli universities seem fairly obvious. The common good of the Islamic University of Gaza cannot be served by bombing it; neither can a university function for the common good if it is established in a settlement area: witness Ariel College, a West Bank campus of Bar-Ilan University, which is now Ariel University Center of Samaria, having acquired fully accreditation in July 2012.[10] Established illegally under international law, on occupied Palestinian territory, it is open only to Israeli academics and students and not to the West Bank Palestinians on whose land it is built. It thus constitutes a separate and unequal apartheid institution. The question undoubtedly becomes, for whose common good are universities established? Whose common good matters? How should the common good be defined in a country under occupation? Once we interrogate the particularity of the common good, it becomes clear that this notion operates under the aegis of a liberal humanism that ignores or even denies colonialism or racial oppression. While both early Zionists and contemporary leaders have been brazen about the settler-colonial nature of Israel's enterprise, the AAUP's statements are all noteworthy for the complete absence of any mention of Israeli colonialism or its repressive military. Let us reflect on this willful blindness: the words colonialism or occupation simply do not appear in their statements.

Next, the AAUP distinguished censure—"which brings public attention to an administration that has violated the organization's principles and standards" —

from a boycott. "Throughout its history," the AAUP claimed, it had "approved numerous resolutions condemning regimes and institutions that limit the freedoms of citizens and faculty," but only in the case of South Africa had it supported resolutions both of condemnation and of divestment. The AAUP not only censured South Africa but also actively supported the divestment movement against apartheid. Now it refuses even the censure of Israel.

Inconsistent as this is, the contradictions have recently been compounded. Two years after the academic boycott statement, the December 2008 bombing of the Islamic University of Gaza, an institution serving twenty-thousand students and comprising ten faculties including education, religion, art, medicine, engineering, and nursing, drew no comment from the AAUP. Yet the AAUP in 2007 had continued its commitment to condemning institutions that limited the freedoms of students and faculty by censuring four New Orleans universities for closing departments in the aftermath of Hurricane Katrina, and, at its annual meeting in 2008, it condemned the government of Iran for discriminating against and denying educational opportunities to its Baha'i community.[11] In contrast, in 2010, the AAUP, responding to allegations of anti-Semitism at UC Berkeley, UC Santa Cruz, and Rutgers, issued a statement in support of free speech but also suggested university administrators use a working definition of anti-Semitism to monitor individual cases. Part of the working definition includes "denying to Jews the right of self-determination (such as by claiming that Zionism is racism)."[12] This definition, which confuses criticism of a state with hatred of an ethno-religious group, itself participates in the larger climate of censorship that we remarked on above. But given that the AAUP accepts the idea that settler-colonialism is self-determination, and implicitly denies the freedom to criticize Israel to the US-based Palestinian students its policies so drastically affects, should we be surprised that the organization has refused to censure Israeli universities, crucial instruments in the extension and maintenance of Israel's regime of dispossession and settlement?

Instead, the AAUP has satisfied itself by condemning criticisms against individuals' writings as part of protecting the speaking of truth. At the 2007 annual meeting of the AAUP, Joan A. Berton, the plenary speaker, portrayed attacks against scholars Norman Finkelstein, Stephen Walt, and John Mearsheimer as simply part of the taboos against speech about Israel and Palestine and presented these, using a tactic of normalization, as "mutually destructive reductionism. . . which prevents recognition of alternate views."[13] The report of the speech stressed the need for competing perspectives to foster discussion, thus equating the politics of settler-colonialism and Palestinian protest and assuming that both sides are heard equally in the United States. In the spirit of this condemnation of individual acts—as if they were aberrant from the US government's support of the Israeli state and its institutions—the AAUP recognizes only the right of individual faculty not to cooperate with institutions, while it opposes any systematic boycott that "threatens the principles of free expression and communication on which we collectively depend."[14] It is crucial to repeat that the academic and cultural boycott is against Israeli *institutions*, all of which are complicit in occupation and create conditions under which the freedoms imagined by the AAUP cannot exist. The boycott does not extend to individual Israeli speakers invited to speak in the United States or individual scholars writing a paper together. The point of the boycott is structural and is meant to challenge the state of exception through which Israel has escaped reprimand or penalty, and that has created conditions under which the rights of Palestinian scholars, academics, and students are routinely suppressed. In this context, it becomes a luxury for North American academics to appeal to a distinctly one-sided and restrictive version of the principles of academic freedom while accepting complicity in the denial of those rights not just to individuals but to whole populations.

We would do well to remember the words of Howard Zinn, in a lecture in South Africa during apartheid: "To me, academic freedom has always meant the right to insist that freedom be more than academic—that the university, because of its special claim to be a place for the pursuit of truth, be a place where we can challenge not only ideas but the institutions, the practices of society, measuring them against millenia-old ideals of equality and justice."[15] If academic freedom is, indeed, a universal value, not one restricted to a few who are privileged by geography and colonial histories, then the Palestinian call for academic and cultural boycott of Israel becomes, as South Africa was in the 1980s, a test case for our intellectual and moral consistency. If we or the AAUP refuse to endorse that call, then the commitment to academic freedom becomes vacuous and meaningless, an assertion of privilege and entitlement, not of fundamental values. Palestinian education, like Palestinian culture and civil society, has been systematically targeted for destruction: it is no longer a matter of the infringement of the free speech of a few individuals, but a case in which, in the time-honored manner of settler-colonialism, a powerful and well-armed state seeks to extinguish the cultural life and identity of an indigenous people. Not only is the boycott movement the only practical possibility for Palestinian survival, its application is also principled and defined in its scope and ends. No clearer case has existed for the extension of an academic boycott since the African National Congress made their similar call for boycott and divestment in the struggle against South African apartheid. To continue to duck what is increasingly one of the defining moral and political struggles of our time would be not merely inconsistent, but intellectually and ethically bankrupt. The oldest US organization representing academics and scholars can do better than that, and it is time for it to do so. We must cease to make an exception of Israel.

7

Boycotts against Israel and the Question of Academic Freedom in American Universities in the Arab World

Sami Hermez and Mayssoun Sukarieh

How can we understand academic freedom in the Arab world today when it comes to the question of Palestine and Israel? What does the concept mean, practically speaking, for a US university in the region? And how should it be deployed? These universities operate today in the context of a colonial present[1] and serve to promote values not dissimilar to those imagined by US missionaries in the 1820s. Instead of an explicit resort to discourses of backwardness, or a mention of defects of the natives,[2] US university presidents today speak of promoting values that are "uniquely American," such as "a sense of mutual respect, tolerance for people of very diverse backgrounds" or solving problems "without recourse to violence."[3] One can only assume that this implies such values do not exist where these universities are operating. What kind of agendas, then, does academic freedom promote when invoked by US universities in what could be called a neocolonial context? How might it be employed for or against collective struggle in the region? And what role can such universities play in advancing or obstructing an academic boycott of Israel?

The Arab–Israeli conflict has meant that, with few exceptions, most Arab countries have not had diplomatic relations with Israel. This state-imposed Arab boycott has provided legal protection as one line of defense against the normalization of Israel's ongoing violations of international law against the Palestinian people, but underlying this is an even more crucial ethical claim against any dealing with Israel, whether economic, cultural, or, for our purposes, academic. It is an ethical claim that leaders of US universities in the region do not seem to consider when they regard the only obstacle to Arab–Israeli academic exchanges as being visa issues, and "hope that in time that we can have exchange relationships," as Winfred Thompson, former chancellor of the University of Sharjah, remarked at a public forum at the Council for Foreign Relations.[4]

The ethical claim against dealing with Israel rests on the fact that Israel continues to occupy Arab land (Palestinian, Syrian, and Lebanese) since 1967; to deny Palestinians their right to return to their homes, as they are legally bound under UN Resolution 194; and to practice a system of institutionalized discrimination (also known as apartheid) against Palestinian citizens of Israel. As a more powerful line of defense, Palestinian civil society has come together in an overwhelming consensus to call for boycott, divestment, and sanctions (BDS), and, even more importantly, has defined Arab normalization with Israel as "the participation in any project, initiative or activity, in Palestine or internationally, that aims (implicitly or explicitly) to bring together Palestinians (and/or Arabs) and Israelis (people or institutions) without placing as its goal resistance to and exposure of the Israeli occupation and all forms of discrimination and oppression against the Palestinian people."[5] This is the minimum required to combat normalization, but people in other Arab countries, such as Lebanon, may opt, and indeed have done so, to define this along stricter lines. The BDS movement considers such normalization to be "a 'colonization of the mind,' whereby the oppressed subject comes to believe that the oppressor's reality is the only 'normal' reality that must be subscribed to, and that the oppression is a fact of life that must be coped with."[6] A significant aspect of Palestinian and Arab nonviolent resistance, then, is to struggle against powerful influences attempting to normalize oppression and to force them to accept the occupier's terms of peace. It is within this context and through these ethical considerations that any notion of academic freedom operates in the Arab world.

THE CASE OF THE AMERICAN UNIVERSITY OF BEIRUT

The American University of Beirut (AUB) offers a strong case through which to explore questions of academic freedom at US institutions in the region. AUB has, in the last few years, repeatedly invoked this principle in order to stifle or shut down protests launched against a series of administrative decisions serving, intentionally or not, to counteract the academic boycott of Israel. In 2011, campus activists successfully opposed an administrative decision to grant an honorary doctorate to James Wolfensohn because of his involvements with complicit Israeli institutions.[7] In 2012, a second petition was launched against granting an honorary doctorate to Donna Shalala,[8] who has been a strong supporter of partnerships with Israeli universities, a strong opponent of the academic boycott, and prior recipient of three doctorate degrees from Israeli universities deeply enmeshed in discriminating against Palestinian students, supporting the Israeli military, and developing weaponry used against Palestinian and Lebanese civilians.[9] In defending its position in both instances, the administration claimed that AUB "is deeply committed to upholding the essential values,"[10] of academic freedom.

Concerns about academic freedom have followed BDS campaigners in many countries, especially in the United States.[11] There are at least three issues that arise when claims of academic freedom are invoked to counter proponents of academic boycott. First, what does the discourse of academic freedom sanction in such situations? Judith Butler calls on us to question "the classically liberal conception of academic freedom with a view that grasps the political realities at stake, and see that our struggles for academic freedom must work in concert with the opposition to state violence, ideological surveillance, and the systematic devastation of everyday life."[12] It seems even former AUB president John Waterbury and other current and past leaders of American universities in the region would concur, as they agree that such institutions "seek to encourage responsible, free speech [sic] and of course responsible academic freedom."[13] What such responsibility entails becomes a matter of political debate rather than a question of an absolute decontextualized and depoliticized principle of academic freedom.

A second and related issue confronting supporters of the academic boycott of Israel around the world is whether academic freedom is being used as a defense to shut down dissent, silence controversy on campus, or promote one set of views or policies over others (for instance, administrative views over faculty ones). As an example, at the 2011 AUB commencement, president Peter Dorman spoke about commitment to academic freedom, claiming that it was a "defining principle," that freedom of expression "is an obligation," and that AUB provides "the freedom and the intellectual space for young generations to imagine the unthinkable and debate the undebatable."[14] Yet this contrasted with how he himself had responded to concerns over violation of the Lebanese boycott law[15] by describing faculty as "deliberately slanted to serve narrow interests regardless of facts. Co-opting the opinions of fellow faculty, students, and alumni by a pretext of authority," and dubbing the campaigns as "fundamentally dishonest" and a diversion from AUB's "commitment to the pursuit of knowledge as grounded in intellectual integrity."[16] Rather than argue over the premise of the original concerns regarding Israel, which were based on both legal and ethical claims, the administration depicted faculty as dishonest and as abusing their authority, thus shutting down debate and offering the administration's position as the final word.

In the case of AUB, a third issue arises over the invocation of academic freedom, which has to do with AUB's status within Lebanon and the broader region. AUB receives US federal funds, is run by an American leadership, and has close cultural, ideological, and political ties with a range of American institutions, including the US Embassy in Lebanon, not to mention the expressed interest of its administration in promoting American values. All of this contrasts markedly with the typical situation of universities in the global north, which tend to be firmly embedded within their home and host-nation states. Hence, all the key questions that inevitably arise in conflicts over academic freedom in the global north—knowledge for what, and freedom for whom and from whom—take on another dimension in neocolonial contexts in the global south. Thus, while AUB's administration framed their arguments on the basis that AUB is an "American" university that respects American traditions of academic freedom, critics of the administration responded by insisting that AUB is an American university "of Beirut," and thus needs to respect the concerns of broader Lebanese and Arab society.

Invocation of academic freedom by the AUB administration not only served to promote the viewpoints and values of the administration and its supporters but also took on an air of cultural condescension, in which the administration purported to know the best interests of a people, whose values and insights seemed subordinate. In this fashion, president Peter Dorman explained that AUB abided with the American notion of academic freedom and that he knew who the friends of Arabs were: "Let us acknowledge that ours is a complex region that is undergoing unprecedented change, and that it needs people, like James Wolfensohn…who has taken a courageous stance in defense of Palestinian rights…. The Arab world needs more friends like him."[17] Academic freedom was here used instrumentally to make a case for the decisions of the administration, who knew the best interests of the Arab world; those who did not agree with the administration could, thus, be said to be hindering not only academic freedom but even what was best for the Arab world.

The appeal to academic freedom by the administrations of American universities in the region also distracts attention from their position serving and supporting US foreign policy above the policies and interests of a broader Arab society. This supporting role has, at times, included university ties to the CIA.[18] Today, AUB works closely with the US Embassy, USAID, the State Department's Middle East Partnership Initiative, and the Congress-funded National Endowment for Democracy. The AUB administration's indifference to the ethical concerns of normalization with Israel fits perfectly within the policies of the US government, but it conflicts with both Lebanese law and the moral commitments and political interests of broad swaths of Lebanese and Arab society. However, as soon as the principle of academic freedom is invoked, this basic conflict is obscured.

There seems to be an insistence that employees and students of AUB act solely as university representatives and leave their other identities at the campus gate; in this sense, BDS campaigns were seen as "campaigns to ruin the reputation of AUB."[19] In response to such campaigns, one heard rhetoric such as "I care for AUB, and we should protect our university." In such discourse, there is a sort of radical detaching of the university from the concerns of the surrounding society. Hence, rather than being part of the larger society and serving it, AUB—and, we argue, other US universities in the region as well—stands outside and against it. Lebanese community groups who have backed BDS campaigns, as well as AUB's own faculty and students who supported these campaigns, were positioned as outside agitators. In a letter addressed to the AUB community in response to BDS campaigns, President Dorman stated that he defended the right of those who took a position criticizing the administration for awarding an honorary degree to individuals who did not adhere to academic boycott guidelines.[20] He claimed, "It is a principled stance, and one that many feel passionate about. Yet institutional decisions cannot be subordinated to an absolute litmus test imposed by the demands of outside groups."[21] While this is a tension in all university-state-community relationships, it becomes particularly problematic when the university itself is quite literally a foreign body, not embedded in the society it claims to serve.

The AUB administration seems to operate with an understanding that academic freedom is a concept foreign and alien to much of the Arab world, and, as such, AUB is seen by its American administrators, along with other universities in the region, as "ambassadors of the US system of higher education and academic freedom."[22] These university administrators ignore the prevalent notion that the support and protection of rigorous, committed, and independent academic scholarship tends to be framed in the region by a concern for freedom of speech and expression, which extends to all members of society, not just academics. One can argue that imposing the notion of academic freedom in the region is part of a longer colonial discourse about bringing light and freedom to the natives.[23] In the early days of AUB, Butrus al-Bustani, a major figure in Arab intellectual and cultural life in the second half of the nineteenth century, proposed the concept of freedom of conscience, instead of the intellectual freedom proposed by the Protestant missionaries, because for him it was a "way of life," a means for humans to "overcome their temporary differences and unite around their essential sameness."[24] In the twentieth century, academic personalities such as Kamal Nasser and Constantine Zurayk insisted that recognizing the principle of "freedom of thought does not negate the organic relation that ties the university to the society it serves," and tried, unsuccessfully, to present more socially engaged and integrated ideas of freedom, not the reductive version of academic freedom as we have come to know the concept today.[25]

AUB's isolation from the society it serves is not new, and this case may be an indication of how other American institutions relate to their surroundings. As Betty Anderson argues, in the early history of AUB, "Conflicts arose repeatedly over the level of authority students could actually wield over their campus and curricular lives," but for the students and the community AUB served this meant precisely bringing the world of Arab politics inside the university, for that is how they could make their university and education useful to their broader society.[26] Subsequent generations of AUB faculty found themselves struggling to bring the politics of the Arab world inside the main gates, while the American leadership of the administration has tried to keep regional politics outside, especially that which conflicted with US policy interests, and balked at the seeping of Arab politics into campus life: "In this administrative perspective politics had to be kept outside of the campus walls because they could only disrupt the education process."[27] Hence, it seems that the notion of academic freedom as advocated by the AUB administration does not include the freedom of involvement of AUB students in the politics of the region. Is it not time to move on from the notion of academic freedom to the notion of freedom of thought that integrates universities into the larger struggle of their communities?

CONCLUSION

The broader role of US universities in the Arab world can be examined through the lens of AUB's experience with academic freedom and active boycott campaigns against Israel. The considerations of these universities and their constituents in the pursuit of academic inquiry will necessarily be different than those of universities in the United States. What this highlights, however, is that academic freedom cannot be regarded as absolute; it is highly contextual and contestable. In the Arab world today, it cannot be divorced from other ethical claims of the right to life and the right to live free of various forms of oppression, whether from Israel, US neocolonialism, or local dictators.

However, in the way that academic freedom has been deployed by current and past university presidents to counter people's legitimate, nonviolent, and ethical resistance in the form of boycott, one is led to conclude that the concept is invoked in the service of US interests rather than in the interest of local people's struggles—it is used in support of power rather than to speak truth to power.

As we see academic freedom being used in US universities abroad to support US hegemony—specifically, to soften the normalization of Arab–Israeli relations and to force this normalization by means other than a comprehensive peace treaty—we return to the crucial moral question of how anyone should relate to Israel so long as it continues its violations of international law against the Palestinian people. In this sense, whether it is legal or not to collaborate with Israel should not be of concern; rather, the question should be whether this collaboration should exist on moral grounds. And if we agree that it shouldn't take place (and there is such agreement in many quarters in the Arab world) then, in such contexts, is it an attack on academic freedom to speak out against such collaboration? Or, in so doing, are we not merely placing such freedom within a responsible framework? Which, if we wish to follow American university leadership and American values, is part of Waterbury's own philosophy of encouraging "responsible academic freedom." We take this encouragement to mean, at minimum, a responsibility not to infringe on a people's right to struggle for a better world and against forms of colonialism, occupation, and apartheid.

8

THE GHOSTS THAT HAUNT US: USACBI AND THE SETTLER UNIVERSITY

SUNAINA MAIRA

The US Academic and Cultural Boycott of Israel (USACBI) was formed in response to the call for an academic and cultural boycott of Israel that was issued by Palestinians in 2004. However, it was not until 2009 and the war on Gaza that winter that a group of academics, part of the network California Scholars for Academic Freedom, mobilized to form an official structure for building a national academic and cultural boycott movement and to recruit US academics to endorse the call by the Palestinian Academic and Cultural Boycott of Israel (PACBI). Today, six years and two more wars on Gaza later, USACBI has 1,200 academic endorsers and an expanded organizing collective that includes scholars, students, and activists from across the United States. At the time of USACBI's founding, there were just a dozen scholars and activists, mostly based in California, who felt a sense of urgency about Israel's genocidal violence and were concerned that the discourse of academic freedom was not enough to address the lockdown on criticism of the Israeli state in the academy. Rather than simply defending US scholars from attacks by Zionist groups, some of us felt that we needed to do more, as our colleagues in Palestine had asked us to do, following on the model of refusal of complicity with South African apartheid.

I was part of the group of scholars that launched USACBI, and we faced intense resistance to our call for academic boycott at the time and for years after, not just from Zionists within and beyond the academy but also from allies of the Palestinian struggle. I want to note that USACBI focuses on both academic and cultural boycott campaigns, but the academic boycott movement has faced much more vicious resistance and backlash than the cultural boycott, with legislative campaigns in several states attempting to crack down on faculty who support the academic boycott and with well-funded, highly organized national campaigns of lawfare, intimidation, censorship, and racist propaganda. In the debates about both the academic and cultural boycott there exists a similar lacuna: that is, the missing figures of Palestinian academics or artists and Palestinians in general who cannot attend world music festivals or conferences in Tel Aviv or Jerusalem.

In this essay, I want to address two major issues: one, I examine the anxieties about the boycott as illuminating the political paradigm that is at the heart of the boycott and the racial and class wars in the US academy. Two, I will discuss those whom the discourse around the boycott has disappeared but whom the boycott movement aims to recenter—that is, Palestinian scholars and students—and touch briefly on the impact the boycott has on them. Much has been written about the implications of the boycott for the US academy, especially since the historic American Studies Association (ASA) resolution, so, in this essay, I would like to shift our attention to the absent figures in this debate, those of Palestinian academics, and to their absent freedoms that haunt this discussion. The challenge to the lockdown on discussion of the Israeli occupation in the US university waged by the boycott is very significant, but the focus of the boycott is ultimately the freedom and justice missing for our colleagues and comrades in Palestine. It is also important to note that the censorship and policing the BDS movement faces in the United States, including the attacks on faculty who mobilize in support of the boycott, is deeply intertwined with the Zionist apparatus of repression in Israel/Palestine.

CHALLENGING THE SETTLER UNIVERSITY FROM WITHIN

The academic boycott has long been considered the third rail of academic politics in the charged discourse about Palestine, Israel, and Zionism. The arguments we faced from detractors when we launched USACBI was that the academy in particular, and the United States in general, were not "ready" for the academic boycott, that it was counterproductive, and that we should focus on divestment. This opposition to the academic boycott began to crumble after the historic 2013 boycott resolutions overwhelmingly supported by the Association of Asian American Studies (AAAS) and, especially, the ASA, which spawned campaigns in numerous other associations and academic labor unions, such as the University of California graduate student workers in 2014. As this wall of resistance started to break down, after years of chipping away at the counterarguments, many of the detractors have actually joined the academic boycott movement and even begun to publicly advocate for boycott. This dramatic shift is a major political victory for the movement in the United

States, as one of its goals has always been to change the discourse about Palestine in the academy, not just to win votes in boycott campaigns in associations; that is, we have been waging a war of position, not just a war of maneuver, in Gramscian terms. But I think this antiboycott anxiety is important to disentangle and theorize, if we are to have a clear political paradigm for the boycott movement as it rapidly expands and becomes if not an acceptable at least a legible component of the political landscape.

Intense national campaigns against the academic boycott have been orchestrated and funded by Zionist organizations, such as the Anti-Defamation League, AIPAC, the Israel on Campus Coalition, the AMHCA Initiative, and the Zionist Organization of America. This backlash only underscores that the boycott poses a real challenge to the material apparatus of Zionism and the ideological framework necessary to maintain Israel's policies of annihilation and racial violence over decades. Zionist organizations such as the Reut Institute, an Israeli government think tank, have long claimed publicly that BDS and the boycott are a strategic if not existential threat to Israel.[1] I would like to press further on this acknowledgment of the effectiveness of the boycott as a tool to challenge Zionism by pointing out that there is an important antiracist challenge waged in the work of USACBI. It is this race politics that has made the boycott a challenging front on which to recruit US scholars, who have long had an uneasy and ambivalent relationship to the repressed race politics of settler-colonialism in Israel/Palestine, even if this race politics and racial violence have been in plain view.

The legacy of the South African boycott and divestment movement is significant here, for it is striking that many academics who supported BDS in opposition to South African apartheid are much more uneasy about BDS for Palestinians and worry that it is somehow anti-Semitic or singles out the Jewish state. There is a problematic racial politics at work here that I want to parse out. The rationale for the academic and also cultural boycott rests first and foremost on the delegitmization of the institutional projects that the apartheid state uses to uphold its impunity and legitimize its deprivations of freedom to racialized populations, so the boycott rests on an anticolonial and also antiracist logic. Academic and cultural institutions are key to shoring up the self-image of the Israeli state as an extension of Western democratic modernity in a sea of "enemy" populations who are antidemocratic and anti-Western, if not barbaric, violent, and repressive, as also portrayed in the mainstream US media. But the underlying logic of the boycott leads to the conclusion that Israel is a rogue state that violates the precepts of international human rights law and the principles of liberal Western democracy. (This is why I think the common question challenging the boycott, "Why not boycott China," or "What about Egypt?" is fundamentally a racist question. One never hears the question, "Why not boycott France?" for example, even when France has banned protests against the war on Gaza and violated civil rights).

But this logic that challenges the core nature of the Israeli state—as undemocratic, racist, and colonialist—also explains why, in my view, it has been more difficult to mobilize support for USACBI in the United States, relative to divestment or consumer boycott. These campaigns, which focus on withdrawing economic support from the military apparatus of the state, do not foreground Israel's apartheid nature extending beyond the occupation. In fact, one of the arguments that was used against the academic boycott resolution in the ASA, including by progressive-left supporters of Palestinian rights, was that divestment was a more appropriate call to support. Boycott in its various forms and divestment are, of course, all important tactics, and each has its role in a particular context and moment as part of the larger BDS movement. But in my view it is because the academic and cultural boycott exposes the fundamental character of the Zionist state, and not just its military occupation in the West Bank and Gaza, that it took much longer for USACBI to become a legitimate campaign.

This is also why the focus of USACBI continues to be unsettling for defenders of Israel, both on the left and the right, for, in addition to highlighting Zionism, it addresses the role of academics and artists—those subjects who are ineluctably modern, cosmopolitan, and liberal—in legitimizing and upholding a settler-colonial state based on racial exclusion. In other words, the academic boycott does not simply take aim at soldiers in combat fatigues (although all Israeli citizens are conscripted into the military, barring Palestinians and Orthodox Jews, so academics, too, do military duty) but concerns the role of subjects in Israel who supposedly are like *us*. There is a global class identification here that the boycott disrupts, and that makes it deeply discomfiting to scholars here who also believe, perhaps, that the university is not complicit with militarization and racial dispossession here *or* there.

In this regard, it is worth noting that one of the counterarguments that impeded the academic boycott campaigns in the ASA and also the Middle East Studies Association (MESA) was the anxiety that the boycott would be "divisive" for the associations. That is, a possible risk to the fate of these national professional academic associations superseded the ethics of solidarity with Palestinian academics—whose right to participate in the conferences of these very associations is violated by an apartheid regime. In other words, the credibility and status of these academic institutions trumped the call to withdraw our support from academic institutions allied with the Israeli state, backed unconditionally by our own government. The boycott challenges these circuits of academic privilege and institutional power, and forces us to ponder the meaning of the word "association," if some subjects are denied the right to associate freely with others.

Palestinians are ghosts in the US academy, constantly eclipsed by the hypothetical figure of the Israeli scholar presumably denied academic freedom, or sometimes juxtaposed with the embodied presence of Israeli scholars at conferences—which proves that the boycott is not targeting Israeli individuals, that it is not racist. The constant need to reference the few Israeli scholars who support the boycott and testify to their existence performs a similarly paradoxical racial move, that is, the need to disprove the alleged racism of an antiracist campaign by continually highlighting those who continue to enjoy academic, and human, freedom, while invisibilizing the bodies that are encaged and disappeared. This is not to discount the vicious attacks on Israeli scholars who support the boycott from within, but to point out that the racial politics of the boycott movement have been muddied by an inability, even among progressive US scholars, to have a clearer racial analysis of Zionism centered on apartheid and settler-colonialism as a *racist* project, and thus a more explicit politics of antiracist, if not anti-Zionist, solidarity. This politics was evident in the campaign waged in the ASA as critical race studies and settler-colonial studies scholars voiced their solidarity with Palestinians calling for boycott in unapologetically antiracist and anticolonial terms. Hence, of course, the campaign of wrath that was hurled at the ASA in the wake of the boycott victory.

The racialized institutional logic of antiboycott arguments is also relevant to the challenges to the ASA's boycott resolution in 2014. Claims by opponents of the boycott that Israeli and Jewish scholars were being excluded from the annual ASA conference make transparent US academics' investment in the figure of the Israeli scholar, and what her/his academic freedom looks like in a post-boycott world. Amjad Barham, who is the head of the major Palestinian academic union, the Palestinian Federation of Unions of University Professors and Employees (PFUUPE), one of the first signatories of the call for BDS, comments trenchantly:

> Is upholding the academic freedom of Israeli academics a loftier aim than upholding the freedom of an entire people being strangled by an illegal occupation? Do Palestinian universities somehow fall outside the purview of the "universal" principle of academic freedom? Israeli academics who argue for the protection of their access to international academic networks, grants, visiting professorships, fellowships and other benefits of the academic system, have paid scant attention to the total denial of the most basic freedoms to Palestinians, academics or otherwise.[2]

In the debate about whether the boycott deprives Jewish Israelis of their academic freedom, there are no Palestinian academics or students who must travel through checkpoints and Israeli borders in order to get a permit to go to Jerusalem simply to apply for a visa to travel to the United States, then face racialized restrictions, interrogations, harassment, and detention at checkpoints and airports and settler roads along the way. There are no Palestinian students being targeted by racially discriminatory policies that shut down their political events or facing physical assaults at Israeli universities.[3]

Yara Sa'adi, a young Palestinian activist who was a student at the Hebrew University, has been involved in organizing with other Palestinian youth in Israeli universities against repression, racism, and militarization.[4] She states, "I believe the [boycott] movement around the world has a big impact on Israeli universities decisions regarding punishing Palestinian students for protesting within the campuses and other activities." Palestinian students are regularly punished, disciplined, threatened, and attacked for protesting Israeli wars on Gaza or in solidarity with Palestinian prisoners. Sa'adi observes that the international pressure generated by BDS campaigns plays an important role in challenging the disciplinary regime of Israeli universities who have come under increased scrutiny and censure as universities allied with the settler state, not as the "pluralist" institutions they claim to be. Samia Botmeh, a Palestinian scholar at Birzeit University in the West Bank and a member of PACBI's steering committee, observes that the academic boycott resolutions in the United States put "pressure on the Israeli academy, which is the first step in alerting this academy that the world is not going to accept its role in repressing the Palestinians." She adds eloquently, "Undermining the unethical privileged position of the Israeli academy has a tremendous impact on the everyday lives of the Palestinians. The ASA's decision empowers the Palestinians to continue with their struggle against repression and injustice. It helps turn the experience of survival under colonialism to an experience of resistance on the path towards freedom and justice." Indeed, PFUUPE leader Barham argues that isolating Israel till it complies with basic human rights is a crucial political strategy, and isolating the Israeli academy is central to this war of legitimacy, which helps explain why the Palestinian call for academic and cultural boycott actually preceded the call for BDS at large.

The academic boycott movement and USACBI's campaigns have also had an impact on Palestinian politics and civil society. Haidar Eid, a PACBI organizer in Gaza (and a contributor to this volume), says of the ASA resolution:

> The impact was huge in Palestine, Gaza in particular because it became clear that a taboo has been shaken in the US...victories achieved by the academic and cultural

boycott movement have drawn the attention of mainstream political organizations and the PA [Palestinian Authority] to the movement so much so that BDS activists have been asked to hold meetings with political leaders and ministers, including the late Ziyad Abu Ein [who was killed by Israeli soldiers in December 2014], to discuss the best ways of enhancing the BDS campaign.

Similarly, Lisa Taraki, a cofounder of PACBI and a scholar at Birzeit (also a contributor to this volume), points to the role of the boycott in challenging the Oslo paradigm of national politics and the collusion and repression of the PA: "The success of the boycott movement, particularly in the US, has had the effect of pushing more and more of Palestinian 'officialdom' (both in the PLO and the PA) into acknowledging the boycott's great potential in the Palestinian liberation strategy, and adopting some of its tactics. After years of post-Oslo consciousness, this is something that has to be remarked upon."

Clearly, the boycott has ramifications for the Palestinian national struggle and lends support to those on the ground struggling to revive resistance movements, in the wake of the decline of mass mobilization after Oslo. These transformative political shifts on the ground are important to note in response to counterarguments that suggest that academic boycott resolutions are simply "symbolic" and do not have a significant impact on Palestinian lives. On the contrary, Botmeh observes, "Palestinian academics and civil society feel empowered by the solidarity expressed by colleagues in associations internationally or individually. This enables us to continue with our everyday lives which are characterized by extremely harsh conditions, but also strive towards ending oppression through applying pressure on Israel and the Israeli academy." Some critics of the boycott have argued that it is not radical enough because it rests on the liberal principles of international human rights. This is true, but the boycott is a tactic, not a political horizon for struggle, and it is clearly an effective political tool that has the power to effect significant material and ideological change for Palestinians. This is what matters.

BOYCOTT BATTLES: RACIAL AND CLASS WARS

The academic boycott movement also demonstrates that Palestine is at the center of challenge to the US academic "establishment" and the neoliberalization and restructuring of the university. The unprecedented "de-hiring" of Steven Salaita by the University of Illinois at Urbana–Champaign, who was a leading advocate of the boycott and a fellow organizer of USACBI, underscored the ways in which the Palestine question is a funnel of academic repression and cuts to the core of the precarity of academic labor. The renewed firestorm over the ASA boycott resolution in 2014, a year after it was passed, and the ongoing attacks on academic boycott campaigns in other associations, such as the Modern Language Association (MLA) or the American Anthropological Association (AAA), reveal the racial and class politics at work in the battle over the boycott.

After the ASA adopted the boycott in 2013, the vitriolic letters and editorials by opponents of the academic boycott rested on the argument that the boycott was anti-Semitic, without any mention of the anti-Palestinian racism upheld by US support for Israel. The politics of the American Association of University Professors (AAUP) and its president, Cary Nelson, in relation to Palestine and Zionism were exposed in their public denunciations of the boycott and concerted pressure on the ASA to uphold the dominant institutionalized definition of academic freedom as precluding the right to education and freedom of Palestinians. Nelson's Zionist politics became even more apparent in his later attacks on Salaita. Some critics denounced the ASA for not being respectful of past (white) presidents of the ASA who opposed the boycott, charging that it emerged only from a "small but vocal minority" within the association. Other statements were more overtly racist, elitist, and homophobic in attacking an association that had become a space for radical scholar-activists, notably academics of color and those in critical race studies and queer scholars (including those in the ASA leadership who endorsed the resolution). This is not surprising, given that Zionism is a racist, colonial ideology, but the campaign by Zionist sympathizes made clear what the lines of battle were.

The academic boycott is a new front in the attempt to challenge Zionist settler-colonialism and apartheid and to confront US complicity in imperial and racial violence, linking Palestine to broader structures of racism and annihilation. Barham says, to those of us privileged to work in the US academy: "We urge you to do everything within your means to make sure that you are not condoning or rewarding colonial domination and [Israel's] grave violations of international law." USACBI's work helps challenge the self-censorship and silence around Palestine and Zionism in the academy, which is why the presence of Palestinian scholars and students at the ASA and other academic conferences is so important (the MESA conference in 2014 featured not a single Palestinian scholar from a Palestinian university but twenty Israeli scholars from Israeli universities). This is not just about moving bodies across Israeli and US borders to present at conferences but about drawing on *Palestinians'* knowledge production about Palestine, as settler-colonial subjects who know best the structure of Israeli coloniality and their own practices of decolonization.

CONCLUSION

I want to point out that the academic boycott movement did not emerge out of thin air and boycott resolutions were not passed spontaneously. They were the result of years of hard work by USACBI organizers, asking academics to endorse the boycott one by one, educating colleagues and students about Palestinian academics' lack of freedom, and organizing in the inhospitable trenches of the academy. BDS is indeed an autonomous, decentralized movement, but the academic boycott has required years of (unpaid) organizing labor, deep commitment, and the willingness to take professional risk and face backlash and defamation.

The boycott interrupts a liberal multicultural discourse in the settler university about cross-cultural "dialogue" between Palestinians and Israelis, Jews and Muslims, which elides Zionism and anti-Palestinian racism. Doing so raises the specter of Palestinians gone missing—dead, encaged, displaced, or fighting—and forces us to confront US settler-colonial mythologies and ongoing imperial violence in the darker regions of the world. The academic boycott movement, and USACBI, has expanded precisely because of the work of scholars and organizers who have addressed these circuits of colonial violence, policing, and rescue but who have often done so at a great price. In a moment when academic employment seems ever more precarious, and Zionist groups aid in the neoliberal university's war on tenure and repression of student movements, I think we must situate boycott at the center of organizing to take back the university and reenergize our antiracist struggles within and across settler states.

III. THE ACADEMIC BOYCOTT OF ISRAELI UNIVERSITIES IN HISTORICAL CONTEXT

9

PALESTINIAN SOLIDARITY IN SOUTH AFRICA AND THE ACADEMIC BOYCOTT OF ISRAEL: THE CASE OF THE UNIVERSITY OF JOHANNESBURG AND BEN GURION UNIVERSITY

SALIM VALLY

On August 9, 2014, between 150,000 and 200,000 South Africans marched in Cape Town against the latest round of atrocities in Gaza, calling for full sanctions against Israel. It was the biggest march in South Africa's history and a continuation of the intense solidarity activity in support of the Palestinian struggle since the first South African democratic elections in 1994. Highlights of these activities have included the following: a ten-thousand-strong march in Durban during the 2001 UN World Conference Against Racism, where the "second antiapartheid movement" was declared and a boycott, divestment, and sanctions (BDS) campaign against Israel was adopted by representatives of South African civil society, led by prominent liberation movement veterans; an equally strong march at the 2002 World Summit on Sustainable Development in support of the Palestinian struggle and against the presence of an Israeli delegation that included Shimon Peres; the 2009 refusal of dock workers in the port city of Durban to off-load an Israeli ship in the wake of Israel's Operation Cast Lead assault on Gaza; and, in 2011, the decision by the senate of the University of Johannesburg to sever ties with Ben Gurion University. In keeping with the theme of this book, the latter campaign will be described in more detail, as well as the ensuing debates around an academic boycott.

For more than sixty-five years Palestinians have alerted us to one outrage after another, injustices piled upon injustices without the commensurate scale of global solidarity required to make a significant difference to their lives. The recent slaughter of Palestinians in Gaza, including eight long years of a medieval-like siege, adds to the urgency of taking political action. It should be viewed together with the ongoing theft of Palestinian land in the West Bank and the Naqab (Negev), the discrimination against Palestinians in Israel, and the misery of millions of Palestinian refugees. The Israeli state is not interested in a just peace but rather the pacification and ethnic cleansing—or, as many are increasingly concluding, using the UN definition—genocide of Palestinians.

For South Africans, as for many others, support for Palestinian human rights has become the emblematic solidarity movement of our time and places in sharp relief the response globally of academics and intellectuals today.

ISRAELI SUPPORT FOR THE ERSTWHILE APARTHEID REGIME IN SOUTH AFRICA

The Palestinian struggle does not only exert a visceral tug on many consciences around the world. A reading of imperialism shows that apartheid Israel is needed as a fundamentalist and militarized warrior state, not only to quell the undefeated and unbowed Palestinians but also as a rapid-response fount of reaction in concert with despotic Arab regimes, to do the Empire's bidding in the Middle East and beyond.

Over the years this has included support for the mass terror waged against the people of Central and South America and facilitation of the evasion of international sanctions against apartheid South Africa. Besides providing a ready supply of mercenaries to terrorize a populace—whether in Guatemala, Iraq, or New Orleans—Israel also trains police forces and military personnel around the world, lending its expertise in collective punishment and mass terror. For instance at least two of the four law enforcement agencies that were deployed in Ferguson, Missouri, after the police killing of unarmed eighteen-year-old Michael Brown—the St. Louis County Police Department and the St. Louis Police Department—received training from Israeli security forces in recent years.[1]

The foundations of the Israeli economy were founded on the special political and military role that Zionism then and today fulfills for Western imperialism. While playing its role to ensure that the region is safe for transnational companies, it has also carved out today a niche market producing high-tech security essential for the day-to-day functioning of the global status quo. The weaponry and technology the Israeli military-industrial complex exports around the world are field-tested on the bodies of Palestinian men, women, and children.

Throughout the apartheid years in South Africa there were individuals and groups who identified and stood in solidarity with the Palestinian people and their struggle for freedom. The Palestine Liberation Organization (PLO) became a symbol of resistance for most South Africans. South Africans struggling against apartheid policies and realities agreed with the words, if not the sentiment, of apartheid prime minister Hendrik Verwoerd when he approvingly stated, in 1961, that "Israel, like South Africa, is an apartheid state."[2] Unlike Verwoerd, they considered this a violent abuse of human rights rather than a reason to praise Israel. In 1976, during the Soweto Uprising, a watershed year in the resistance against apartheid, South African prime minister John Vorster was invited to Israel and received with open arms by the likes of Yitzhak Rabin and Shimon Peres.

In addition to identifying with the struggle of Palestinians, South Africans also recognized that Israel was playing a role in their own oppression. For instance, Israel was an important arms supplier to South Africa despite the international arms embargo, and as late as 1980, 35 percent of Israel's arms exports were destined for South Africa. Israel was loyal to the racist state and clung to the friendship when almost all other relationships had dissolved. During the 1970s this affiliation expanded into the field of nuclear weaponry, when Israeli experts helped South Africa to develop at least six nuclear warheads, and, in the 1980s, when the global anti-apartheid movement had forced states to impose sanctions on the apartheid regime, Israel imported South African goods and re-exported them to the world as a form of inter-racist solidarity. Israeli companies, subsidized by the South African regime, were established in a number of Bantustans.

BOYCOTTING THE APARTHEID ACADEMY

The university in South Africa played a critical role in reproducing the structural inequalities and injustices found in that society. Universities in South Africa, including the "liberal" ones, were closely linked to the state: they received much of their funding from the state; they provided the scientific, commercial, and intellectual bases for the state to continue functioning; and they were the prime knowledge producers for the state and its bureaucracy. Moreover, a large number of academics were directly linked to the state, furthered the apartheid agenda at universities, conducted research on specific issues as the state required, and even spied on other academics and students. The university also provided some of the basis for the security forces' military operations against neighboring countries and liberation movements.

Of course, there was resistance to this, and the university was, as we called it, an important "site of struggle."

The Israeli university is not that much different from what the South African one was. Israeli universities and a number of individual Israeli academics play key roles in providing the intellectual support for the Israeli state and its endeavors. Certain Israeli universities have very strong links to the military establishment, including various forms of support to those serving in the military. A number of Israeli academics provide the practical and ideological support necessary for the maintenance of the occupation and even for the ethnic cleansing of Palestinians, extrajudicial killings, racial segregation, and land expropriation. Palestinian colleagues, through the Palestinian Campaign for the Academic and Cultural Boycott of Israel (PACBI), have compellingly shown how Israeli academic institutions collude with the occupation, ethnic cleansing, and racism in practical terms, whether through engineering, geography, demography, hydrology, or psychology, among other disciplines.

A few years back, in responding to the American Association of University Professors' (AAUP) invitation to debate the issue of the academic boycott, some South African and Palestinian colleagues argued that Israeli institutions in the main consistently violated the AAUP principle that "institutions of higher education are conducted for the common good . . . [which] depends on the free search for truth and its free exposition."[3] The "common good"—whether "common" includes only Israelis or both Israelis and Palestinians—is not served when universities and individual academics support racism, ethnic cleansing, and the continued violation of international law. Can we ask colleges and universities to be "institutions committed to the search for truth and its free expression" when they willingly support a state and military complex that promotes discrimination among their student bodies and when they have no regard for their fellow academics (Palestinian and dissenting Israeli academics), whose academic freedom is trampled and denied at every turn by the patrons of these colleges and universities?

In South Africa the academic boycott was never regarded as a privileged strategy nor academics regarded as an exceptional category. First, the strategies adopted by the liberation struggle placed onerous conditions on millions of individuals and many institutions in society, some more than others. Particularly for workers and the poor, the sacrifices they were asked to make exceeded those of other social classes, and in some cases it meant not only the loss of jobs, family, and health but also direct physical confrontation with a brutish state. Second, academic boycotts were supported by the majority of those academics who understood their role to be engaged and socially committed intellectuals. Academics so engaged did not regard themselves as privileged when it came to making sacrifices, even though their sacrifices were, relative to those of others, less onerous and demanding. Third, we simply did not regard intellectual work as outside of accountability. Finally, the call for an academic boycott was considered a legitimate and necessary extension of the freedom struggle into other arenas of social and political engagement and practice.

The "objective test" by which the issue of an academic boycott or any other such strategy must be evaluated can only arise from a consideration of the conditions of each case. That is, it is determined contextually, not a priori or ahistorically. Academic freedom in the conditions of civil war, violent occupation, genocide, or conquest and subjugation must surely bear some reference to these very conditions for the criteria of its determination. Failure to recognize this will mean that the very concept of freedom more generally, and academic freedom in particular, becomes both meaningless and bereft of any practical possibilities. Professor Hilary Rose, a sociologist of science, reminds us of academics, including liberal and left geneticists, who actively collaborated with their German counterparts who provided the specious "scientific" basis for the ugly concept of "lives not worth living" and *Russenhygiene* (ethnic cleansing). She says, "Here, an absolutist principle of academic freedom ... [facilitated] the eugenic project of the Final Solution."[4] It is instructive that Rose is a prominent member of the British Committee for the Universities of Palestine and a supporter of the academic boycott campaign against Israel.

Today, despite the corporatized debasement of higher education—which casts public space as a commodified sphere—intellectual work must recover its connections with political realities. These include issues of solidarity and our responsibility as academics to being citizens in the broader world beyond the confines of the academy.

THE UNIVERSITY OF JOHANNESBURG AND BEN GURION UNIVERSITY

The precursor of the University of Johannesburg was the Randse Afrikaanse Universiteit (RAU), established by the apartheid regime in 1966 as the academic hub for Afrikaners in Johannesburg. In 2005, RAU merged with the Technikon Witwatersrand and the Soweto and East Rand campuses of Vista University to form the University of Johannesburg (UJ). UJ has an enrollment of fifty thousand students spread over four campuses. RAU, like other similar institutions in South Africa, enjoyed close working relations with Israeli state institutions through the research those institutions provided to South Africa's booming military-industrial complex.[5]

In late 2009, at the urging of a local donor and prominent Zionist,[6] UJ attempted to resuscitate a general apartheid-era agreement with Ben Gurion University (BGU), ostensibly to use BGU's water purification technology and micro-algal biotechnology research to reuse waste water in South Africa. UJ intended to partner with Mekorot, the Israeli water authority responsible for implementing discriminatory water policies against Palestinians. A Memorandum of Agreement between BGU and UJ was quickly and stealthily drawn up and signed. A group of academic staff members were alerted to this development, and, together with progressive student organizations, Palestinian solidarity activists and trade unionists began mobilizing against the Memorandum of Agreement. After a series of mass meetings and seminars, as well as concerted pressure on the university's managers, a special meeting of the senate was convened in May 2010 to discuss the issue. The senate established a committee, which met on five different occasions in the ensuring months and concluded that, inter alia:

> There is significant evidence that BGU has research and other engagements that supports the military and armed forces of Israel…. As a university embedded in a highly militarized Israeli society, BGU's obligation to implement state policies, and its research and other relationships with the Israeli armed forces does have a significant impact on the society, and therefore on the continued subjugation of the Palestinian population….

The senate recommended that "UJ should not continue with the MOU [Memorandum of Agreement] with BGU as it stands. Instead…our institutional response should be guided by the following principles":

> In support of the principle of solidarity with any oppressed population (a defining principle emanating from our own history), we should take leadership on this matter from peer institutions among the Palestinian population. Our engagement must encourage reconciliation and the advancement of human dignity and human solidarity.[7]

Attempts were made to amend the MOU "to include one or more Palestinian universities chosen on the basis of agreement between BGU and UJ." Palestinian colleagues alerted to this disingenuous attempt to continue with the agreement easily rebuffed maneuvers by both BGU and some of the managers at UJ. The latter also received various threats from donors such as the hospitality mogul Sol Kerzner's Sun International Group.[8] The partnership was defended in the senate meeting by professor Ilan Troen, Ben Gurion's founding dean of humanities and social sciences. Troen's participation was organized by the South African Associates of Ben Gurion University, the president of which, Bertram Lubner, is also vice chairperson of Ben Gurion's board of governors.

Finally, a decision by secret ballot to end the agreement with BGU was supported by the overwhelming majority of senate members.[9] It came after an eighteen-month debate involving committees, task teams, fact-finding missions, and lengthy council and senate deliberations. It involved massive mobilization and had the support of the vast majority of UJ's students and staff members, leading intellectuals in South Africa, Palestinian academics, and Palestinian and Israeli nongovernmental organizations (NGOs), which played a critical role in providing information about BGU and the ways in which water is used as an instrument of oppression. NGOs included LifeSource, the Palestinian Hydrology Group, and others affiliated to the Palestinian Environmental NGO Network (PENGON).[10]

The campaign for ending relations with BGU also benefited from the comprehensive report issued by Amnesty International in the same week UJ signed the agreement with BGU. The report, entitled *Troubled Waters—Thirsting for Justice: Palestinians' Access to Water Restricted*,[11] meticulously detailed Israel's discriminatory water policies. Through the campaign against BGU and the publicity it received in the mainstream press, thousands of South Africans began to understand the details of one aspect of the daily injustices confronting Palestinians.

They learned how Israel permits Palestinians access to only a fraction of the available water, which is held mainly in aquifers under the occupied West Bank, while Israeli settlements receive a virtually unlimited supply. In the Gaza Strip, 90 to 95 percent of the water from the Coastal Aquifer, its only water resource, is contaminated. The siege of Gaza has prevented the import of basic building materials, spare parts, and energy for the treatment of wastewater. Chemicals necessary for desalinating the brackish water are prohibited by Israel. These restrictions are compounded by Israel's frequent bombing sprees against infrastructure, utilities, and Gaza's only power plant. Israel has also imposed a complex system of permits that the Palestinians must obtain from the Israeli Army and other authorities in order to carry out water-related projects in the occupied Palestinian territories. According to the Palestinian NGO LifeSource, even when on the rare occasion a permit was received to build the Salfit Wastewater Treatment Plant, the Israeli military vetoed the project. In light of this and many other egregious instances, it is not surprising that, on August 5, 2010, the UN Human Rights Committee found Israel guilty of directly violating Palestinian human rights to water and sanitation.

More specific to BGU, researchers showed that BGU's water research and biotechnology institutes and laboratories have clear links with Elbit Systems, Israel's largest private military contractor, and the Jewish National Fund, which has expropriated vast properties belonging to millions of Palestinians. Despite the hubris, patronization, and spin of the pro-Israeli lobby, who made the highly publicized, spurious claim that South Africa's water problems would have been solved by Israeli expertise,[12] the truth is that our water woes have less to do with a lack of technology and expertise than with the historic and ongoing negative role of the mining industry, issues of privatization, and the maintenance and provision of water infrastructure, to name just a few key areas. The proposed, small-scale UJ–BGU partnership in water research was far removed from these contextual issues.

In an age of the neoliberal "knowledge economy," where there is mere rhetorical support for social justice, where research and teaching related to this purpose are seen as "ornamental," ending the aparthied-era agreement with Ben Gurion was a significant victory, even more so given the antecedents of UJ.

Today, twenty years after the first democratic elections in South Africa, difficult but necessary questions are being posed about our trajectory of development. Struggles persist and there are continuities and discontinuities, antinomies and ambiguities in policy and practice, and considerable contestation. Higher education in South Africa has not escaped, under the behest of corporate globalization, the impact of marketization on the academy. In this situation, neoliberal policies and the seduction of money and lucre often trump solidarity. The possibilities and extent of the academy and intellectuals in South Africa to live up to Edward Said's imperative of "taking a principled stand" will be shaped not only by the nature and changes in the political economy but just as importantly by the character and mettle of human agency inside and outside the academy. Support for the BDS campaign against apartheid Israel, as it did against apartheid South Africa, can only assist such agency.

10

STRUCTURAL VIOLENCE ON TRIAL: BDS AND THE MOVEMENT TO RESIST ERASURE

NOURA ERAKAT

Walking to the home of Rifqa Al Kurd (Umm Al Kurd) is a journey into violence. To visit the ninety-two-year-old matriarch, one must navigate through a narrow walkway, past a dwelling that she owned until 2009. She built a concrete two-bedroom home for her eldest son and his family adjacent to her own. She had envisioned a residential space for her family, adorned by green grass, a garden of plants and flowers, and an outdoor patio. Today that grass is mostly dirt with yellowed shrubs, the walls are splashed with graffiti commanding her to leave, and the patio furniture is soiled with feces and urine.

In 2009, a group of Jewish Israeli settlers walked into Umm Al Kurd's home and declared it their own by divine decree. To the unknowing eye, they appeared as if they were going on a camping trip. In the East Jerusalem suburb of Sheikh Jarrah, however, these young men, funded by the Israeli state and protected by its police forces, are taking over Umm Al Kurd's home one inch at a time, thereby expanding and entrenching Israel's settler-colonial project.

Umm Al Kurd is originally from Haifa but was forced to flee her home in the course of Israel's establishment in 1948, what Palestinians regard as their *Nakba*, or catastrophe.[1] She has been living in Sheikh Jarrah since 1956, when Jordan built residential dwellings for Palestinian refugees atop an olive grove. Sheikh Jarrah, along with Beit Safafa, Issawiyeh, Silwan, Beit Hanina, Wadi al-Joz, and Jabal al Mukabbar, are all Palestinian suburbs of East Jerusalem that stand in the way of Israel's master plan to Judaize the city and complete its de facto annexation in contravention of UN Security Council resolutions, the International Court of Justice's jurisprudence, international humanitarian law, and even the diplomatic dictates of the United States.

In a YouTube video of the takeover,[2] Umm Al Kurd musters all the energy her aged body and spirit have to scream for the men to "Get out!" She tugs on the shirts of the settler men, who see her as an insignificant obstruction, a puddle to step over in order to reach her door's front steps, where they will plant themselves and expand Israel's exclusionary jurisdiction. Umm Al Kurd's male relatives hold her to make sure she does not fall as she futilely commands the settlers to leave. The Palestinian men dare not intervene themselves, because, should they do so much as touch the settlers, the Israeli state—which deems them trespassers in their own homes—will criminally prosecute them. There are no police to whom Umm Al Kurd can turn; there is no state that recognizes her claims; there is no law to depend on or morality that will prevail.

In all the uproar since the American Studies Association (ASA) endorsed the academic boycott of Israel, not a single article has been written about Umm Al Kurd or about the thousands of Palestinians like her.[3] In fact, well before the boycott resolution, mainstream media outlets similarly failed to describe this grotesque condition of displacement and dispossession—endemic features of Palestinian life. While Western audiences may only hear about or see images of Palestinians during intermittent episodes of kinetic violence, Palestinians endure structural violence that threatens their lives, families, and livelihoods on a daily basis. The erasure of this violence, and of Palestinian subjectivity more broadly, has had a profound and devastating impact.

Such erasure facilitated Israel's original colonization of Palestinian lands, which Zionist mythology continues to recall as "a land without a people for a people without a land." Today, that erasure facilitates the ongoing forced population transfer of Palestinians from East Jerusalem, the Jordan Valley, Area C (approximately 62 percent of the West Bank), and within Israel itself—most prominently in the Negev region.[4] And the vehement campaign against the boycott, divestment, and sanctions (BDS) movement threatens erasure of yet another feature of Palestinian life under attack: their political agency.[5]

The US-based conversation about BDS, and the Israel/Palestine conflict generally, is framed as either a discussion about US national interests in the Middle East or as an intra-Jewish conversation about the future of Zionism. To the extent that Palestinians are discussed at all, they are depicted as hapless victims, nominal tokens, or looming terrorist threats. However, if one recognizes that the settler takeover of Umm Al Kurd's home is not an outlier but a central feature of Israel's matrix of control, aimed at forcibly removing Palestinians from their homes and implanting Jewish settlers in their place, the conversation is suddenly, and irreparably, disrupted.

By centralizing Palestinian claims, the BDS movement scrutinizes the legitimacy of Israel's structural violence. That is why the recent critical response to the ASA boycott resolution has not challenged the allegations made against Israel but instead has sought to censor and shut down the conversation all together. Legislative efforts within the New York, Maryland, and Illinois state assemblies proposed rescinding funding from American studies departments at public universities that endorsed the boycott. University provosts and presidents across dozens of campuses unilaterally condemned the boycott resolution without so much as consulting their respective faculties.[6] Most recently, Israeli prime minister Benjamin Netanyahu closed his address at the AIPAC conference by decrying BDS as a manifestation of anti-Semitism rather than a grassroots political tactic aimed at applying pressure on a state where diplomacy has failed.[7]

Not surprisingly, and notwithstanding this national fervor, no state assembly, no university president, and no heads of state have called for a debate or a dialogue. They have simply sought to suppress a Palestinian-centered narrative and to incapacitate a movement. Surmounting these silencing tactics is critical to understanding Palestinian claims.

East Jerusalem is a microcosm of the forced population transfer that characterizes Palestinian life. It is unique because, unlike other Palestinian cities dominated by Israel in 1948, it was occupied in 1967 and is therefore a designated part of the inchoate state of Palestine; specifically, its capital. But, unlike other cities in the occupied West Bank and the Gaza Strip, Israel unilaterally annexed East Jerusalem in 1980 and has steadily worked to remove it from the purview of political contestation. It has tried to make it another "fact on the ground" to be dealt with pragmatically, without the cumbersome and distracting reference to law, rights, or morality. Thus, East Jerusalem is a contemporary case study that illustrates the historical transformation of Palestinian cities such as Safad and Haifa and Yaffa and Lydd and Lifta and Ramle and Ikrit and Bir'im, whose indigenous peoples have mostly become exiled refugees; whose remaining Palestinian communities are second-class citizens; whose histories have been rewritten in Israeli textbooks to elide the presence of Palestinians prior to Israel's establishment; and whose future is beyond the reach of the peace process despite the fervent claims of Palestinian refugees seeking to return. I examine East Jerusalem both to show the legal and policy mechanisms used to diminish and marginalize the Palestinian population as well as to demonstrate why BDS is an insufficient but necessary tactic.

Colonizing Jerusalem and Forcibly Removing the Palestinian Jerusalem Population: 1948 to the Present

Since its inception, Israel has considered the Palestinian population in areas adjacent to Jerusalem as an obstruction to the territorial contiguity between the Jewish populations in Jerusalem and those in the coastal areas.[8] Within months of the collapse of the UN Partition Plan, the western areas of Jerusalem were transformed from a mixed urban setting to one where Jewish predominance was absolute.[9] To achieve this dramatic transformation, Zionist armies evicted nearly eighty thousand Palestinians from West Jerusalem, reducing their original population by half.[10]

In the immediate aftermath of the 1967 war and the occupation that followed, Israel issued the Municipalities Ordinance (Amendment No. 6) Law, which effectively annexed approximately seventy square kilometers of the West Bank and integrated it into the Israeli municipality of Jerusalem.[11] Israel sought to incorporate the maximum amount of Palestinian land with the least number of Palestinians. The state thus bestowed upon East Jerusalemite Palestinians the legal status of foreign permanent residents rather than citizens, with the aim of undermining their ability to remain in the area.[12]

Permanent residency, indicated by blue identity cards, is a special category of permit that affords residents the right to vote in municipal elections but not in national elections, and their residency is in a permanent state of temporality.[13] By legislative means, Israel made Palestinian residency in Jerusalem a privilege rather than a right and transformed their status from an indigenous population to a foreign one. Palestinian Jerusalemites have thus been at extreme risk of arbitrary removal.

In December 1995, without forewarning, the Israeli Ministry of Interior issued a "center of life" policy directive and revoked the residency of all Palestinians who had not lived in Jerusalem for seven consecutive years.[14] Until then, Palestinian Jerusalemites had been able to live in the occupied West Bank outside of the Israeli-defined municipal boundaries of East Jerusalem and cohabitate seamlessly with their Palestinian counterparts. In 2008 alone, based upon this directive, which applied to Palestinians only, Israel revoked the residency permits of 4,577 Palestinian Jerusalemites.[15] Together with other policies aimed at diminishing the Palestinian population, Israel revoked the residency of more than 14,000 Palestinian Jerusalemites between 1967 and 2012.[16] Although the implementation of the "center of life" policy, which amounts to "quiet deportation," has abated since 2008, it remains in effect.[17] It has significantly altered the demographic composition of Jerusalem in the furtherance of Israel's demographic policy goals.

In its most recent municipal master plan, "Jerusalem 2000," Israeli authorities expressed a desire to maintain a balance in the city of 70 percent Jews to 30 percent Arab.[18] Moreover, because trends project a ratio of 60:40 by the year 2020, the plan proposed a number of measures aimed at maintaining a "Jewish majority in the city while attending to the needs of the Arab minority."[19] These policies take on two dimensions: the privileged treatment of Jewish nationals and citizens and/or the discriminatory treatment of Jerusalem's Palestinian residents. Such discriminatory treatment is evidenced in zoning and planning policy, home demolitions, inadequate municipal services, and a lack of due process within Israeli courts.

The Jerusalem municipal government rejects Palestinian applications for planning schemes almost as a matter of policy.[20] While Israel provides the services of urban planners to its Jewish residents free of charge, Palestinian neighborhoods must hire and pay for planners to develop plans intended for review by municipal authorities. In its report *Separate and Unequal: Israel's Discriminatory Treatment of Palestinians in the Occupied Palestinian Territories*, Human Rights Watch notes that, to date, municipal authorities have not approved any of these plans.[21]

The state deliberately limits the land eligible for zoning for Palestinians, one-third of East Jerusalem's population, to 13 percent of all available land. For areas of Jerusalem that Israel has not zoned for construction, building permits are impossible to obtain. As an example, in 2008 Israeli municipal authorities issued only 125 building licenses for 400 housing unit requests.[22] In order to accommodate their natural population growth, Palestinian Jerusalemites are forced to build residential and commercial structures without permits. In turn, Israel has destroyed all property built "illegally" without a permit and displaced thousands of Palestinians.[23] Between 2000 and 2008, Israeli authorities demolished 670 Palestinian homes for lacking a building permit.[24]

Jewish Israeli citizens also build their homes without building permits, but Israel's review of housing laws disproportionately harms its Palestinian population. From 1996 to 2001, 82 percent of building violations in Jerusalem were in Jewish neighborhoods as compared to 18 percent in Palestinian ones; however, 80 percent of enforcement actions were taken in Palestinian neighborhoods whereas only 20 percent occurred in Jewish ones.[25]

The disproportionate resources the state affords its Jerusalem residents, according to national and religious origin, are further evidence of Israel's blatantly discriminatory planning policy. In June 1967 Israel annexed 70,500 dunams (1 dunam = 1,000 square meters) of East Jerusalem land, one-third of which was privately owned Arab property, to develop residential construction. According to the Israeli human rights group B'Tselem, "By the end of 2001, 46,978 housing units had been built for Jews on this land, but not one unit for Palestinians who constitute one-third of the city's population."[26] Additionally, one thousand parks, thirty-four public swimming pools, and twenty-six libraries serve Jerusalem's Jewish population. In contrast, Palestinians living in the east part of the city have forty-five parks, two libraries, and no public swimming pools.[27]

The state also works hand in hand with Jewish settlers to intimidate and remove Palestinian families where it seeks to expand its colonial jurisdiction. Such has been the case with Umm Al Kurd and at least five other Palestinian families in Sheikh Jarrah.[28] In most cases, removal of Palestinian Jerusalemites from their homes begins with a court proceeding seeking eviction of the family for failure to provide original land deeds, failure to obtain building permits, or failure to comply with arbitrary laws applied disproportionately against Palestinian Jerusalemites. Once the court has issued its decision, it becomes a matter of time before Israeli police forces forcibly remove the Palestinian families. To prevent the families from returning to and/or remaining in their homes, the state supports Jewish settlers willing to live in those homes amid Palestinian neighbors who rightfully see them as a dangerous threat. Israel dedicates US$19.2 million (70 million NIS) for the security of its settlers in East Jerusalem alone, where they enjoy complete legal impunity for any harm they inflict upon Palestinians.[29] To date, Israel and these settlers have completely driven away the Hanoun and Al Ghawi families, who lived in makeshift tents in front of their homes for months before searching for more suitable shelter elsewhere. As of this writing, settlers have taken over part of Umm Al Kurd's home, and the Shamasneh, Sabbagh, and Hijazi families have been issued eviction orders.

Like Umm Al Kurd, these families have challenged their evictions in Israel's highest courts and lost. The decisions all turned on a dubious precedent set in 1982, wherein an Israeli attorney named Yitzhak Toussia-Cohen, who represented seventeen of Sheikh Jarrah's twenty-eight families, failed to challenge the ownership claims by two Jewish groups that asserted the land belonged to them based on religious and historical claims.[30] The Toussia-Cohen agreement permitted the families to stay in their homes as "protected tenants" of the two Jewish groups.[31] The Israeli High Court refused to nullify this agreement despite its questionable origins and the families' inadequate legal representation.

Israel's courts, its police forces, and its armed civilian settler population work in tandem to alter the demographic composition of East Jerusalem. The forced population transfer of these Palestinian families is thus inevitable.

BDS: RESISTANCE AND NARRATION

Umm Al Kurd's unsuccessful legal challenge fits within a mosaic of equally futile legal and diplomatic efforts to thwart Israel's ethnic cleansing campaign in East Jerusalem. In response to Israel's unilateral annexation of East Jerusalem in 1980, the UN Security Council passed Resolution 476, reiterating "that all such measures which have altered the geographic, demographic and historical character and status of the Holy City of Jerusalem are null and void and must be rescinded in compliance with the relevant resolutions of the Security Council."[32]

In protest of the annexation, no state, not even Israel's benefactor and strongest ally, the United States, moved its embassy to Jerusalem. Despite the universally disapproving response, Israel suffered no real consequences, and it continued its settler-colonial expansion without pause.

Far from helping to resist it, the Oslo peace process enabled Israel's expansionism. Oslo's elision of international law conveniently shelved Article 49 of the Fourth Geneva Convention, prohibiting settlement activity; Article 147, deeming it a war crime; and numerous UN Security Council resolutions prohibiting the transformation of East Jerusalem. Governed only by politics of the strong, Oslo considered 54 percent of Israeli settlements Jewish "neighborhoods" and thus legal at the time of its signing in 1993.[33] Not surprisingly, and the under the veneer of a peace process, the settler population in the West Bank, including East Jerusalem, tripled from two hundred thousand in 1993 to nearly six hundred thousand today.

In February 2011, the Palestinian leadership drafted a UN Security Council resolution to condemn the settlements, using language that mirrored US policy on settlements. The Obama administration issued its first veto in the council to block the measure. Susan Rice, US Ambassador to the United Nations at the time, explained:

> For more than four decades, Israeli settlement activity in territories occupied in 1967 has undermined Israel's security and corroded hopes for peace and stability in the region....Continued settlement activity violates Israel's international commitments, devastates trust between the parties and threatens the prospects for peace...[but the adoption of the resolution would risk] hardening the positions of both sides.[34]

However, in its capacity as peace broker, the United States has acted systematically to protect Israel from rebuke, thereby providing it no incentive to modify its position or reevaluate its colonial logic.[35] Even in those exceptional instances when it has objected to Israel's activities, the US domestic political landscape has impeded its efficacy. During Vice President Biden's 2010 visit to Israel, he urged Israel to freeze its settlement expansion for the sake of renewed peace talks. In the same visit, Prime Minister Netanyahu announced plans for 1,600 new settlements. An embarrassed Biden issued a statement objecting to the timing and substance of the announcement and emphasized that "unilateral action taken by either party cannot prejudge the outcome of negotiations on permanent status issues."[36]

In response to its public reprimand, no less than twenty-three members of Congress publicly chastised the Obama administration. Representative Todd Tiahrt described President Obama's public row with Israel as "disrespectful."[37] Representative (now Indiana governor) Mike Pence explained, "The American people consider Israel our most cherished ally and we her closest friend and guardian.... As I just told the Prime Minister [Netanyahu], I never thought I'd live to see the day that an American administration would denounce the State of Israel for rebuilding Jerusalem.... The American people and the American Congress in both parties support the State of Israel."[38] Rather than stand off with its Congress, the Obama administration responded to the incident by significantly chilling its interest and investment in resolving the conflict.

On July 9, 2004, the International Court of Justice (ICJ) issued an Advisory Opinion on the case, *Legal Consequences of the Construction of a Wall in the Occupied Palestinian Territory*.[39] Israel began building the Separation Wall in 2002. By the time it is projected to be complete in 2020, 85 percent of it will run through the West Bank, confiscating 13 percent of West Bank lands.[40] The meandering route not so coincidentally circumscribes East Jerusalem and its mammoth Jewish Israeli settlement enterprise. The court held that the while Israel could build a wall on the 1949 Armistice Line, the route of the wall, insofar as it has altered the territorial integrity of the occupied territory, was illegal. In a vote of 14 to 1, the justices held that "All States are under an obligation not to recognize the illegal situation resulting from the construction of the wall and not to render aid or assistance in maintaining the situation created by such construction."[41]

In essence, the ICJ called for international sanction of Israel in regard to its settlement enterprise. White House spokesperson at the time, Scott McClellan, dismissed the decision and explained, "We do not believe that [the ICJ is an] appropriate forum to resolve what is a political issue."[42] No state responded to the ICJ's call, and the Palestinian leadership, under the tutelage of the United States, dropped the watershed decision like a heavy brick.

On the one-year anniversary of the Advisory Opinion, July 9, 2005, and after nearly sixteen years of a counterproductive peace process, the largest swath of Palestinian civil society organizations, individuals, and political parties took their lives into their own hands. The Boycott National Committee (BNC) issued a call for global solidarity to boycott, divest, and sanction Israel until and when it ended its occupation of Arab lands, afforded equality to its Palestinian citizens, and promoted the right of return of Palestinian refugees.[43] The call circumvents the intransigence of the unequivocal US support for Israel as well as the consequential impotence of the international community.

In its short existence, without a central leadership, and with barely any funding, the global BDS movement has achieved significant milestones: Denmark's largest bank blacklisted the Israeli bank Hapoalim for its involvement in settlement construction[44]; Netherlands' largest pension fund company divested from Israel's five largest banks[45]; South Africa's University of Johannesburg severed its ties to Ben Gurion University[46]; Naomi Klein, journalist and author of *The Shock Doctrine* refused to allow sales of her books to Israelis benefit the Israeli economy[47]; musician Elvis Costello refused to perform in Israel[48]; Stephen Hawking, the world's most famous scientist, refused to attend the Israeli Presidential Conference[49]; British film director Ken Loach declined an invitation to Haifa Film Festival[50]; and most recently, in the United States, the Association of Asian American Studies (AAAS),[51] the Native American and Indigenous Studies Association (NAISA),[52] and the American Studies Association (ASA)[53] have all endorsed the academic boycott of Israel. These are but a few of the BDS victories achieved in less than nine years of the movement's existence.[54]

While none of these victories have changed the reality for Palestinians on the ground, they have changed the decades-long attitude that Israel can act with impunity, and they have helped put Israel's structural violence on trial. More importantly, the BDS call has restored a sense of political agency for Palestinians.

Umm Al Kurd cannot use force to resist the takeover of her home because the state has delegitimized her claims and criminalized her protest. She cannot avail herself of juridical justice because the state privileges the narrative and well-being of her Jewish counterparts as a matter of law. She cannot rely on international relations or legal processes because of the vested interest of the United States in Israel. Among her limited options is her ability to ask for solidarity. Truly, it is an unfortunate condition, because it places her fate in the hands of others who may or may not choose to believe her story; who may or may not choose to empathize with it; and who may or may not choose to do something about it on her terms.

Liberal Zionist supporters of BDS, for example, insist that the tactic should target only Israel's occupation but not the state itself, thereby truncating the BNC's tripartite call.[55] What these fair-weather friends fail to note, however, is that this harrowing tale of ethnic cleansing in Jerusalem has stark corollaries within the state, both past and present. Between 1948 and 1953, for example, Israel established 370 new settlements for Jews only within the nascent state.[56] Of those, 350 were located on land confiscated as "absentee" property that belonged to exiled Palestinian refugees.[57] Today, Israel seeks to remove 70,000 Bedouin Palestinians from their homes in the Negev region to build a Jewish-only settlement and plant a forest.[58]

The BDS call represents the interests of all Palestinians and not just the one-third of their population resident in the occupied territories. It is a Palestinian call made on behalf of a Palestinian nation. Negating its legitimacy effectively usurps Palestinian agency to define themselves and their aspirations for themselves.

But perhaps this liberal Zionist position is the best-case scenario. In the worst case, detractors such as AAUP head Cary Nelson insist that supporting BDS is politically misguided because it "hardens the extremists on both sides, and moves us further away from peace."[59] Nelson's appeal not only equates the messianic settlers who took over Umm Al Kurd's home with Umm Al Kurd herself, but it also disingenuously suggests that he and others like him have been working tirelessly to thwart Israel's forced population transfer of Palestinians, and they simply take issue with boycott as a tactic. In fact, Nelson is actually an ardent supporter of Israel, using academic freedom as a proxy for his protest.[60]

In *The Origins of Totalitarianism*, Hannah Arendt explains that the fundamental violation of liberty is the deprivation "not of the right to freedom, but the right to action; not of the right to think whatever they please, but of the right to opinion."[61] Israel's matrix of control together with US hegemony has denied Palestinians of the right to action. The attack on BDS threatens to deny Palestinians of their right to opinion and further restrict their right to action.

Umm Al Kurd and thousands of other Palestinians like her from Al-Araqib, Yaffa, Hebron, Sidon, and beyond would like to do something for themselves to effectively remedy their condition, but they cannot. Condemning BDS risks telling them that they cannot even appeal for international support. Doing so would force Umm Al Kurd and her counterparts to capitulate and to accept their condition as part of a normal order, when, in fact, it is within the realm of the absurd. BDS may be insufficient on its own to realize Palestinian freedom, but it is a form of resistance nonetheless. I do not know who said it first, but it bears repeating: to resist is to exist.

11

THE BOYCOTT WILL WORK: AN ISRAELI PERSPECTIVE*

ILAN PAPPÉ

I have been a political activist for most of my adult life. In all these years, I have believed deeply that the unbearable and unacceptable reality of Israel and Palestine could only be changed from within. This is why I have been ceaselessly devoted to persuading Jewish society—to which I belong and into which I was born—that its basic policy in the land was wrong and disastrous.

As for so many others, the options for me were clear: I could either join politics from above or counter it from below. I began by joining the Labor Party in the 1980s, and then the Democratic Front for Peace and Equality (Hadash), when I declined an offer to join the Knesset.

At the same time, I focused my energies on working alongside others within educational and peace NGOs, even chairing two such institutions: the left-Zionist Institute for Peace Studies in Givat Haviva, and the non-Zionist Emil Touma Institute for Palestinian Studies. In both circles, veteran and younger colleagues alike sought to create constructive dialogue with our compatriots in the hope of influencing present policy for future reconciliation. It was mainly a campaign of information about crimes and atrocities committed by Israel since 1948, and a plea for a future based on equal human and civil rights.

For an activist, the realization that change from within is unattainable not only grows out of an intellectual or political process, but is more than anything else an admission of defeat. And it was this fear of defeatism that prevented me from adopting a more resolute position for a very long time. After almost thirty years of activism and historical research, I became convinced that the balance of power in

* This essay was published previously in *The Case for Sanctions Against Israel*, edited by Audrea Lim (Verso, 2013).

Palestine and Israel preempted any possibility for a transformation within Jewish Israeli society in the foreseeable future. Though rather late in the game, I came to realize that the problem was not a particular policy or a specific government, but one more deeply rooted in the ideological infrastructure informing Israeli decisions on Palestine and the Palestinians ever since 1948. I have described this ideology elsewhere as a hybrid between colonialism and romantic nationalism.[1]

Today, Israel is a formidable settler-colonialist state, unwilling to transform or compromise, and eager to crush by whatever means necessary any resistance to its control and rule in historic Palestine. Beginning with the ethnic cleansing of 80 percent of Palestine in 1948, followed by Israel's occupation of the remaining 20 percent of the land in 1967, Palestinians in Israel are now enclaved in mega-prisons, Bantustans, and besieged cantons, and are singled out through discriminatory policies.

Meanwhile, millions of Palestinian refugees around the world have no way to return home, and time has only weakened, if not annihilated, all internal challenges to this ideological infrastructure. Even as I write, the Israeli settler state continues to further colonize and uproot the indigenous people of Palestine.

Admittedly, Israel is not a straightforward case study in colonialism,[2] nor can the solutions to either the 1967 occupation or the question of Palestine as a whole be easily described as decolonization. Unlike most colonialist projects, the Zionist movement had no clear metropolis, and because it far predates the age of colonialism, describing it in that way would be anachronistic. But these paradigms are still highly relevant to the situation, for two reasons. The first is that diplomatic efforts in Palestine since 1936 and the peace process that began in 1967 have only increased the number of Israeli settlements in Palestine, from less than 10 percent of Palestine in 1936 to over 90 percent of the country today.

Thus it seems that the message from the peace brokers, mainly the United States ever since 1970, is that peace can be achieved without any significant limit being placed on the settlements, or colonies, in Palestine. True, settlers have periodically been evicted from Gaza settlements and some other isolated outposts, but this did not alter the overall matrix of colonial control, with all its systematic daily abuses of civil and human rights.

The occupation of the West Bank and the Gaza Strip, the oppression of the Palestinians inside Israel, and the denial of the refugees' right of return will continue as long as these policies (occupation, oppression, and denial) are packaged as a comprehensive peace settlement to be endorsed by obedient Palestinian and Arab partners.

The second reason for viewing the situation through the lens of colonialism/ anticolonialism is that it allows us a fresh look at the raison d'être of the peace process. The basic objective, apart from the creation of two separate states, is for Israel to withdraw from areas it occupied in 1967.

But this is contingent upon Israeli security concerns being satisfied, which Prime Minister Netanyahu has articulated as the recognition of Israel as a Jewish state, and the rest of Israel's political center has articulated as the existence of a demilitarized future Palestinian state confined only to parts of the occupied territories. The consensus is that, after withdrawal, the army will still keep an eye on Palestine from the Jewish settlement blocs, East Jerusalem, the Jordanian border, and the other side of the walls and fences surrounding the West Bank and the Gaza Strip.

Whether or not the Quartet—the UN, the United States, European Union, and Russia—or even the current US administration seeks a more comprehensive withdrawal and a more sovereign Palestinian state, no one in the international community has seriously challenged the Israeli demand that its concerns first be satisfied. The peace process requires a change only in the Palestinian agenda, leaving the Israeli agenda untouched.

In other words, the message from abroad to Israel is that peace does not require any transformation from within. In fact, it even leaves Israel room for interpretation: the Israeli government, apprehensive of the reaction of hardline settlers, was unwilling to evict them from isolated posts in the occupied territories. That even the weak Palestinian leadership has refused to accept this rationale has allowed the Israelis to claim that the Palestinians are stubborn and inflexible, and thus that Israel is entitled to pursue unilateral policies to safeguard its national security (the infamous "ingathering policy," as coined by Ehud Olmert).[3]

Therefore, it seems safe to conclude that the peace process has actually deterred the colonizer and occupier from transforming its mentality and ideology. As long as the international community waits for the oppressed to transform their positions, while validating those upheld by the oppressor since 1967, this will remain the most brutal occupation the world has seen since World War II.

The annals of colonialism and decolonization teach us that an end to the military presence and occupation has been a condition sine qua non for meaningful negotiations between colonizer and colonized even to begin. An unconditional end to Israel's military presence in the lives of more than three million Palestinians should be the precondition for any negotiations, which can only develop when the relationship between the two sides is not oppressive but equal.

In most historical cases, occupiers have not decided to leave. They were forced out, usually through a prolonged and bloody armed struggle. This has been attempted with very little success in the Israel/Palestine conflict. In fewer cases, success was achieved by applying external pressure on the rogue power or state in the very last stage of decolonization. The latter strategy is more attractive. In any case, the Israeli paradigm of "peace" is not going to shift unless it is pressured from the outside or forced to do so on the ground.

Even before one begins to define more specifically what such outside pressure entails, it is essential not to confuse the means (pressure) with the objective (finding a formula for joint living). In other words, it is important to emphasize that pressure is meant to trigger meaningful negotiations, not take their place. So while I still believe that change from within is key to bringing about a lasting solution to the question of the refugees, the predicament of the Palestinian minority in Israel, and the future of Jerusalem, other steps must first be taken for this to be achieved.

What kind of pressure is necessary? South Africa has provided the most illuminating and inspiring historical example for those leading this debate, while, on the ground, activists and NGOs under occupation have sought nonviolent means both to resist the occupation and to expand the forms of resistance beyond suicide bombing and the firing of Qassam missiles from Gaza. These two impulses produced the BDS campaign against Israel. It is not a coordinated campaign operated by some secret cabal. It began as a call from within the civil society under occupation, endorsed by other Palestinian groups, and translated into individual and collective actions worldwide.

These actions vary in focus and form, from boycotting Israeli products to severing ties with academic institutes in Israel. Some are individual displays of protest; others are organized campaigns. What they have in common is their message of outrage against the atrocities on the ground in Palestine—but the campaign's elasticity has made it into a broad process powerful enough to produce a new public mood and atmosphere, without a predetermined focal point.

For the few Israelis who sponsored the campaign early on, it was a definitive moment that clearly stated our position vis-à-vis the origins, nature, and policies of our state. But, in hindsight, it also seems to have provided moral sponsorship, which has been helpful for the success of the campaign.

Supporting BDS remains a drastic act for an Israeli peace activist. It excludes one immediately from the consensus and from the accepted discourse in Israel. Palestinians pay a higher price for the struggle, and those of us Israelis who choose this path should not expect to be rewarded or even praised. But it does involve putting yourself in direct confrontation with the state, your own society, and quite often friends and family. For all intents and purposes, this is to cross the final red line—to say farewell to the tribe.

This is why any one of us deciding to join the call should make such a decision wholeheartedly, and with a clear sense of its implications.

But there is really no alternative. Any other option—from indifference, through soft criticism, up to full endorsement of Israeli policy—is a willful decision to be an accomplice to crimes against humanity. The closing of the public mind in Israel, the persistent hold of the settlers over Israeli society, the inbuilt racism within the Jewish population, the dehumanization of the Palestinians, and the vested interests of the army and industry in keeping the occupied territories—all of these mean that we are in for a very long period of callous and oppressive occupation. Thus, the responsibility of Israeli Jews is far greater than that of anyone else involved in advancing peace in Israel and Palestine. Israeli Jews are coming to realize this fact, and this is why the number who support pressuring Israel from the outside is growing by the day. It is still a very small group, but it does form the nucleus of the future Israeli peace camp.

Much can be learned from the Oslo process. There, the Israelis employed the discourse of peace as a convenient way of maintaining the occupation (aided for a while by Palestinian leaders who fell prey to US–Israeli deception tactics). This meant that an end to the occupation was vetoed by not only the "hawks" but also the "doves," who were not really interested in stopping it. That is why concentrated and effective pressure on Israel needs to be applied by the world at large. Such pressure proved successful in the past, particularly in the case of South Africa, and pressure is also necessary to prevent the worst-case scenarios from becoming realities.

After the massacre in Gaza in January 2009, it was hard to see how things could get worse, but they can—with no halt to the expansion of settlements, and continuing assaults on Gaza, the Israeli repertoire of evil has not yet been exhausted. The problem is that the governments of Europe and especially the United States are not likely to endorse the BDS campaign. But one is reminded of the trials and tribulations of the boycott campaign against South Africa, which emanated from civil society and not from the corridors of power.

In many ways, the most encouraging news comes from the most unlikely quarter: US campuses. The enthusiasm and commitment of hundreds of local students have helped in the last decade to bring the idea of divestment to US society—a society that was regarded as a lost cause by the global campaign for Palestine. They have faced formidable foes: both the effective and cynical AIPAC and the fanatical Christian Zionists. But they offer a new way of engaging with Israel, not only for the sake of Palestinians but also for Jews worldwide.

In Europe, an admirable coalition of Muslims, Jews, and Christians is advancing this agenda against fierce accusations of anti-Semitism. The presence of a few Israelis among them has helped to fend off these vicious and totally false allegations. I do not regard the moral and active support of Israelis like myself as the most important ingredient in this campaign. But connections with progressive and radical Jewish dissidents in Israel are vital to the campaign. They are a bridge to a wider public in Israel, which will eventually have to be incorporated. Pariah status will hopefully persuade Israel to abandon its policies of war crimes and abuses of human rights. We hope to empower those on the outside who are now engaged in the campaign, and we are empowered ourselves by their actions.

All of us, it seems, need clear targets, and also need to remain vigilant against simplistic generalizations about the boycott being against Israel for being Jewish, or against the Jews for being in Israel. That is simply not true. The millions of Jews in Israel must be acknowledged. Israel's Jewish population is a living organism that will remain part of any future outcome. However, it is first our sacred duty to end the oppressive occupation and to prevent another Nakba—and the best means for achieving this is a sustained boycott, divestment, and sanctions campaign.

12

CHANGING MY MIND
ABOUT THE BOYCOTT

JOAN W. SCOTT

In 2006, I was one of the organizers of an aborted American Association of University Professors (AAUP) conference on academic boycotts. The point was to open a conversation about the utility—past and present—of such political actions; to understand what was actually involved in the choice of that strategy; to conduct a conversation in a setting above the fray—in this instance at the Rockefeller Conference Center in Bellagio, Italy—and to learn what we could from the various different points of view (South Africa, Cuba, Yugoslavia, as well as Israel) we hoped to represent at the conference. Idealistically, we imagined the conference to be an exercise in academic freedom, the fulfillment of the best of AAUP principles. In fact, our experience was anything but the fulfillment of AAUP ideals. From the outset, defenders of right-wing Israeli politics—with professor Gerald Steinberg of Bar-Ilan University in the lead—sought to prevent the meeting, expressing their "concern" in the name of academic freedom that "illegitimate" voices would be included in the group. Soon the then leadership of AAUP—Cary Nelson and Jane Buck—joined the opposition, notifying the funders of the conference that it did not have official AAUP approval. (They did not notify the conference organizers of their actions.) At that point the conference was canceled. The full story, as well as some of the papers that would have been presented at the conference, was published in a special report in *Academe* (September–October 2006).[1] The published papers are not representative of all who were invited to the conference, because those demanding the exclusion of critics of Israel withdrew their submissions.

Those of us who organized the conference were not promoting academic boycotts; we were simply interested in debating the issue, in order to better understand and evaluate the strategy of the boycott. In fact, at the time, I agreed with the prevailing view at AAUP—that academic boycotts were contrary to principles of open exchange protected by academic freedom. I have now reconsidered that view. Even at the time, in the heat of the controversy about our conference, it began to seem to me that inflexible adherence to a principle did not make sense without consideration of the political contexts within which one wanted to apply it. Indeed, given the vagueness of the principle of academic freedom, its many different uses and applications, knowing how to apply it required understanding the different functions it served in practice. If the conference was meant to achieve that understanding it was thwarted, for we had clearly walked onto a political minefield—the so-called defenders of Israel were going to prevent us from exercising our rights to free speech (to discussion and debate), just as they were preventing their critics within Israel from doing the same by threatening and firing those who represented dissenting views. What did it mean, I wondered, to oppose the boycott campaign in the name of Israeli academic freedom, when the Israeli state regularly denied academic freedom to critics of the state, the occupation, or, indeed, of Zionism, and when the blacklisting of its critics is the regular tool used by state authorities against its own academic institutions?

If anything, the power of the Israeli right and the oppression of Palestinians have increased since 2006—even the supposed "weakening" of the Netanyahu regime has increased representation for far-right parties. The country that claims to be the only democracy in the Middle East has put in place a brutal apartheid system, its politicians talking openly about the irrelevance of Arab Israeli votes in elections and developing new methods for testing their loyalty to the Jewish state. Its legal system is one that rests on inequality between Jewish and non-Jewish citizens; its children are regularly taught that Arab lives are worth less than Jewish lives; its military interferes with Palestinians' access to university education, freedom of assembly, and the right to free speech; its Council of Higher Education, now an arm of the Likud Party, has elevated a religious college in the settlements to the status of a university, accredited a neoconservative think tank to grant BA degrees to students, and conducted inquisitions among critical university faculty, seeking to harass, demote, or fire dissidents—that is, to silence their speech. David Remnick's *New Yorker* article of November 17, 2014, extensively documents what he calls "the decline of tolerance in Israel," citing, among other things, the brutal treatment of critics of current state policy.[2] The hypocrisy of those who consider these to be democratic practices needs to be exposed. An academic and cultural boycott seems to me to be the way to do this.

Such a boycott refuses to accept the façade of democracy Israel wants to present to the world. It refutes the argument that there is an equal power relationship between Israel and its Palestinian neighbors. The inequality of that relationship was dramatically evident in the death and destruction visited upon Gaza during the summer of 2014—a response entirely out of proportion to the damage done by rockets fired upon Israel. The boycott is not directed at individuals on the basis of their national citizenship, quite the contrary. It is an institutional boycott, aimed at those cultural and educational institutions that consistently fail to oppose the occupation and the unequal treatment of non-Jewish citizens. It demands evidence that these institutions provide and support academic freedom to Arabs as well as Jews, Palestinians as well as Israelis, within the borders of Israel, the occupied West Bank, and Gaza. It says that, in the face of an apartheid that violates both the principles and practices of equality and freedom for all, a principled opposition to boycotts as punitive or unfair makes no sense. In fact, such an opposition only helps perpetuate the system. The boycott is a strategic way of exposing the unprincipled and undemocratic behavior of Israeli state institutions; its aim might be characterized as "saving Israel from itself."

The US academy has been particularly complicit in perpetuating the fiction of Israeli democracy—its leaders seeking to protect Israel from its critics, even as they seek to protect themselves from the wrath of the organized lobbies who speak on behalf of the current Israeli regime and its policy of establishing academic outposts in illegal settlements. The complicity is evident most recently in the firing of Steven Salaita at the University of Illinois at Urbana–Champaign after lobbyists and donors objected to his comments on the Gaza war. The chancellor and the chairman of the Board of Trustees justified their capitulation to those who would silence criticism of Israel as consistent with the university's commitment to academic freedom! In fact, of course, those who would silence criticism of Israel on US campuses are practicing a politics here (and defending a politics in Israel) that is at odds with the best values of the US educational system and of US democracy more generally. Paradoxically, it is because we believe so strongly in principles of academic freedom that a strategic boycott of the state that so abuses it makes sense right now.

IV. SCHOLARS AND STUDENTS IN THE STRUGGLE, UNDER ATTACK

13

AN INTERVIEW
WITH RABAB ABDULHADI

DAVID FINKEL AND DIANNE FEELEY

INTRODUCTION

Professor Rabab Abdulhadi is founder and Senior Scholar at the Arab and Muslim Ethnicities and Diasporas Initiative (AMED) at San Francisco State University (SFSU). A longtime scholar and a lifelong activist for Palestinian freedom, her account, "Living Under Occupation," was published in the July–August 2012 issue of *Against the Current*.[1]

After leading a January 2014 academic and labor delegation to Palestine and Jordan, Dr. Abdulhadi has come under sustained attack from the right-wing, McCarthyist AMCHA Initiative, which describes itself as "a non-profit organization dedicated to investigating, documenting, educating about, and combating anti-Semitism at institutions of higher education in America."[2] AMCHA accused Abdulhadi of securing university funding on a false pretext of attending a conference of the Center for American Studies and Research (CASAR) at the American University of Beirut. In fact, as she explained in detail in a response to AMCHA's charges: "To my dismay, I was unable to attend the conference in Beirut because of university delays in approving my travel authorization request. Because SFSU and CSU (California State University) delayed funding approval for my travel to areas that the State Department defines as 'high-risk,' I was not able to confirm my attendance to conference organizers by their deadline."

Ken Monteiro, the dean of the SFSU College of Ethnic Studies confirmed, after additional review, that "Dr. Abdulhadi's travel claim is correct and appropriate," that "her travel involved meetings and discussions with people who are related to her research, that "her past, current and in preparation publications evidence publicly that her travel is the basis for her scholarship, scholarship that is internationally regarded," and that "the College of Ethnic Studies does not censor any of our scholars, nor does the college condone such censorship."

"We hired Dr. Abdulhadi explicitly for her work in Palestine and with Palestinians in the Diaspora including, but not limited to, the USA," Monteiro added. He continued,

> The reference to Dr. Abdulhadi indicating "Unfortunately my name was dropped from the Beirut conference" was a polite indication that because our process takes so long to confirm travel to areas like Lebanon and Palestine, the conference planners had to drop her participation because she was not able to confirm before their deadline. This was no fault of hers. It is just an operating fact based on our need for due diligence regarding travel to high risk areas as defined by our State Department. I would note that Israel is not a high risk area, though almost all nations surrounding it are and the portion of Israel designated as Palestine also is, which may be part of the unclarity in the attached email.

Dean Monteiro's repudiation of "censorship" is a response to AMCHA's allegation that the delegation met with "terrorists," including Leila Khaled and Sheikh Raed Salah. Further pursuing its vendetta against Dr. Abdulhadi and San Francisco State, on June 25, 2014, AMCHA issued a letter demanding "that California State Controller John Chiang conduct a state audit of SFSU."[3]

The letter's cosigners include StandWithUs, a heavily funded campus-oriented Zionist advocacy group, the extreme right-wing Zionist Organization of America, and the Simon Wiesenthal Center. The latter is sponsoring the building of a museum (of tolerance) on the land of the historic Palestinian cemetery Mamilla.

In response to AMCHA's attack on Dr. Abdulhadi's work and reputation, a wide assortment of groups and individuals has rallied to her defense. David Finkel and Dianne Feeley interviewed Dr. Abdulhadi by phone for *Against the Current* (ATC).

A COORDINATED ATTACK
ATC: HOW SERIOUS IS AMCHA'S ATTACK ON YOU AND THEIR NEW DEMAND FOR A STATE AUDIT OF THE UNIVERSITY?
Rabab Abdulhadi: It's serious on the one hand, not because of their size—AMCHA is two or three people, and most of the other groups they list are tiny—but they are very well-financed, including by Sheldon Adelson.[4] And they're part of the network around the Reut Institute in Israel, which came out with a big report in 2010 describing how to target pro-Palestinian activities and stop what we're doing.[5]

They're not a little grassroots organization, so it's serious when they ask the State Controller to investigate. They, AMCHA and company, requested and received all the documentation from the university regarding my travel authorization request and reimbursements, both of which, I might add, have been fully reviewed several times by SFSU and CSU before it was authorized. In its May 27 letter AMCHA copied also the California attorney general, trying to get me implicated in criminal charges and "terrorism."

In addition to Dean Monteiro's report on May 28 immediately following AMCHA's latest attack, SFSU Counsel reported to me and my lawyers on June 4 that the university had thoroughly reviewed my documents and found no wrong doing. On June 24, SFSU President Wong cleared me and further said that AMCHA's false allegations had no merit and reported this on the university website.[6]

Although I knew all along that I did not violate any SFSU or CSU guidelines, nor did I do anything wrong from a legal standpoint, what's disturbing is that AMCHA has targeted so many other scholars. Needless to say that they haven't succeeded in a single case. However, they continue to try to raise the cost of speaking up on Palestine.

I believe that AMCHA's strategy is to try to get me fired, investigated on criminal charges and charges of aiding and abetting terrorism, and to ultimately destroy AMED as an academic program whose mission is to produce knowledge for social justice, including intimidating SFSU from signing any collaborative agreements with Palestinian universities. A California colleague reported that she, too, was attacked during her sabbatical.

Using McCarthyist-era tactics, they really want to make me an example to other people and scare everyone so they won't dare get involved in the struggle for justice in/for Palestine. They started by saying I was teaching students to kill Jews.[7] That did not work because folks know me and know that I live by the principle of the indivisibility of justice, in other words, opposition to hatred and racism against any people. As a result we received overwhelming support from our broader communities.

Their next line of attack was to target the NAAL (North American Academic and Labor) delegation by selectively drawing from the blog of my colleague, Joanne Barker, who wrote about our activities. For example, although we met with 189 individuals, in its smear campaign AMCHA chose to focus only on two, Leila Khaled and Sheikh Raed Salah, exploiting the anti-Palestinian, pro-Zionist standpoint of US dominant circles, on one hand, and the widespread influence of Islamophobia, on the other. Then they attacked our report-back event by asking the university to cancel it.

After we held a very successful and standing-room-only event, AMCHA and its ilk made false allegations anew, but, in addition to attacking me this time around, they also spelled out their goals of undermining our plans to formalize collaboration between SFSU and Palestinian universities, calling them "terrorist." They also claimed that our event harassed Jewish students.

In fact, and as our videos of the event show, we had a beautiful discussion, with everything transparent and where all members of the audience were allowed to raise questions and debate the issues with no coercion.[8]

The campaign has escalated to accusing me of "anti-Semitism." The *Jacobin* article by Selma James and Sara Kershnar[9] as well as the letters sent to President Wong, including that by Sherry Gorelick published on *Mondoweiss*,[10] have been beautiful responses to such false claims. More recently, there is also the letter signed by over five hundred Jews from the United States, Israel, and around the world.[11]

SOCIAL JUSTICE LINKAGE

AMCHA's attack did not stop after President Wong exonerated me of all wrongdoing. Rather, they have now started a new campaign directed at the California controller, claiming again that I misused public funds and demanding another investigation. The bottom line is that they are arguing that public dollars shouldn't be used to advocate for social justice.

I'm saying the opposite—that we need to produce knowledge for social justice. That's the mission of AMED, and it is supported by the College of Ethnic Studies and SFSU. This was the reason why I accepted the position at San Francisco State— to teach, research, and write about social justice issues and not only for Palestine, but all over the world, including the United States.

This is not unreasonable: For every US resident who pays taxes—that includes undocumented workers, who pay taxes too—a portion goes to subsidize Israeli colonization of Palestine and violation of Palestinian rights.

ATC: WHEN WE TALK ABOUT BDS (BOYCOTT, DIVESTMENT, SANCTIONS), IT SEEMS IMPORTANT TO FIND PARTICULAR CAMPAIGNS THAT HAVE RESONANCE WITH PEOPLE'S CONCERNS. THE G4S COMPANY THAT BUILDS PRISONS IN ISRAEL IS ALSO INVOLVED IN PRIVATE PRISONS HERE, FOR EXAMPLE, SO THERE'S A POWERFUL CONNECTION WITH DENYING PALESTINIAN RIGHTS.

RA: We make the connection all the time, not in an opportunistic fashion but within the framework of what I define as the "indivisibility of justice." That's how we conceptualize everything we do.

In the case of G4S, through our campaign, "From Pelican Bay and Guantanamo to Palestine," we highlighted the struggle of prisoners on hunger strike in Pelican Bay, California; Guantanamo Bay, Cuba; and Israeli jails. It is instructive to know that G4S and the security industry operates prisons in all these locations.[12]

If we understand global political economy, we can see the connections everywhere, and note how much is being spent on bombs and drones and prisons instead of the necessary investment in human needs in the United States and elsewhere in the world, including in Palestine.

ATC: Do you think the right-wing attacks are growing now because there's growing support on campuses for Palestinian rights, BDS, and criticism of Israel?

RA: Yes. The racist and right-wing forces are freaking out over what's going on. The Presbyterian General Assembly has just voted to divest church funds from Caterpillar, Hewlett-Packard, and Motorola Solutions.[13]

United Methodist Church divested its pension funds and the United Church of Christ is discussing divestment. The Association for Asian American Studies (AAAS), the Native American and Indigenous Studies Association (NAISA). and the American Studies Association (ASA) have all responded positively and decided to join to the call by the Palestinian Academic and Cultural Boycott of Israel (PACBI). The Gates Foundation has withdrawn its investments in G4S.

What's happening today with regards to Palestine brings to mind the "South African moment" of the mid-1980s. Israel has always sought to present itself as exceptional, humane, and wonderful. That lie is being exposed in broader publics and communities. As Israel's apologists feel the pressure, they have started spending millions of dollars to counter our advocacy for justice in/for Palestine as part and parcel of justice for all.

We can observe the Israeli and Zionist arrogance of power in their shock that someone has dared to challenge their monopoly of public space, especially in the United States. It is as if they are saying, "How dare you build a movement against us? This space belongs only to us!" This reminds me of the climate in the United States immediately after the September 11, 2001, attacks. The attacks of course were horrible but the American mindset at that time obliterated any possibilities of critical thought and public discussion.

BRIDGES OF SOLIDARITY

ATC: The "South African moment" came at a time when the tide of the liberation movement there was clearly rising. The upsurge today in support of Palestine comes at a very difficult moment for the

PALESTINIAN STRUGGLE, AND CERTAINLY AT A POINT WHEN ITS LEADERSHIP IS WEAK AND DIVIDED.

RA: There are definitely severe problems with the official Palestinian leadership. This places an ultimatum to the PLO to either reform itself and act like a true leadership of an anticolonial resistance movement or becoming totally irrelevant and face the possibility of the emergence of a new leadership that will replace it.

Unfortunately and as we know, growing solid leadership takes much longer time than a single uprising—especially when we take into consideration the fact that Israel has, since the 1960s, assassinated one leader after another, not excluding PLO Chairman Yasser Arafat in 2004.

At the same time, there are encouraging signs in Palestine today—from squatter movements of young people refusing to move from Palestinian lands confiscated by the Israeli military for the use of Jewish colonial settlements, to struggles of Palestinians inside Israel, including Druze and Christian Palestinians who refuse to serve in the Israeli Army that oppresses their people. Palestinians are really resisting and mobilizing, even though there is indeed a huge vacuum of official leadership.

Right now, the disappearance of the three settlers[14] has been a pretext for a huge Israeli effort to further harass the Palestinian population under occupation, deepen the blockade and starvation of Gaza, and destroy the Palestinian unity government. The United States and Israel have definitely participated in undermining the Palestinian leadership. Yes, things would be so much different if we had an effective leadership. But the Palestinian people are in struggle and seeking their self-determination, and receiving grassroots support around the world.

As we learned from revolutionary history and history of social movements, people have always risen against injustices. This is what's happening in Palestine today and in due time we will see real leadership emerging and navigating people's mobilization toward a qualitative change.

ATC: PART OF YOUR PURPOSE, AS DESCRIBED IN YOUR REPORT ON THE DELEGATION, WAS TRYING TO BUILD CONNECTIONS BETWEEN SFSU AND BIRZEIT UNIVERSITY IN THE WEST BANK. CAN YOU DESCRIBE THE PROGRESS OF THAT WORK?

RA: We are working to establish a Memorandum of Understanding (MOU) between SFSU and An-Najah University[15] first, and then with Birzeit. These are my strongest connections—I have been collaborating with both universities for a very long time. I was a student at Birzeit, as well as a visiting professor in 1998.

My collaboration with An-Najah University goes back to 2005, and more recently An-Najah coordinated the full program for the Indigenous and Feminist of Color Delegation to Palestine. But it's not going to be exclusive to two Palestinian universities; we plan to connect with other universities in Palestine and elsewhere in the Arab world as well as in Muslim-majority countries.

AMCHA calls these Palestinian universities "terrorist." Birzeit, Jenin, and other Palestinian universities have just been raided, which reminds us of the closure of institutions of education and higher education during the First Intifada. We believe that SFSU students can learn from students and professors in Palestine, and Palestinian students could also learn from students and faculty from SFSU, given the leading role of SFSU students, staff, and faculty who led in 1968–69 the longest strike for social justice when they insisted [on] and succeeded in realizing the College of Ethnic Studies.

We also hope to conduct joint research and student and faculty exchanges. The planning has been delayed because of AMCHA's attack but we are serious about developing these MOUs. Also, this is not exclusive to the Palestinian, Arab, or Muslim communities in the San Francisco Bay Area, but the fruits of our collaboration will be enjoyed by what we call AMED's broader community that supports us.

ATC: Was there much of a program in place when you arrived at SFSU?
RA: No. I was actually recruited from the University of Michigan–Dearborn to create it. This was a practical step to implement the recommendations of the taskforce past SFSU President Corrigan formed in order to address the campus tensions in 2002, when the Palestinian students were unjustly sanctioned even though they were attacked by on- and off-campus pro-Israeli groups.

When I arrived in 2007, there were five courses in Arab American and Muslim American studies. Now we have twenty-four new courses, fifteen of which are already certified, and eight are in the queue for approval as part of the general education curriculum that every student at SFSU can take, including in American ethnic and racial minorities, social justice, and global perspectives.

Our proposal for a minor in AMED has been approved in the Race and Resistance Studies Program as well as by the College of Ethnic Studies. There is a real need for an AMED program that would cater to all students interested in learning about Arab and Muslim communities from a justice-centered perspective, not only to Arab and Muslim students. Students who will be the future leaders in the United States need to learn about the genocide and resistance of Native Americans, the kidnapping and enslavement of Africans, as well as the exclusion of Asian Americans and the colonization of Latina/o lands and people. AMED organically fits within this conceptual framework.

This is also why AMCHA has targeted me—they would kill the program if they can wear me out or get me fired. They have also been attacking the College of Ethnic Studies for the same reasons. For example, AMCHA's leader, Tammi Rossman Benjamin, has attacked Black Student Union and other activists who led the 1968–69 strike.[16] She has targeted Dean Monteiro and made several racist comments, some of which have been caught on YouTube.

STRONG SUPPORT

ATC: CAN YOU TELL US ABOUT SOME OF THE SUPPORT YOU'RE RECEIVING?
RA: It's fantastic. A national coalition against McCarthyism and for academic freedom is building around my case as well as providing support for the American Studies Association, various chapters of SJP (Students for Justice in Palestine) including Northeastern, NYU, and UCLA, and other faculty and students who are being targeted by pro-Israeli right-wing groups that employ McCarthyist tactics.

As I said earlier, the Jewish letter has garnered over five hundred signatures. An international academic and public intellectuals' letter that will be released in a couple of days has already more than three hundred fifty names. There is a letter of support from the Palestinian Youth Movement and another initiated by the Malcolm X Grassroots Movement and signed by many scholars and activists in the African American community. The Palestinian, Arab, and Muslim communities have initiated a letter and so did veterans of the 1968–69 SFSU student strike.

While I am gratified that I am receiving support from so many individuals, organizations, and communities, I am thrilled that we are coming together to fight these false allegations and insist on our right to speak up for justice in/for Palestine as an integral part of justice for all.

Colleagues who accompanied me on various delegations to Palestine have been amazing, particularly Joanne Barker, who has been blogging and has also initiated a letter signed by members of the delegation I either led or co-organized.[17]

The National Lawyers Guild, Asian Law Caucus, Center for Constitutional Rights, and the Council on American Islamic Relations have been incredible, and so has Palestine Solidarity Legal Support, who stood by me at every step of the way. My academic colleagues have been great, especially the dean and chairs' council in the College of Ethnic Studies. There's been a strong statement from the SFSU president Leslie Wong.

[*Editors' Note: Dr. Abdulhadi's response to the AMCHA allegations can be read in full at* http://palestinelegalsupport.org/download/Public%20Statement%20-%20 Abdulhadi%20-%20June%202014.pdf.]

UPDATE FROM RABAB ABDULHADI:

Since this interview was initially published in *Against the Current* on July 21, 2014, Israel has escalated its reign of terror against the Palestinian population under its colonial rule, on one hand, and has launched another genocidal war on Gaza, killing more than 2,100 Palestinians—a third of whom were children—on the other. In the United States and elsewhere, the Zionist movement likewise escalated its campaign of intimidation, character assassination, and extortion against advocates for justice in/for Palestine, including Chicago-based leading Palestinian community organizer Rasmea Odeh, and has focused its efforts on college campuses to undermine the growing academic and cultural boycott of the Israeli academic establishment. However, not unlike the defeat Israel has been dealt at the hands of the legendary Palestinian resistance and steadfastness in Gaza, Jerusalem, and elsewhere in Palestine, the McCarthyist and racist Zionist movement also failed to silence us.

In my case, SFSU President Wong issued a press release on June 24, 2014, in which he rejected the Zionist accusations against me as having "no merit," declaring his commitment neither to censor scholars nor "condone censorship by others," and affirmed my right to academic freedom. The dean of the College of Ethnic Studies posted a public statement of support as well as a strongly worded condemnation of AMCHA, describing its actions as bearing "ill intent." Furthermore, the college has also posted statements of support from members of the Jewish community; international academics and scholars; veterans of the 1968 SFSU Student strike; and Palestinians, Arabs, and Muslims, among others.

Zionist groups reacted by rejecting the outcome of the SFSU investigation and President Wong's press release that cleared me of all wrongdoing, launching instead a new campaign that demanded that the controller of the State of California investigate me further. As a result, the university initiated a new audit of my international travel for the last five years. Once again, and as expected, the Zionist attempts to slander me failed.

Moreover, drawing attention to our intention to collaborate with Palestinian universities (labeled by the Anti-Defamation League of B'nai B'rith as "terrorist" universities), failed to produce the results Zionist groups had hoped for, namely, halting any such collaboration. Although we had to develop a full proposal for such collaboration with Palestinian universities that I suspect was not necessarily the case with regard to other universities elsewhere in the world,[18] the SFSU All University Committee on International Programs voted unanimously in favor of establishing formal collaborative relations, an MOU, with An-Najah National University in Nablus, Palestine. This MOU inaugurates SFSU collaborative relations with any institution of higher learning in any Arab or Muslim communities worldwide. We plan to follow up with an MOU with Birzeit University and with other Palestinian universities in the Gaza Strip.

In another development, the faculty senate of California State University, the parent system to which SFSU belongs, passed a resolution on academic freedom that offers a measure of protection for all faculty members—senior, junior, and lecturers—from future Zionist attacks. And the SFSU faculty senate is putting the final touches on academic freedom conversations that will be held in spring 2015.

In short, this well-funded and powerfully orchestrated Zionist campaign that has targeted me, AMED, and Palestinian students[19] since the inception of the program in 2007, and sought to intimidate me so I would halt my political advocacy for justice in/for Palestine at SFSU and beyond, as well as to undermine the creation of an academic program that places knowledge production for social justice at its center, not only failed miserably, it has actually backfired. It probably goes without saying that this attack took a personal toll on my life. Instead of focusing my attention on finishing my book during my sabbatical or preparing my file for promotion to full professor, I had to dedicate all my time to defending myself against false accusations of criminal and terrorism charges and clear my name from the Zionist smear campaign. However and as I've shown, on a political level and insofar as the movement for justice in/for Palestine is concerned, I believe that we scored victories on several levels.

Perhaps the most important lesson to draw here is the necessity to fight back not only defensively to fend off Zionist attacks but also to go on the offensive, outing Zionist intimidation and strong-arm tactics. Zionist and other groups that rely on intimidation, extortion, bullying, and threats (accusations of anti-Semitism, character assassination, attempts at getting me fired by the university and arrested on charges of terrorism) thrive on secret deals and back-alley politics. Standing up to them and refusing to succumb to their bullying exposes their illicit behavior and rallies support in quarters in which little support existed before. In my case, I fought the new McCarthyism while maintaining my activism to advance BDS in general and the academic boycott in particular. In October, along with my longtime Israeli anti-Zionist feminist comrade Simona Sharoni and others such as Matt Meyer and Mark Lance, we were able to convince the Peace and Justice Studies Association

(PJSA) to vote in favor of the strongest BDS resolution with the highest percentage (87 percent) of any academic association. And in November, along with Simona, another longtime comrade (and undergraduate mentor), Rosalind Petchesky, and a collective of fierce feminists, we were able to convince the Executive Board of the National Women's Studies Association (NWSA) to issue a statement in support of BDS, paving the way for a membership resolution next year. Finally, I continued to work with my former students whom I mentored in the SF Bay Area as they delivered the vote in favor of BDS for the fourteen thousand members of the UC student-workers union, UAW Local 2865.

14

HOW TO PRACTICE BDS IN ACADEME

STEVEN SALAITA

I'm no world traveler, but I'm lucky enough to regularly discuss or debate boycott, divestment, and sanctions (BDS)[1] at various universities and academic gatherings. Almost uniformly, somebody in the audience asks me about how he or she might broach the subject when the potential for recrimination is so great. This question is especially pertinent to tenure-track and contingent faculty.

It's true that recrimination against supporters of Palestine is a legitimate possibility. It's a longstanding reality, in fact. Universities are filled with students, faculty, and administrators whose primary focus seems to be policing criticism of Israel that oversteps their stringent preferences.

Through the years my answers to this question have varied. Situations are diverse. Conditions evolve. Minds change. I've thought much about it and finally feel like I'm in a place where I can offer useful feedback. What follows is meant to be a practical but fluid primer for practicing BDS in academe.

HISTORY

It's important to put Zionist intimidation in historical context. We should keep two things in mind: First, this sort of thing has been going on in US universities since their inception. For many decades, speaking in favor of marginalized groups has resulted in denunciation or termination, especially vis-a-vis African Americans and Indigenous peoples. The denunciation is often implicit, articulated through microaggression, ostracism, and debasement, but it can be explicit, too, in the form of tenure denial, censure, or outright dismissal. Other groups affected by this problem include women, queers, ethnic minorities, Marxists, transgender people, Muslims, and Jews, which makes the situation at hand both ironic and depressing. It is myopic to explore the dangers of a pro-Palestine commitment without simultaneously considering the conditions that prevail around race, gender, religion, and sexuality more generally.

Second, academe is inherently authoritarian and conformist. It's difficult to develop this observation in a compact space, but I'm highlighting a particular culture—one that encompasses hiring practices, classroom conduct, standards of collegiality, funding, prestige, campus climate, and tenure rituals—that rewards obeisance and orthodoxy. Many, probably most, workplaces are authoritarian and conformist, but universities bill themselves as bastions of innovative analysis and independent thought. Those bastions have never accommodated systematic criticism of state power. Academe has long been deeply complicit in imperialism, military violence, corporate malfeasance, and neoliberalism. Indeed, it's not a stretch to say that universities themselves function as corporations, replete with fierce emphasis on branding at the expense of introspection and ethical responsibility. Recalcitrant academics are often victims of this reality, but universities cannot function as corporations without a hegemony that constantly reproduces itself through governing practices. Fellow academics play a critical role in enforcing that hegemony.

These two points illustrate that Palestine's supporters are not alone—in ways both good and bad.

FOOD AND SHELTER

Being a professor involves many things: passion, gratification, innovation, mentorship, travel, flexibility. More than anything else, though, it involves livelihood. It's difficult to proffer advice when livelihood is involved because the high-mindedness of counsel never quite matches the gravity of survival.

When we consider the implications of practicing BDS in academe, it's essential to remember the possibility of termination, either through the denial of tenure or simply being fired, sometimes precipitated by the intense lobbying efforts of various Zionist outfits. BDS is also a commitment that might preclude getting hired in the first place. For the safely employed, BDS is often an impediment to promotion or upward mobility. Therefore, while my instinct is to tell everybody to practice BDS, I try to be sensitive to the realities of power in US universities. I'm not arrogant enough to believe that my words can or should play a role in people's life decisions, but being encouraged to act and subsequently deciding against it can evoke the fear of rejection. BDS aims only to make agents of the Israeli state feel rejected. This is the conundrum inherent to practicing BDS in academe. It is a just practice; but precisely because it is based on a commitment to justice, it is precarious and can result in various forms of retribution.

Another major pitfall to practicing BDS is the harassment it entails. It's not unusual for a supporter of Palestinian freedom to receive hateful messages and experience Internet trolling less coherent than what is generally produced by a toddler pounding a keyboard. Zionist groups have put spies in classrooms and aren't shy to approach administrators (often receptive ideologically) to discipline the inadequately compliant. Nevertheless, I adhere to my instinct and would suggest that if somebody has a sincere interest in advocating for BDS on campus, then he or she ought to do it.

Why Do It?

The operative phrase in my suggestion is "sincere interest." If BDS is an issue about which a person feels strongly (in the affirmative), then deferring to the opposition results in an unnecessary capitulation to larger forces of repression, corporatism, conformity, and inequality. People of conscience need to challenge those forces in order to preserve the ethical ideals of the university about which management publicly brags but privately undermines.

From the standpoint of job performance, there is no good time to do something controversial. (To clarify: "controversial" in the sense that gatekeepers of respectability will dislike it, not in the sense of being morally or intellectually dubious.) There is always a reward to chase, a promotion to consider, an award to pursue, not to mention the pressures of collegiality, which tacitly demand compliance to authority. I am skeptical about the notion that one should wait until tenure to raise her voice. Tenure is no panacea, and in many ways it can be the culmination of a six-year acculturation into the commonplaces of overintellectualized timidity.

The plain reality is that any legitimate fight for justice entails personal risk. It is much riskier, however, to leave injustice unchecked.

How to Do It

One needn't be a firebrand or provocateur in order to support BDS. It's possible to maintain a low profile and still contribute. Here are some suggestions I hope accommodate the shy and brash alike:

- Endorse the call to boycott from USACBI,[2] the US Campaign for the Academic and Cultural Boycott of Israel.
- Attend relevant events on campus. Ask questions. The mere existence of supportive people makes the work of BDS easier.
- Encourage your students and colleagues to attend panels and presentations that might provide less conventional points of view about Palestine.

- Express support to student activists, even if only privately. They need faculty backing. They don't always receive it.
- Vote in the elections of scholarly associations. Various referenda about Palestine have been presented across numerous disciplines for member approval in the past ten years, with many more to come. A low percentage of membership traditionally participates in these elections. Voting is a virtually risk-free way to provide an impact. Also: help elect officers favorable to BDS.
- Propose a boycott or divestment resolution to your faculty senate. It might not get very far, but it will force acknowledgment of the university's complicity in the occupation and other Israeli abuses. You'll also be amused by breathtaking displays of indignant dissimulation.
- Work with the local Students for Justice in Palestine (SJP)[3] chapter or its equivalent.
- Organize an event to generate better understanding of why BDS is an appropriate response to Israeli colonization.
- Investigate your school's study abroad program. If there is an arrangement with an Israeli university, it may contravene your school's antidiscrimination policies because Arab or Muslim students could be denied the opportunity to participate due to Israel's systematic discrimination[4] at the borders it controls.
- Hold your university accountable to its inclusionary rhetoric as it pertains to the suppression of Palestinian voices.
- Write an article for your campus paper or for a national publication. There is much interest in BDS these days.

WHAT NOT TO DO

Do not fear the Zionists. Yes, they have inordinate resources and influence. And, yes, their tactics can be vicious. But suppression is not a long-term strategy. It's the tactic of one whose ideology has no merit beyond the force he can summon to impose it on those with less power.

Please do not misread me: Israel's supporters, as they have illustrated for many decades, are perfectly content to rely on suppression as long as it can effectively preserve their colonial fetish, no matter how many constitutional rights they destroy. In order to survive, suppression relies on the anxiety of its targets. It is sustainable, then, only in relation to our quiescence.

Nobody should stop you from articulating a principled critique of unjust power. When that unjust power is Zionism, the impetus to act is even greater, for in so doing we also respond to US colonization, restricted speech, racism, neoliberalism, militarization, ethnocracy, and a host of related issues about which those in our profession should be concerned. Zionists rely on our fear to embolden their tactics of intimidation. It is no small comfort that they fear BDS much more, however.

15

TESTIMONY BEFORE THE FACULTY SENATE BODY, UNIVERSITY OF ILLINOIS AT URBANA–CHAMPAIGN, SEPTEMBER 22, 2014

VICENTE M. DIAZ

My name is Vicente M. Diaz. I am an associate professor in American Indian studies and anthropology. I am also an affiliate faculty member in History and Asian American Studies. I represent American Indian Studies; in fact, I co-chaired the search committee that recommended the hire of Steven Salaita.

I'm here to express moral indignation and outrage at the BOT's [Board of Trustees'] denial of Professor Salaita's hire. Far from over, and even further from correct, our leadership's decision is a wrongheaded and misguided action that has tarnished our university's reputation among academics who know and understand how academia is supposed to work. It has also put us in actual harm's way, some of us more than others. Above all, this administration has willingly placed political expediency and possibly money over academic matters. Indeed, academics is the biggest casualty of our leadership's dereliction of its duties.

This casualty is most clearly visible and palpably experienced when viewed from our vantage point in American Indian studies, the originating unit, where the proverbial rubber meets the road. I begin by addressing a particularly insidious rumor of the sort that can come only from the kind of toxic environment that Chancellor Wise has created and maintained right down to her comments today. It is a rumor that I've already had to lay to rest twice in private emails, namely, that our unit director, Professor Robert Warrior, used his influence and power to hire Salaita, who was a student of his years ago at another university. Warrior did

141

not ask me to address this issue and is not even aware that I'm doing so. In fact, Warrior maintained his distance from Salaita's candidacy, and shame on those of you who are spreading this rumor in order to delegitimize him and my unit.

The fact that I even have to state in public that we did our due diligence, that our process and findings were affirmed at the college, [by the] provost, and even by the chancellor's own vice chancellors, is itself a shameful testimony as to just what kind of environment our leadership has plunged us.

Simply put, this case was a routine academic hire, properly vetted all the way up to where substance matters, and because it concerned tenure, it received additional vetting at the national and international levels. Contrary to the accolades about her courage and bravado, the only courage that Chancellor Wise needed was to simply tell those donors and lobbyists that the case had been properly vetted and that she stands by the academic process. Period. For it was actually she and President Easter and the BOT who opened the floodgates by, in effect, capitulating to external pressure to block Salaita's hire, whether or not she based her decision on their interests.

The simple fact is that she involved herself on nonacademic grounds and made a decision on the most unscholarly of approaches and in the most clandestine of ways, with the blessings of the Board and the president—or was it at their behest? —to indeed block Salaita's hire on decidedly nonacademic terms. Of course, it is precisely the contention of the thousands of scholars and dozens of academic organizations, departments, disciplines, that the real casualty is academic freedom, if not excellence itself.

The chilling effects are now upon us. And this is on the chancellor, not on Salaita. Three weeks ago, I received an email from an individual, unknown to me, inviting me to "discuss" the Salaita case at some undisclosed venue in Danville. Even a cursory read of the letter reveals it to be something other than a genuine interest in civil dialogue, as for instance, when its author addresses me—addresses me—as "foaming in the mouth" in support of a "rabid" Salaita, who is further described as "anti-Jewish" in a sentence that also conflates Palestine with Hamas.

Contrary to a well-orchestrated and financed smear campaign aimed at stopping his hire, it is in fact reductive to equate Salaita's anti-Zionist stance with anti-Jewish or anti-Semitic ideology, or to equate Palestine with Hamas. Apparently, he has also been charged with siding with ISIS, even if he had condemned that group in the same period in which he decried Israel's military assault on Palestinians. Had Salaita only tweeted about ISIS, I dare say that I would not be standing here today, that he would not have been mistreated so.

There was something especially disturbing in that letter's urging me to bring to the meeting (way over there in Danville), "some of the Palestinian students" from UIUC. The targeting of this particular group of students should not be trivialized given how the author equates Palestine with terrorism. Nobody can read this letter and conclude that it intends anything other than something sinister passing as an invitation to dialogue.

I received this letter for no other reason than my public defense of Salaita and my disagreement with the university on academic terms. Precisely because the university musters all of its authority and resources so, we have now arrived at the point wherein to publicly disagree with the university is to be virtually cast as a supporter of terrorism, if not a terrorist.

Neither I nor Professor Salaita are rabid dogs who hate Jewish people. The preponderance of the evidence shows him to be not only a stellar but also a beloved teacher, one fully capable of subordinating or bracketing his politics in favor of student learning and real critical thinking. Passion, of course, is a prerequisite for compassion, and when combined with the demands and rigors of dispassionate analyses, they become ingredients for cutting-edge scholarship.

My claims here are best grasped on academic grounds, and in view of the negative consequences when academic regulations and sensibilities aren't adhered to. Also, and quite tellingly, the chancellor has yet to look us (in American Indian studies) in the eye and explain her actions to us in particular.

I seriously doubt that she would ever have taken such an action were this a case of a hire in one of the STEM fields, or even in one of the traditional disciplinary departments, rather than American Indian studies. I do believe she'd have done it to a partner ethnic studies unit.

I also think she saw us as collateral damage, but underestimated just how damaging her actions would be for the humanities and the social sciences, which probably accounts for her expressions of regret. But these expressions are way too little and way too late.

In closing, like the heads of the sixteen departments, I still don't have confidence in her words, much less on her abilities to safeguard academic integrity. And sure as the saying goes, that "an attack on one is an attack on all," the other side of the coin rings even more true here: that what is good for American Indian studies as an academic unit is also good for the entire institution.

This principle of unit autonomy is the bedrock of shared governance, which is key to proper academic governance, whose ultimate objective is to safeguard academic integrity and excellence. All other concerns must serve this mission because that is what we do and who we are.

And so, when the chancellor and her supporters on campus urge us to pick up the pieces and move on, their words ring as vacuous, as hypocritical, and therefore as outrageous as the administration's reasons for targeting and preempting Salaita's academic hire in the first place, and then doubling down by using civility or teaching unfitness as the excuse.

Thus I call upon the senate to rise and express moral and, if I may coin a term here, academic outrage at the administration's decision to place political and other considerations above academics. And if, under this new regime, civility be the condition for expressing academic freedom and excellence, then let the appropriate expression be that of civil disobedience.

Move on? No. Colleagues, the work of reclaiming this university from those who would sell it to the highest bidder under the suspect mantra of civility has only just begun. Stand up, stand up like Trustee Montgomery, who had the audacity to look at the evidence and admit he was wrong in initially supporting the chancellor. Stand up for academic integrity and the academic excellence that is staked on it.

16

CLIMBING DOWN FROM THE IVORY TOWER: DOUBLE STANDARDS AND THE USE OF ACADEMIC BOYCOTTS TO ACHIEVE SOCIAL AND ECONOMIC JUSTICE

RIMA NAJJAR KAPITAN

This chapter* argues that academic freedom functions within powerful institutions that influence and interact with the broader society and therefore should not be seen as artificially divorced from it. Their interaction must be flexible enough to allow professors to use expressive disassociation to bring about educational, social and political change. In the case of Israel/Palestine, the question that most bothers US skeptics is, "Does the academic boycott of Israel violate the academic freedom rights of Israelis?" The answer to that question hinges in part on how the boycott affects its intended beneficiaries and the individuals participating in the boycott, not merely the institutions and/or individuals being boycotted. I distinguish between academic entitlement and academic freedom. I also present a few snapshots from US history in which scholars grapple with collisions between academic freedom and other rights and duties, and thereby situate the academic boycott for Palestine as part of a tradition of US academic activism.

---

* Sections of this chapter are reprinted from the AAUP *Journal of Academic Freedom* 4. Available at www.aaup.org/reports-publications/journal-academic-freedom/volume-4.

ACADEMIC ENTITLEMENT VERSUS ACADEMIC FREEDOM

Many opponents of the academic boycott mistakenly assume that all of the demands of the boycott movement restrict academic freedom, and they do this by employing a selectively expansive definition of "academic freedom"—one that dictates that American scholars must engage with Israeli ones or else be deemed to have violated the academic freedom of the latter. Because the principle of academic freedom is so important to US academic culture, its invocation should be critically examined.

Responding to pressure from StandWithUs, an organization that works closely with the Israeli government,[1] dozens of US university presidents issued statements condemning the campaign for the academic boycott of Israel, which the American Studies Association (ASA) had just joined. Other academic organizations also recorded or reiterated their opposition to the boycott. Consistent in most of these statements was an avowed concern that the boycott violated the principle of academic freedom.

Israeli professors do not need forced academic cooperation in order to exercise their academic freedom. Cary Nelson and others point out that "a significant number of American, Israeli, and Palestinian faculty are involved in inter-institutional research projects" funded in part by Israeli universities.[2] When addressing this type of collaboration, Nelson broadens the definition of academic freedom to encompass anything that maximizes academic cooperation between Americans and Israelis, but restricts it when addressing Israeli actions that paralyze the educational system in the occupied Palestinian territories.

> In the Israeli context: "Academic freedom includes the right to pursue the research of your choice, *including collaborative research*, and the right to pursue the funding necessary for that work."[3]

> In the Palestinian context: "Academic freedom protects your right to seek infrastructural support, but it does not guarantee that you will get it."[4]

Legislation introduced by a few states and federal congressmen following the decision of the ASA to boycott Israel used a similarly selective definition of academic freedom. The legislation treated as sacrosanct the entitlement of Israeli and American institutions to continue academic partnerships but then imposed severe retaliatory restrictions on American academic individuals and associations which participated in the boycott, restrictions that they apparently did not worry would violate academic freedom.[5] Some of the university administrations who condemned the ASA boycott move took a similar step, cutting ties with the ASA,[6] a move that obviously would hamper the free exchange of ideas. In Nelson's construction, a professor's academic freedom is violated if s/he cannot form a joint degree program with a US university, but academic freedom is not violated when the government detains students without charge or trial,[7] erects checkpoints that make travel to university difficult or impossible, or withholds Palestinians' access to their own tax revenue.[8] But when he is not talking about Israel/Palestine, it is the latter types of restrictions that Nelson argues academic freedom prohibits.[9] As Nelson himself might admit in another context, no academic has an *entitlement* to collaborate with outside academic institutions, unless there has been an open application process for which that academic has qualified. The University of Illinois might choose to establish a joint degree program with the University of Edinburgh but not the University of Glasgow, but that would not violate the academic freedom of the professors at Glasgow. It is not a violation of anyone's "academic freedom" if American institutions freely choose to disassociate from Israeli universities until they cease reinforcing Israeli apartheid, whether or not we disagree with the reasons for the boycott. So, with respect to many of the demands of the boycott movement, academic freedom is not implicated at all.

ACADEMIC FREEDOM DOES NOT FUNCTION IN A VOID

This brings us to the forms of boycott that do limit the academic activity of certain Israeli professors (for example, rejecting the participation in an academic conference of a scholar who is sponsored by the Israeli Ministry of Foreign Affairs).[10] The limitation to which I am referring is the limitation of academic activity to which an Israeli institution or individual would be entitled were it not for their participation in Israeli apartheid. So, while a professor from the University of Glasgow may not be entitled to start a joint academic project with a US university, she might be entitled to participate in an academic conference by virtue of her having met the attendance requirements. It should be emphasized that Israeli scholars do not, by virtue of their nationality, have to participate in such programs, nor does such a boycott impose an affirmative requirement for Israeli professors to join the justice movement (as Martha Nussbaum mistakenly assumes[11]); a professor whose international visit is sponsored by the Ministry of Foreign Affairs is choosing to participate in Israeli state propaganda to promote Zionism and the virtues of the Israeli state in the face of international criticism. Can a US institution refuse to legitimize such a program or must it remain apolitical? In this case, it is not merely the right of the Israeli scholar at stake. The academic freedom of that scholar is conflicting with the rights of others.

Stanley Fish gets around any potential conflict of rights by arguing that it is beneath academics to meddle in the political world. Rather, Fish believes that there should be only one kind of academic—the academic who buries herself in medieval metrics and "brackets out" geopolitical considerations. To apply one's expertise in a way that informs the manner in which the scholar interacts with the scholarly and broader community, according to Fish, would be to "sail under false colors by appropriating the machinery and prestige of the academy for political purposes."[12] The virtuous academic, according to Fish, is the one wearing political blinders (like a soldier who does not think about the moral implications of his actions but merely does his job). If academic freedom is conceived so narrowly, the only academics with any true freedom would be those who are positioned at the top of their profession, such as Fish, who already have political power and need not concern themselves with how their actions and omissions affect themselves and others. We are fortunate that the scholars of the Enlightenment did not subscribe to Fish's narrow view of academic purpose.

But even Fish cannot build a complete wall between institutions of academia and the incarnate world. On the one hand he argues that it is not appropriate for a university to choose to disassociate from "significant figures" such as Margaret Thatcher, because they should separate her significance to society from whether we politically or morally approve of her actions. On the other hand he concedes that we might properly seek to disassociate from significant figures, such as Al Capone and Adolf Hitler (and perhaps Henry Kissinger), who engage in "significant criminality."[13] Fish does not explain how academics buried in the study of medieval metrics are supposed to determine who has engaged in criminality that is significant enough for academic shunning to be acceptable. Nor does he explain why a public figure's significant criminality should concern the university—presumably because a university should be permitted to decline to legitimize or normalize criminal actions, which is exactly what academic boycotters seek to do with Israel. Fish thinks that a narrow conception of academia will protect it from becoming "a place indistinguishable at bottom from the ballot-box."[14] But if academics may not be political actors, they will become political pawns. When the appropriate criteria are met, US academics should be able to choose not to enter into joint academic enterprises with universities that legitimatize and further oppressive regimes.

Fish and Nelson view the academic freedom of Israeli professors in a vacuum. This is a shortcoming that results from their disinclination to reconcile conflicting rights. When academic rights clash with the academic and nonacademic freedoms of others, academic associations and governments have acknowledged that academic freedom must sometimes yield.[15]

DOUBLE STANDARDS: LIMITING ACADEMIC FREEDOM
AND THE ISRAEL EXCEPTION

Even the US legislators who sought to discourage associations like the ASA from boycotting Israel recognized that it would be ludicrous to build a Fish-style wall between academia and the outside world. For example, the proposed New York legislation created exemptions for boycotts against colleges "located in a foreign country that is a state sponsor of terrorism," boycotts connected with labor disputes, and boycotts "for the purpose of protesting unlawful discriminatory practices."[16]

The American Association of University Professors (AAUP) recognizes similar "exemptions." As we will see, they are not really exemptions, but recognition that where there are conflicting rights, academics have to make ethical choices about how to reconcile the conflicts. Although these choices are made throughout academia, I focus primarily on the AAUP, both because of its prominence in protecting academic freedom and its criticism of the academic boycott of Israel. One of the conflicting freedoms that cannot be discounted is the freedom of the boycotting professors themselves. Professors sometimes have a right based in academic freedom to disassociate from discriminatory institutions. The AAUP made this argument in the *SAME v. Rumsfeld* case,[17] as I discussed at greater length in the AAUP's *Journal of Academic Freedom*.[18]

The AAUP views the academic strike as an appropriate tool to effect social change under certain circumstances. It explains that "resort to economic pressure through strikes or other work actions may be a necessary and unavoidable means of dispute resolution," even when it involves actions targeting academic speech, such as asking outside speakers not to come to a campus during a strike.[19] In furtherance of the civil and educational rights of faculty members and others, the AAUP has supported strikes aimed at securing fair working conditions,[20] faculty governance,[21] health-insurance plans,[22] curricular enrichment,[23] and, significantly, an end to administrative practices that increase racial segregation.[24] In those cases, other means could certainly have been employed to further the same ends, such as public condemnation or debate about the administrative policies the faculty members were opposing. But the memberships determined that strike was the best available means of pressure despite the fact that temporary restriction of academic discourse was a casualty.

In contrast to its support of strikes, the AAUP in 2006 summarized its position on boycotts as follows: "Institutions that are not free . . . but in fact suppress freedom . . . should not be boycotted. Rather, they should be exposed for what they are, and, wherever possible, the continued exchange of ideas should be actively encouraged. The need is always for more academic freedom, not less."[25]

It is doubtful that the negative scenario the AAUP warns of will come to pass. As Judith Butler points out, if sacrificing ties with Israeli institutions means helping remove some of the serious obstacles to education Israel imposes, we are doing a service to academic freedom.[26] If the boycott is successful, the result will be a freer and more democratic Israeli society in which education is not under assault. Second, as the AAUP itself acknowledged in its amicus brief to the Supreme Court in the case *Rumsfeld v. Forum for Academic and Institutional Rights*, "Academic freedom 'thrives not only on the independent and uninhibited exchange of ideas among teachers and students, but also, and somewhat inconsistently, on autonomous decision-making by the academy itself.'"[27] Just as faculty unions have the right to bring about better academic conditions through strike, academics working towards freedom in Israel/Palestine should not be confined to the method of merely "expos[ing]" oppressive institutions "for what they are."

In another international case, the AAUP suggests that the use of academic boycott is not only a right but an obligation. The AAUP sent a letter to Yale University reiterating concerns about its collaboration with the Singaporean government in establishing a campus in that country. It asked that Yale ensure that human rights were not undermined by the collaboration, and even suggested total withdrawal from the partnership might be necessary. Its concerns stemmed partly from a worry that the establishment of the campus might bring about unwanted "political implications" because it would entail indirectly "assist[ing] the Singapore government in achieving greater financial strength and cultural legitimacy."[28] For the AAUP, Yale has the obligation to avoid legitimizing countries with "odious" laws, such as laws that criminalized sexual orientation, even if that entailed restricting academic speech in Singapore.[29]

The question remains whether the AAUP will apply these principles in Israel/Palestine, where the United States has much more extensive political, economic and cultural engagement. Like the AAUP in the Singapore case, many of the proponents of the boycott of Israel argue that they do not want to participate in the legitimization and normalization of Israel's apartheid by collaborating with Israeli institutions, which are integral to Israel's *hasbara* (propaganda) project.

CONCLUDING REMARKS

This chapter does not detail the conditions in Israel/Palestine that justify the boycott strategy. Others (including in this book) have made that case persuasively and will continue to do so. To determine whether boycott is defensible in a particular situation, we should consider the extent to which the entity considering boycott is already complacent in human rights abuses through its academic collaborations. We should also consider the likely effectiveness of other means available to achieve the same ends, the restriction of academic discourse to be imposed by the boycott itself, and the seriousness of the violations that are the target of the boycott. Generally though, boycott as a method can be completely compatible with, and indeed even itself may be, an exercise of academic freedom.

In this regard, critics of the boycott should consider climbing down from their ivory towers and stop creating specious definitions of academic freedom that only apply to Israel. Academic freedom is a right that is adequately protected only by considering how actions of academics affect others.

17

BUILDING UNITY AND WRECKING WALLS: CENTERING THE PALESTINIAN RIGHT TO EDUCATION

KRISTIAN DAVIS BAILEY

Mainstream discourse around the academic boycott of Israel often ignores the Palestinian right to education. Opponents of the boycott misdirect attention, decrying the tactic's alleged infringement upon the academic freedom of individuals in Israel. Refocusing the conversation on the academic freedom of Palestinians has strengthened campus-based advocacy for the Palestinian cause over the past year. The fall 2014 Right to Education (R2E) tour not only provides an example of how a focus on students strengthens academic BDS but has also been a point of mobilization for multidirectional solidarity between Palestinians and Black Americans. This essay is a synthesis of two articles I've written—one about education under occupation following a summer 2013 trip to Palestine, and another about R2E students' encounters with St. Louis activists in November 2014. The groundwork for the tour began in Palestine in September 2013, when I remained in Palestine for three weeks following a twelve-day delegation with Interfaith Peace Builders (IFPB). During this time, I had the opportunity to meet with the Right to Education Campaign at Birzeit University and to interact with other Palestinian youth and students.[1]

"God, Kristian, I can't even remember how many times my school closed this semester," Amanda Mansara, a Palestinian university student, wrote to me in January 2014. When Amanda and I met in the West Bank in September 2013, she was supposed to be starting her second year at Al-Quds University, but her classes had been canceled. Her school was closed because the Israeli military had been firing tear gas canisters and rubber bullets at students on campus every day during the first week of the semester.[2] So Amanda and I passed the hours when she should have been learning in a downtown Ramallah café, working on a crossword, playing cards, drinking tea, and smoking hookah with her friends. Days later when I saw her again, the campus was still closed. It took two full weeks before the Israeli Army stopped attacking the university, but even this peace was short-lived: just over a month later, Al-Quds had to close again following a military raid on Abu Dis, the adjacent town.[3] And less than a month after that, students commuting from Abu Dis were among forty people injured by rubber bullets from the Israeli military.[4]

When these attacks occur, Amanda said, the Student Body Council suspends all classes and evacuates campus through the back door if bullets are involved in the attack. Amanda and her peers do not get to make up this lost time.

"Our university has been under constant attack this semester," she said to me. "WE NEED whatever support we can get."

The troubles faced by Al-Quds and other Palestinian universities have never been mentioned by those who have been loudly attacking the American Studies Association (ASA) and other institutions that have recently voted to support the academic boycott of Israel. As reactionary legislatures in New York, Illinois, Maryland, and the US House of Representatives have considered bills to deny public funding to institutions like the ASA for supporting the boycott,[5] the need for critical support of Palestinians' academic freedom becomes paramount. These bills and university administrators' claims that the boycott limits the "academic freedom" of Israelis are distracting and disingenuous to the lived experiences of people on the ground in Palestine, experiences that paint a very clear picture of academic freedom under attack—from kindergarten all the way through college.

THE UNIVERSITY UNDER OCCUPATION

Earlier in September 2013, I had spent an afternoon at Birzeit University meeting with Sundos Hammad, a recent graduate and the coordinator of R2E. Sundos said that Birzeit has been closed by Israeli military order more than fifteen times throughout its history.[6] The longest stretch lasted four and a half years. Students have also faced restriction of movement and imprisonment.[7] The occupation has compromised education for generations of Palestinians. Resisting this oppression, students at Birzeit launched R2E in 1988, which today calls for student and faculty unions and other institutions to affirm the right of Palestinian students and academics to pursue an education free from Israeli occupation. By last September, the campus was preparing for closure again—not from a military threat but from students striking against tuition hikes.

The strikes happen regularly, as Birzeit relies on student tuition to cover up to 60 percent of its operating costs.[8] Neither families nor the Palestinian government can afford these costs. The World Bank estimates that the occupation has cost the West Bank economy $3.4 billion,[9] while unemployment in the West Bank is 20 percent across the territory but as high as 41 percent among young adults aged twenty to twenty-four.[10] The Palestinian Authority (PA), which is expected to provide a certain amount of the budget, has been hindered by reductions in foreign aid and Israel's withholding of Palestinian tax revenues as political punishment.[11] PA budget cuts reduced contributions to Birzeit from $2 million in 2008 to $120,000 in 2013.[12] Universities across the West Bank and Gaza are in financial crisis.[13]

Beyond financial woes, Sundos highlighted how the infrastructure of Israel's occupation limits Birzeit and other universities through its control of borders and entry and its checkpoints inside the West Bank. While visiting faculty and students at Birzeit receive a three-month visa upon entry to Israel, the Israeli border control frequently denies visa renewals to academics,[14] disrupting coursework in the middle of the semester. Sundos said this tends to discourage academics in the Palestinian *shatat* (diaspora) from becoming involved with the university, which limits academic discourse available on campus.

"The meaning of the university is to have universal thoughts on everything. And we don't have that," Sundos said. She was also sure to connect her compromised education to its larger context: "The occupation is the disease and what's happening in Palestine are the symptoms."

EDUCATION BEYOND THE UNIVERSITY

University education does not exist in a vacuum, and so before looking at academic freedom for those in the highest levels of learning we must also examine primary and secondary education. The entire structure of Israel's occupation, siege, and discrimination against non-Jews in the West Bank, Gaza, and Israel all prohibit any true access to education.

During my IFPB delegation, we met with people in a Jahalin Bedouin village in the Jordan Valley, a part of the West Bank that Israel's deputy foreign minister has said Israel will not give up under a two-state solution.[15] In the 1980s, the Israeli military declared the land to be a closed military zone under its control (as 60 percent of land in the West Bank is classified) and the residents of the Khan al-Ahmar village found their water, electricity, and even road access cut off.[16] Eid Abu Khamis, one of the villagers, focused the majority of his conversation on education.

Until a few years ago, children had to travel between eighteen and twenty kilometers to school in Jericho or Azariya. Because the PA still had not provided the buses they promised in the late 1990s, students had to walk, Eid said. Due to the distance, families would not send their daughters and some of their sons would live at school for the week. Some parents discovered their children would hide near home rather than attending classes; others grieved for children either killed or handicapped by vehicles during their travel. The village soon decided to build their own school, which now holds 110 pupils and has an Israeli relocation order against it since the village is unrecognized.[17] Eid called this a war crime. "Education is a human right—only here is it forbidden," he said.

Just over the hill from where we sat with Eid was Ma'ale Adumim, a massive Is-raeli settlement with running water and electricity, an Israeli-approved school, and even an Ace Hardware store. Three members of the Knesset live in the settlement, Eid said, as well as the former ambassador to the United States and the administra-tor of the Allenby Bridge to Jordan.

In the Aida Refugee Camp directly outside Bethlehem, our guide from the Lajee Center[18] walked us past a UN school where the Israeli military's shooting had killed a teacher inside in 2005. The bullet holes were still visible on the exterior of the building.

To the north, in Nablus, we learned that, until 2008, there were no schools for the six thousand residents of the New Askar Refugee Camp, where more than 55 percent of residents are children. Though the UN recognized the refugees living in New Askar as refugees, they did not view the camp as distinct from the Old Askar camp, two kilometers away.[19] So instead of going to school close to their homes, children had to walk back and forth each day. People like Amjad Rfaie, manager of the Social Development Center,[20] work to fill the void of education in the camp.

On a later visit to the camps, one of my friends showed me the end result of education in the camps: unemployment. Pointing to a group of his friends standing around in the narrow streets of Old Askar Camp, he said: "These are the people of the camp and all they are doing is standing, watching each other. This is the only thing people can do."

Youth Against Settlements (YAS)[21] in Hebron has responded to a similar need for schools in its own neighborhood. Between late August and September 2013, I made repeated trips to visit YAS, which is run by Issa Amro and, at the time, Badia Dwaik. Issa and Badia live and work in "H2," the heart of Hebron that has been under Israeli control and closed to Palestinians since 2000 to protect the more than seven hundred settlers living there illegally. What used to be the thriving center of the city is now a ghost town, with nearly all Palestinian shops closed and roads only accessible to settlers and foreigners. The majority of families have since moved out, leaving thousands of abandoned buildings. For those who remain, YAS visits families to see what resources they can provide.

In one case, a school was needed. So over multiple visits over the course of a week, I witnessed Issa, Badia, and roughly a dozen other young and grown men rehabilitate one of these abandoned houses into a kindergarten that they had been planning for months.

"I believe in this more than I believe in the protests," Issa commented.

Rights beyond Education

Around the same time the kindergarten opened up in Hebron, news from Tel Aviv showed that the city had approved separate public schools for the children of Eritrean and South Sudanese refugees.[22] Many discussions of Israeli racism tend to focus on anti-Palestinian policies, but as tens of thousands of asylum seekers demonstrated beginning in December 2013, Israel's systemic issues extend far beyond that. Universal human rights become an even more imperative goal in the region.[23]

As many have said already, we cannot talk about "academic freedom" without recognizing the material rights that are tied to it, such as movement, protection from discrimination, political imprisonment and military violence, and control on economics and civilian infrastructure. While Israel has allowed only three Gazans to study in the West Bank since 2000[24] and has denied travel to Fulbright scholars,[25] its assaults on academic freedom cut to the core. When fuel and electricity shortages caused by Israel (with help from Egypt) force students to take exams by candlelight,[26] academic freedom is threatened. When 42 percent of post-traumatic stress cases in the Gaza Strip are in children under the age of nine,[27] following two Israeli military bombardments on the territory, academic freedom is compromised. And when 128 Palestinians refugees living in Syria's Yarmouk Camp have died of starvation[28] since last July, academic freedom becomes meaningless. Having the freedom to live free from occupation and siege, having the freedom to leave the camps and return home, having the freedom to live free from Israeli discrimination—*those* will all create a world where Palestinians can enjoy true academic freedom, and these are all freedoms supported by the boycott, divestment, and sanctions (BDS) movement.

As discussions of Palestinian and Israeli academic freedom become a mainstay in the American academy, everyone must consider academic freedom in its fuller context. Education is a fundamental human right that is not just limited to the realm of PhDs. We must protect it at all of its levels. So even when the academy or political elite do not agree with the methods of BDS, they have been presented with facts and with a call from a suffering people to do something.

The question is no longer whether or when to act, but how will we respond now?

Following my trip to Palestine, and as part of the steering committee of National Students for Justice in Palestine (SJP), I coordinated a speaking tour for ten members of the R2E campaign from Birzeit University in November 2014. The tour was organized under the theme "Building Unity, Wrecking Walls," which Ahmad Shweiki, R2E coordinator and a first year master's student in law, described as follows:

> The first part is "Building Unity" because we believe that our struggle as Palestinian and as students is not something isolated. It's something that people everywhere around the world suffer from. 'Wrecking Walls' also has to do with wrecking walls that people sometimes try to build to isolate us from our rights because we know that since the struggle is one, this struggle is against walls that prevent us from accessing our rights including our right to education.

The students split into five teams and visited more than forty campuses across the United States over two weeks. All of the teams advocated BDS as one step concerned students could take toward supporting Palestinians' right to education. Some R2E members were able to directly support the divestment at UCLA, addressing student senators the night of the 8 to 2 to 2 resolution vote. They also supported academic boycott work with members of UAW 2865 at UC Riverside, whose campus and statewide members voted overwhelmingly to endorse BDS in December 2014. One thousand one hundred twenty-six UAW members personally pledged to support the academic boycott in this vote.

But perhaps the most exciting development from the tour was its contribution to ongoing Black–Palestinian solidarity. Support between Palestine and Ferguson, Missouri, came to the forefront during the summer of 2014, first with tweets of support in each direction, and followed by the participation of a Palestine contingent at "Ferguson October," the national weekend of resistance. Emerging out of these developments, the natural starting place of the R2E tour was connecting Palestinian students with the epicenter of youth resistance in the United States: Ferguson. The students had a two-day orientation in St. Louis and the opportunity to connect with youth organizers across the city.

For Shatha Hammad, a third-year English literature student, the unity of the St. Louis community in the face of violence and oppression reinvigorated her commitment to student activism in Palestine. "It was an experience that renewed something inside me," Hammad said. "As a Palestinian I see people every day getting killed and all my rights are violated. I don't have any rights basically. For a moment there I got used to it. But at the vigil when I saw everything and heard the people talk, something woke up inside me and said 'You suffer from that and these people suffer from that, so you better stand next to each other and do something.'"

Mahmoud Doughlas, a senior in electrical engineering, said he felt a lot of resonance with the Black struggle in the United States: "We tried to connect the dots between the struggles between the African American society and the Palestinians and we found this major solid ground that we share together—it's that we are not allowed to narrate our own history."

Jonathan Pulphus is an African American studies major at St. Louis University and member of Tribe X, a group that seeks to counteract global injustices and systemic racism through issues organizing, education, empowerment, and building strong alliances. For Pulphus, meeting Palestinians was an eye-opening experience about the Israeli occupation of Palestine and its connections to issues facing Black people in the United States. "Shatha told us how, to this day, Israel receives billions of dollars from the United States to illegally occupy Palestinian land," he said. "Meanwhile, the majority Black spaces in the United States, such as St. Louis City and Ferguson, face poverty and disinvestment, neglect."

Since returning to Birzeit, the R2E students have hosted a number of events and demonstrations to educate their campus about Black American struggles and resistance. In December 2014, students placed posters of Black resistance figures around campus—Angela Davis, Toni Morrison, Huey Newton, and Malcolm X. The posters featured captions in English and Arabic, along with the hashtag #BlackLivesMatter. The students also placed a picture of Michael Brown's parents on their memorial to Saji Darwish, the eighteen-year-old Birzeit student whom Israeli forces killed in March 2014.[29] Later in the month, R2E hosted an event at Birzeit about raising solidarity with the Black struggle before an audience of one hundred students. The following week, R2E staged a silent demonstration at Birzeit, holding signs including the Assata Shakur chant: "It is our duty to fight for our freedom / It is our duty to win / We must love and support each other / We have nothing to lose but our chains."[30]

In this same week, the Florida-based racial justice group Dream Defenders (who hosted some of the R2E students in Florida) unanimously passed a resolution supporting the BDS movement, just two weeks before the Dream Defenders leadership departed for a weeklong delegation to Palestine with people from Ferguson and other organizations.

These actions constitute a new chapter in the rich and ongoing history of solidarity between Black and Palestinian resistance. For some of the Birzeit students, the tour and subsequent events have offered a welcomed challenge to the "bubble of victimization" they say feels pervasive on campus.

The foregrounding of Palestinian students and the right to education proves to be rich ground for building mutually empowering solidarity. As academics, students, and cultural workers continue to pursue boycott and divestment campaigns, we should consider how to take this solidarity and build mutually liberating projects of co-resistance.

18

STANDING FOR JUSTICE: CHALLENGES AND VICTORIES OF STUDENTS FOR JUSTICE IN PALESTINE

NERDEEN MOHSEN

What does it feel like to be aiding and abetting your own erasure, to be an accomplice in the cleansing of your people? That is how I felt growing up as a Palestinian in the United States, which provides billions of dollars in military aid to Israel through taxpayer funds, and shields it from accountability on the level of international organizations. The relationship between the United States and Israel was reflected on a societal level while I was growing up, as "Palestine" was a dirty word, and any criticism of the state of Israel was unacceptable. My family was forcibly expelled in the 1948 *Nakba* and then fled again, out of fear, before the war in 1967. The first time, our village, Beit Iksa, was cleansed by Zionist militias; later on, the land was returned to the indigenous population as part of an exchange deal. My paternal grandparents came back after years of moving around, so my father was also born in Beit Iksa, but when he was just three years old, they fled again, knowing that they would not be able to build a life there. They were right: as of now, almost all of my village was seized for building illegal settlements and the Apartheid Wall. I grew up my whole life listening to stories of dispossession and suffering, in a country that plays one of the largest roles in allowing it to occur. I have dried my grandparents' tears for years, while they lamented all that was lost. To this day, the remains of their destroyed homes stand, awaiting their return. They have passed on to me the keys, older than the state of Israel, to open doors that no longer exist.

I clearly remember knowing about the Palestinian struggle and that it was directly part of my identity as far back as kindergarten. I was between the ages of six and ten during the Second Intifada, and the television would always be tuned to the news, bringing pictures and videos to the stories I heard. Through the scenes I saw I was able to better understand what it meant to be a Palestinian living in Palestine, and to recognize that in many ways I had it a lot better. Faces and stories of pain were etched into my memory, like that of Muhammad Al-Durrah, whose look of sheer terror was televised moments before he was killed. I did not feel that it was fair for me to escape many of the harsh realities that my fellow Palestinians faced, still living under occupation and in refugee camps. It was immoral to live comfortably as an American, contributing to the loss of my own people.

Although my identity and experiences have played a large part in shaping my understanding of Palestine, my principle of standing for justice is what led me to become involved with Students for Justice in Palestine (SJP) during my freshman year of college. I have been attending lectures, events, and rallies for as long as I can remember, but it was in college that I was able to materialize and focus my activism. It is my place in the United States, with the privilege of being able to speak out and not having to face living under occupation in my everyday life, and my responsibility to hold my government accountable, that pushed me into student activism. Anyone in the United States who is not actively challenging our government's egregious loyalty to Israel to the farthest extent of their capabilities is a part of the problem. Every single American has a moral responsibility to challenge our government's unwavering protection of Israel. Why Israel? It is imperative that we all stand against injustice everywhere; however, when our government has a direct responsibility in allowing this injustice to occur, we have a direct responsibility in standing against it. The United States aids Israel with UN vetoes, preferential trade agreements, and over eight million dollars every single day in military aid. Furthermore, US involvement with and support for Israel directly contributes to domestic repression that we face here. Israel and the United States share a mutually beneficial relationship when it comes to militarization, surveillance, and policing. The FBI, the ICE (Immigration and Customs Enforcement), and police forces from all across the United States receive Israeli training; the NYPD even has a branch there. The St. Louis County police chief, for example, received training in Israel. He is from the same department that killed Michael Brown and put Ferguson under siege during protests in the summer of 2014. The experience was very much related to what Palestinians face, as protesters from Ferguson and Palestine were sharing messages of solidarity and tips on how to deal with crowd control tactics. The racism and brutality endemic to our police forces are not new; however, the recent hypermilitarization of police in the United States is strongly linked to this collaboration.

There are clear ways in which we can make change. The boycott, divestment, and sanctions (BDS) movement is a clear-cut rubric that provides specific ways in which we can act. Palestinians have called on us, the international community, to be a part of this movement. Everyone can play a part in promoting BDS: it can be as simple ask asking their university, church, organization, and so on, to divest from corporations that enable the occupation and apartheid system. If such campaigns are successful, we are no longer invested in human rights violations. If not, at least awareness of the issue has been raised, as, in this case, silence is consent. Upholding BDS is upholding human rights and international law; the call only asks to respect the systems already in place. It does not ask for anything more than the very least—to cease aiding the ongoing ethnic cleansing of the Palestinians. At a minimum, do no harm. We live at a time in which all the information we need is at our disposal, and we cannot claim ignorance. We are able to challenge our government's role in Israel's human rights and international law violations, and failing to do so is complicity. This is why now, more than ever, SJP branches are rapidly growing on campuses nationwide. We all witness the atrocities that the Palestinian people face, we know what part we play in it, and there are concrete ways carved out for us to take action.

SJP chapters differ from one to the next; however, those at the City University of New York (CUNY) generally share a similar basis of organizing. Our main goal is to raise awareness about the human rights violations that Palestinians face every single day. We want to build solidarity for the Palestinian people based on human rights, justice, freedom, equality, self-determination, and the right of return. We endorse the BDS movement called for by Palestinian civil society, to the best of our ability. They have asked the international community to boycott, divest, and sanction Israel until it complies with international law and Palestinians are granted their rights. If we claim to side with human rights and justice, then we must heed this call that the Palestinian people are asking of us. As students on US campuses our taxes and tuition dollars go into violently oppressing the Palestinian people. At CUNY, the interim chancellor, William P. Kelly, released a statement condemning the American Studies Association's (ASA) decision to boycott Israeli academic institutions. Individual campuses on CUNY have echoed this sentiment, as our university has ties and partnerships with Israeli universities. Our academic institutions have only served to reify the status quo, so we take it in our hands to hold them accountable for their actions.

As organizers in the belly of the beast, CUNY SJPs face massive repression on an administrative level. Public universities already have many issues that curtail student organizing, from lack of funding to limited space availability. However, SJPs have been actively repressed at a level that no other student group within CUNY faces. After the ASA voted to endorse BDS, the New York State Senate passed a bill that would prevent colleges and universities from using public funding for groups that boycott Israel. The forms of repression are very visible, calculated, and persistent among every CUNY college with an SJP chapter. It got so bad that, at the beginning of the 2014 fall semester, faculty from sixteen colleges in the CUNY system sent an open letter to the CUNY administration, asking that all CUNY SJPs be treated exactly like other student organizations. CUNY's administration was not helpful; they instead suggested contacting the president of each individual campus on this issue. When we did so at the College of Staten Island (CSI), we received no response.

Although the forms of repression are different, their ultimate goal is to stifle and silence those organizing for justice in Palestine. At Brooklyn College (BC), the administration is very blatant in their efforts to repress SJP, from cutting their budget—yet forcing them to pay for unwanted security—to the invasive metal detectors, pat-downs, and searches every single BC SJP guest is subjected to before an event. They make no effort to hide it, either. I recently went to a BC event only to be met with a sign at the door that said, "SJP event attendees please use east gate entrance, all other BC events enter here," since only those going to a pro-Palestine event had to be searched. In fall 2014, Brooklyn politicians attempted to shut down an SJP event with Steven Salaita: they wanted to silence a dissenting event on silencing dissent. Fortunately, these attempts were unsuccessful, and, in October 2014, thanks to the help of Palestine Solidarity Legal Support (PSLS), the unconstitutional policy of making SJP pay for their security was suspended. Hunter College SJP has experienced room cancellations hours before events were to take place, and are sometimes even denied access to their own club room. At John Jay, the college president wrote a public letter relating the rise of anti-Semitism around the world to the work that John Jay SJP is doing. At City College, SJP students are regularly prevented from distributing educational flyers and information about events. At CSI, SJP students face issues of surveillance and the creation of arbitrary and improvised rules. Such policies that are usually used solely with SJP severely limit the resources, time, and energy of student organizers, effectively diminishing SJP's ability to function.

As president of Students for Justice in Palestine at the College of Staten Island, the amount of repression SJP faced made it extremely difficult for me to organize.

At every event we had an overwhelming presence of campus security, either in uniform or plainclothes, even though we never needed them. Many times during or after an event, students asked what we had done wrong or what had happened, instead of discussing the actual topic of the event. During closed meetings, we would have security officers posted outside of our door, making many students feel uncomfortable being under surveillance. We have also experienced excessive delays in the approval of our events; in one case I submitted an event and space request weeks ahead of time, but it was not approved until five minutes before it was set to take place. I was also called into meetings with the administration and security officials every single time we planned an event, even when it was something straightforward, like a talk with Ali Abunimah or a panel of our own CSI professors. The administration has come up with new and arbitrary rules on the spot to distance SJP from the university. We were forced, for example, to put disclaimers on our flyers specifying that our views were our own and were not reflective of the college. This policy was created when we wanted to advertise our first major event and has been implemented since. We were also required to make a similar announcement before events. We asked other student groups whether they experienced similar treatment from the administration, and no other club reported such experiences. The behavior of the administration made it very difficult to organize events and activities, and it discouraged students from learning about this very important issue. SJP was effectively singled out for harassment and differential treatment from CSI because we affirm Palestinian rights, equality, and freedom. We were increasingly silenced and ostracized as we became more active, and we were prevented from engaging in academic discourse at an academic institution. It turned out that the provost of CSI had sent a letter to all department chairs denouncing the ASA's decision to boycott Israel and encouraged "similar outrage by protesting" any endorsement of their view. And, of course, SJP was the only student group on campus to endorse BDS. It is ironic that an influential and powerful presence at CSI tried to impose his political views on his colleagues and denounced a student organization in the name of academic freedom.

At CSI, we are up against the provost, the administration that is swayed by him, and Hillel on our campus. It is common for pro-Palestinian groups on campus to face Zionist groups who lobby the administration to suppress SJP while working simultaneously to delegitimize Palestine solidarity work. Sometimes, this is disguised as efforts to promote "coexistence," to normalize relations between Palestine and Israel. However, Hillel's Zionist stance is antithetical to what SJP aims to accomplish on campuses. At CSI and many other campuses, Hillel is the only student organization that has paid staff on campus, usually in advising positions. Hillel was very eager to work with our SJP; however, when their efforts were consistently denied, they resorted to labeling us as anti-Semitic for refusing to normalize their racist ideology. Yet when our faculty advisor, professor Sarah Schulman, approached Hillel about having an event on dissenting Jewish voices on Israel, they refused. Although they were eager to work with us, regardless of our differing political stances, they turned Professor Schulman away—even though she shared our same views on Palestine—since she was also Jewish.

The vice president of student affairs of our campus went so far as to compel SJP to work with Hillel as well. When I explained our political differences and our stance of antinormalization, she went on to create hypothetical situations, asking, "Would you do Sandy relief with them?" The administration was adamant in their efforts to have us work together until I made the comparisons of a university asking a climate change club to work with climate change deniers or an LGBT group to work with a homophobic organization. Their passive aggression cloaked in false coexistence is evident when they invite SJP to celebrate the anniversary of "Israel's independence." For Palestinians this marks our Nakba, in which more than 700,000 Palestinians were forcibly expelled by Zionist militias, among them my grandparents as well as relatives of other CSI SJP students. Palestinians and those who advocate for justice in Palestine should not be forced to work with groups who believe that this massacre and expulsion were justified. We were able to overcome their attempts to distort our message by focusing on what SJP aimed to do on campus and not allowing them to derail us, nor engaging with them in any way.

There are many hurdles that students organizing Palestine solidarity work on campuses must overcome. Whether they come from the administration, other groups on campus, or even the government, they establish a threat to SJPs and the work we do. One of the key elements we learned while organizing that can help SJPs overcome or deal with many of these issues is building a network of support that is readily available when needed. This includes people on and off campus as well as organizations. At CSI, our faculty advisor, Professor Schulman, is not just someone who signs off on papers and lends her name to our organization. She actually advises us, gives us her time, provides us with connections, intervenes on our behalf with the administration, and rounds up other professors who will do the same. It is really valuable to have faculty and administrative representation in the face of adversaries: it sends a message that we have support. In addition, it is important to find someone who cares about the same things SJP does, because it is the type of student organization that will actually need its faculty advisors. Another step we have taken is reaching out to other organizations, on or off campus, to provide additional protection and resources. Local chapters of Al-Awda, Jewish Voice for Peace, and Adalah, to name a few, are often very helpful in providing materials, promoting actions/events, and offering services to student groups. Building connections with other student groups on campus can amplify SJP's voice as well as allowing us to stand in solidarity with other groups and learn about other issues, as solidarity does not end on ethnic lines. Reaching out to local SJPs to defend one another when they are under attack or promote awareness regarding their repression has proved to be incredibly helpful.

CUNY SJPs and professors have been working to create a network that provides a regionally and institutionally focused group of people working for the same goal. Out of this we have created CUNY for Palestine, a group of professors, students, faculty, and even community members who want to build Palestine solidarity at CUNY and beyond. CUNY for Palestine has been a great network, helping SJP on their respective campuses, and fostering a broader atmosphere for Palestine solidarity activism in New York in general. Although we are still relatively new, CUNY for Palestine has been able to mobilize quickly on issues SJP has faced, for example, when the John Jay SJP chapter was slandered by Zionist publications and groups on campus, and the administration attempted to censor SJP. CUNY for Palestine quickly released and signed statements that served to alleviate some of the pressure on John Jay SJP. These types of support systems are an invaluable resource to student organizers, as they are ready to stand with SJP when the administration tries to crack down.

One of the most crucial groups to have provided guidance, assistance, protection, and a source of strength has been Palestine Solidarity Legal Support (PSLS). I was first introduced to them when we had a legal question as to whether pursuing a particular action could get us in trouble. Not only did they provide legal advice and take the time to learn about our SJP, but Radhika Sainath, the staff attorney of PSLS, also came to our campus to educate us on our rights and issues concerning surveillance, media law, campus activism, and more. She has played an essential role in ensuring our rights are protected and helping to advance campus activism overall. With the issues CSI SJP has faced over the years, Radhika has kept a record of all the ways we have been repressed and helped us overcome much it by providing the language, resources, and knowledge we needed to resist it. It is as if we have become our own lawyers, making sure we keep a record of every exchange between us and the administration and holding them accountable to everything they say. PSLS works with SJPs nationwide and documents so many instances of repression that their experience and ability to support SJPs is unmatched. Their work is not limited to when an SJP is in hot water, as they also share tips for organizing. Much of the time we find ourselves on the defensive, as SJP is always struggling to simply have the right to speak. When we are able to have our voices heard, we must ensure that we make the best of it. Because of this, when PSLS came to our campus to give a "know your rights" workshop, they brought along members of the Institute for Middle East Understanding (IMEU) to give a media workshop. It is easy for SJP to be put in compromising situations because everything we say is scrutinized to the very last detail, making it extremely important to be mindful of language when participating in organizing such events/actions. We should also take advantage of media coverage by contacting school and local newspapers about upcoming events and even write op-eds that allow SJPs to have their own narrative. The IMEU offers detailed resources, advice, and experience in media that are essential to SJP's portrayal. With their help we have been able to reclaim our narrative of what we do as CSI SJP, endorsing our views in the public sphere while remaining safe from having our message misconstrued.

It is time to get past fighting our repression and actually focus on endorsing BDS and launching campaigns on our campuses that contribute to the movement. The curtailment of academic freedom in the United States when it comes to Palestine is blatant and pervasive, so much so that people are taking notice and standing up against it—if not yet endorsing or standing with the Palestinian cause, then standing against censorship and obstruction of our freedom of speech. After all, the fact that university administrations are trying so hard to silence us means that we are doing something right. It means our actions actually have an impact, and we are changing the discourse surrounding Palestine and the BDS campaign. Academic institutions are one of the most important site of this developing shift, and Students for Justice in Palestine is at the forefront of advancing the struggle.

V. New Horizons for the Academic Boycott Movement

19

NORMALIZATION: SUPREMACY IDEOLOGY MASQUERADING AS REALITY

SARAH SCHULMAN

If we believe that, by virtue of being born, all human beings are inherently equal, then we uphold that we all deserve opportunity, expression, and recognition. Yet, negative group relationships emerge in which some people bond around a practice of superiority in order to feel whole. They use false accusation and undeserved punishment to elevate their sense of self. This is "normalization": casting the net of an artificial reality in which cruelty is falsely depicted as natural and value free, when actually it is constructed and filled with value. In order to puncture this façade, those of us who resist are obligated to go through a process of coming to consciousness in which we first refuse and then reframe supremacist terms.

We have seen this ideological weapon of distorted thinking used consistently in every corrupt system of supremacy: whites, men, heterosexuals, the bourgeois and the rich, the colonizer, and the bully have used the arenas of couple, family, street, employment, health care, housing, education, sex, art, entertainment, media, neighborhood, community, race, religion, nation state, law, national identity, and the state apparatus to pretend at superiority. They use shunning, exclusion, projection, misrepresentation, threat, incarceration, violence, and genocide to impose this artificial story of their own goodness, to pretend that something elaborate and kept in place by force is actually objective and neutral. Normal.

In Israel, we see both classic and innovative terms of this supremacy ideology. On one hand, there is the traditional Superman construction: Jews are always right. Arabs are always wrong. Judaism is good, Islam is bad. Jews have moral values. Palestinians do not. Therefore everything Jews do is justified. No deliberations. This mode contains a particular continuum variant: Arab Jews are wrong unless they pass by changing their names, refusing to speak Arabic, and redeem their Arab-ness by enacting European racism against Palestinians. Christian Palestinians are less wrong than Muslim ones, and they can be successfully divided from each other through legislation by the occupying force.

On the other hand, there is the specifically Jewish, innovative spin on this supremacy ideology: Super Victim construction. Jews are victims who are defending themselves. Jews are always wronged, Jews must always be afraid. Jews must always punish or else we will be destroyed. Palestinians are predators who are in a constant state of threatening and abusing Jews. Therefore, any tactic, strategy, or action to hurt Palestinians is justified.

As early as November 1948, Albert Einstein, Hannah Arendt, and others wrote in the *New York Times* that they saw a "Fascism" emerging in Israel, embodied by Menachem Begin and the Irgun. They cited murders of Palestinian citizens in what we now call the *Nakba*, specifying the massacre at the Palestinian village of Deir Yassin.[1] So these classic tendencies are as old as the nation-state itself and are intrinsically connected to the poison of nationalism. Only those who control the state apparatus can convince themselves that they deserve to do so. Feeling superior from a place of subordination is quite materially different than being able to act out one's feelings with the full power of the state.

There is a lot here to undo. Like all bullies' self-concepts, this Israeli construction demands full and complete obedience. It does not tolerate critique, resistance, or analysis. It can't negotiate or acknowledge contradiction. Since it is a house of cards, any nuance or acceptance of mutual experience would collapse it. Hence we have totalitarian modes of maintenance.

In 2011, PACBI (Palestinian Campaign for the Academic and Cultural Boycott of Israel) described the lived experience of existing under systems of Israeli supremacy from the Palestinian point of view: "It is helpful to think of normalization as a 'colonization of the mind,' whereby the oppressed subject comes to believe that the oppressor's reality is the only 'normal' reality that must be subscribed to, and that the oppression is a fact of life that must be coped with."[2]

In this way, PACBI lays out the task of dismantling occupation values: first, to understand that just because the Israeli state and its supporters make claims does not mean that those claims are true or need to be abided by. That, in fact, being forced to engage within those paradigms is part of the tactic of control. In this way, we have the power to reject their rules. Second, even though they pretend that their point of view is God-given, in other words, unquestionable, actually nothing about this construction of reality is neutral or unchangeable. It is all subjective and imposed by force.

Normalization is thus a tactic in which Palestinians are asked to enter into these false constructions and re-enforce them through their active participation. So, for example, one very common form of normalization is to use the term "both sides." "Both sides are hurting." "There are wrongs on both sides." This falsely implies that Israel and Palestine are two equal forces, with equal strength and equal resources. Obviously, this is false. Israel is a nuclear superpower, funded by the United States, while Palestine is a divided land, and most Palestinians are in exile, many under dire living conditions. The West Bank is occupied and Gaza is under siege, its people living in abject poverty and subject to violence daily by Israeli forces. Even more important to the inequality of positions is that Israel, as an occupying power, is in violation of key tenets of international law, and Palestine is the victim of those violations. For example, the UN Charter forbids acquisition of land by force, the Geneva Convention forbids banning refugees from returning to their homes, UN resolutions, the Geneva Convention, and international law charters forbid occupying armies from settling their populations on seized territory. And so on. Yet, Palestinians in the diaspora are often invited to panels, debates, and "dialogue" groups that are constructed around the myth of two equivalent "sides." According to the principle of antinormalization, Palestinians can refuse to participate in those spectacles rather than re-enforce false concepts of equity.

PACBI breaks down normalization into three categories relevant to boycott, divestment, sanctions (BDS), as approved by the Boycott National Committee (BNC).

1. In Palestinian and Arab contexts: "As the participation in any project, initiative or activity, in Palestine or internationally, that aims (implicitly or explicitly) to bring together Palestinians (and/or Arabs) and Israelis (people or institutions) without placing as its goal resistance to and exposure of the Israeli occupation and all forms of discrimination and oppression against the Palestinian people."[3] These kinds of projects, for example, a joint Palestinian/Israeli dialogue on hummus, on LGBT cinema, on architecture, or the like, create the illusion that "coexistence" can lead to the end of oppression.

PACBI continues, "In the process, Palestinians, regardless of intentions, end up serving as a fig leaf[4] for Israelis who are able to benefit from a 'business-as-usual' environment, perhaps even allowing Israelis to feel their conscience is cleared for having engaged Palestinians they are usually accused of oppressing and discriminating against."[5] Instead PACBI proposes "co-resistance," appearing with, working with and dialoguing with others about how to achieve the goals of BDS: end to occupation, full and equal rights, right of return for refugees.

2. Palestinian citizens of Israel: Colonized, indigenous Palestinians who live within Israel are obligated to cooperate with Israeli systems. They must pay taxes, they must obey laws, they must maintain employment and educational requirements. They have to read and write and speak Hebrew, carry Israeli passports and use Israeli currency. But, as compelled by PACBI's definition of normalization, Palestinian citizens of Israel are asked to not act internationally as representatives of the Israeli state. In other words, not to represent Israel at the Oscars, Eurovision, international conferences, or sports events.

> When Palestinians engage in such activities without placing them within the same resistance framework mentioned above, they contribute, even if inadvertently, to a deceptive appearance of tolerance, democracy, and normal life in Israel for an international audience who may not know better.... The absence of vigilance in this matter has the effect of telling the Palestinian public that they can live with and accept apartheid, should engage Israelis on their own terms, and forgo any act of resistance.[6]

3. In the international context: International supporters of BDS are asked not to participate in events that "morally or politically equate the oppressor and the oppressed." In this context, "dialogue" is often presented as an alternative to boycott. Yet, "dialogue" on these terms positions coexistence or status quo as a substitute for ending oppression. In South Africa, forgiveness processes and "healing" rituals only occurred *after* the dismantling of apartheid.[7]

One concrete example of the nuances and complexities of normalization occurred on my campus, the College of Staten Island of the City University of New York (CSI/CUNY), where I am the faculty advisor to a strong and effective chapter of Students for Justice in Palestine (SJP). Our SJP is almost entirely Palestinian. Our campus has 20 percent Muslim students and 2 percent Jewish students, yet international Hillel pays the full-time salary of a person to staff campus Hillel. This may seem odd for a campus with almost no Jewish students, but this trend is expanding nationally, as we see Hillel pay the salaries of staff embedded on Catholic campuses, Historically Black Colleges, and other schools with little or no Jewish student body. In our case, the CSI administration granted free office space to Hillel inside the Interfaith Center, along with a Catholic priest and a Methodist minister. The number of Methodist students is miniscule; there is no imam. In this way, Hillel is the only outside partisan political organization that is allowed free office space on campus. And the Hillel staff person is the only person (students, staff, faculty, and administration) who has not been vetted before being admitted to campus in an official capacity. It's a strange, inexplicable exception. Would Right to Life, the National Rifle Association, or the International Socialist Organization be awarded the same privileges?

Part of the reason for the unique situation is that some members of our administration are confused about the role of Hillel. They view it as a bipartisan religious organization instead of as a highly sectarian political order representing the interests of the Israeli government. This concretizes or normalizes pro-Israel hegemony as a Jewish position on campus. At the same time, other members of the administration are staunchly Zionist and hold supremacist views vis-à-vis Israel and Palestinians.

In 2014 I received a phone call from the only African American member of the administration informing me that the leadership of CSI wanted SJP to do a joint event with Hillel. I explained to her that Hillel does not represent all Jews, which she did not know. I also explained the principle of normalization. The SJP discussed the offer and turned it down based in antinormalization committments. I, however, approached the staff member and the two of us had lunch. I proposed to her that I do an event with Hillel, in order to present the variety of Jewish perspectives on the occupation.

I want to explain why I felt that for me to appear with Hillel is *not* normalization, while for the Palestinians in SJP to do so would be. As PACBI makes clear above, if SJP were to appear in a "dialogue" event with Hillel, they would be re-enforcing the false argument that there are "two sides" that are equal. And that "dialogue" between these "sides" would lead to a lessening of oppression, when it is clear that Hillel, which supports the occupation, was actually trying to use SJP to make themselves appear to be "fair" and liberal. However, as a member of Jewish Voice for Peace, the only mainstream Jewish organization to fully oppose every element of the war on Gaza, it is my *responsibility* to engage the rest of the Jewish community, no matter how daunting or frustrating. This is not the job of Palestinians or pro-Palestinian groups such as SJP. It is my job. Ironically, Hillel refused my offer because of their national policy of not creating platforms for Jews who oppose Israeli government policy.

Ironically, this closed-mindedness on the part of Hillel sparked the creation of a renegade Jewish student movement called Open Hillel on the campuses of Harvard, Swarthmore, and Wesleyan, three ruling-class institutions. I attended the first national Open Hillel conference at Harvard in October 2014 and conducted a workshop on the question of normalization.

It was a difficult and tense conversation. While many of the students who participated were clear, open, and supportive of antinormalization strategies, not everyone felt that way. There was a spectrum of frustration on the part of some of the Jews who attended my workshop about how antinormalization was obstructing their wishes and conceptualizations of their relationships with Palestinians. Three stand-outs remain in my memory:

A young man from a Midwestern state school said, "We invited the Palestinian students to our Shabbat dinner, but they didn't want to come." I asked him, "Why do you want them to come to your Shabbat dinner?" "Because we want to hear what they have to say." I suggested that his group ask them what the best forum would be for *them* to convey to his group what they have to say.

A young woman from an elite university said she wanted to "approach Palestinian students" but she didn't know how. She did not belong to a group or organization, was just acting as an individual. I asked her, "What are you offering them?" She didn't know. I said, "Because if you are not offering them anything, then you are basically asking them to take care of you." She seemed hurt and taken aback by my answer, but did acknowledge that perhaps working with an organization that could offer support would be more constructive.

A rabbi affiliated with Harvard Hillel actually attended my talk. He was aggressive, in a style that is very, very typical in these kinds of conversations. He would "ask" questions that were not questions but were actually attempts to "trick" me or force me into making statements that he could later use to undermine my point of view. It was a familiar and tedious trope. He could not understand why Palestinian students or their organizational representative, SJP, would not cooperate with invitations to do events with Hillel. I asked him what the purpose of these events was. He answered something like "To exchange views." Or "To hear each other's views." I pointed out that Palestinians speak in Boston regularly and he had many opportunities to hear their views. But it became clear that he really wanted them to hear *his* views. Even though his views are already very well known to them, as they live under the consequences of those views every day.

I found the resistance to Palestinian refusal to reflect a combination of factors. To be generous, there is a Jewish tradition of discussion; Judaism is a dialogic religion and the idea of debate and commentary is culturally consistent. Unfortunately I also think that this particular element of the community is very entitled, privileged, and used to being heard. A kind of enraged indignation comes to the surface when the idea of speaking is replaced by the idea of listening. There was not a realistic self-conception as members of the oppressor group, and so the subsequent responsibilities inherent in that position were refused. As usual, the beneficiaries of these kinds of encounters are the bystanders, the witnesses to the debate, who have the opportunity to contrast views and draw their own conclusions. And they are the most crucial factors in creating a critical mass of support for dismantling US military aid to Israel, the "S" in BDS: sanctions. In the work to transform US ideology and practice in relation to Israel/Palestine, this tactic, of reaching bystanders by engaging those who are rigidly fixed, is a crucial one. And for that reason I was reconfirmed in my belief that while, on the one hand, Palestinians should not be subjected to normalizing "dialogue" about whether or not they deserve full human rights, Jews, on the other hand, who oppose these crimes against humanity absolutely must take up the responsibility to refute any claim that the occupation, apartheid, or Jewish supremacy are normal, instead of pathological, practices.

20

THE WALL IS CRUMBLING: WILL LABOR FOLLOW THE UNIVERSITIES?

ANDREW ROSS

The fog of war creates uncertainty for combatants, but it also obscures the vision of onlookers, erasing their memories of the moral landscape, now altered by military violence, that preceded it. By most accounts, Israel's latest, brutal offensive on Gaza was aimed, in the short term, at subverting the prospects of the Hamas–Fatah unity initiative announced in the spring of 2014. In the long term, the assumptive goal was to force the mass flight of Palestinians from Gaza and parts of the West Bank, further diluting the demographic strength of Arab populations in the region. With respect to Gaza and the West Bank, the Israeli policy of divide and rule depends on preserving the antagonism between the two Palestinian governments. Any show of reconciliation threatens the ongoing campaign of annexation, displacement, and ethnic cleansing that is the everyday reality of the occupation.

Israel's military managers and their political taskmasters know that the harsh clarity of this policy cannot be allowed to take hold in the international public mind, and especially not in the United States. Destabilization of opinion is essential, and for many casual onlookers the tricked-out national security threat of Hamas's rockets and tunnels proved sufficient. Ever since 9/11, the American media frame has been disposed to respond sympathetically to over-retaliation on the part of the United States and its Middle Eastern proxy to even the semblance of minor threats.[1] The ostensible massacre of civilians (the "uninvolved" is the preferred Israeli euphemism) is never easy to explain away, but, in the case of Gaza, Washington's response demanded nothing less than the rationalization of such atrocities as a direct by-product of Hamas intransigence.

While Israel now faces stepped-up condemnation and widespread boycott measures in nations around the globe, its political majority continues to behave as

179

if Washington's steadfast support is the only vote that counts. In response, the US political class, fully abject across the entire partisan spectrum, rushed to appease the lobbyists by passing senate resolutions in support of the Israeli Defense Forces' (IDF) barbarous operations. Yet when the fog of war lifted, the gulf between state policy and many sectors of civil opinion in the United States had widened appreciably. Jewish American sentiment, in particular, is now sharply polarized, and revulsion at Israel's war crimes has further skewed the distribution to the anti-Zionist left. Support for the burgeoning BDS movement is building in strength, especially because it involves private actions that circumvent the grisly stalemate of state-to-state diplomacy (a Bermuda Triangle between Washington–Jerusalem–Ramallah) that has allowed Israel's expansion to proceed unchecked.

For those in official positions, the formidable sway of pro-Zionist lobbying continues to be disturbingly effective, and nowhere more so than on Capitol Hill, where not one politician has been able to utter a word of public reproach for Israel's repeated violations of international law. While it was a milestone of sorts, the Democrat revolt against Benjamin Netanyahu's address to a joint session of Congress in March 2015 was presented more as an opportunity to reframe support for Israel than as a dissenting stance on its policies. But public acceptance of this lockstep positioning is no longer guaranteed. In February 2014, for example, after the news leaked out about New York City Mayor Bill de Blasio's off-the-record assurances to AIPAC that part of his "job description is to be a defender of Israel" and that "City Hall will always be open to AIPAC," he had to face down the public wrath of the city's progressive Jewish communities. So, too, the scope and degree of street protests, direct actions, and petition-building in response to the Gaza offensive was more intensive than ever before. Disgust at the atrocities committed by the IDF had a particular impact on younger people who get their news directly from online sources and social media. Liberals, long inclined to observe the fiction of symmetry between Palestinians and Israelis, on and off the killing fields of combat, are more responsive now to the pressure to take the side of the oppressed party.

THE ACADEMIC FRONT

A prescient pre-Gaza example of this pushback against the US–Israeli continuum was the fierce debate that followed the membership votes of several academic associations to support a boycott of Israeli universities: American Studies Association (ASA), Association for Asian American Studies, Native American and Indigenous Studies Association, Association for Humanist Sociology, Critical Ethnic Studies Association, Arab American Studies Association, and the African Literature Asso-

THE WALL IS CRUMBLING 181

ciation. The backlash against the ASA resolution on the part of official elites (including hundreds of university presidents) and organized Zionist groups was particularly virulent, though it should have surprised no one. Less predictable was the widespread mobilization *against* the backlash, which even included individuals and organizations, such as the American Association of University Professors (AAUP) and the American Civil Liberties Union (ACLU), that were opposed to the boycott itself. In the New York State legislature, a bill aimed at penalizing ASA membership (I am an ASA member) was pulled even before it moved out of committee.[2] This was almost unprecedented for legislation sponsored by Sheldon Silver, the powerful Speaker of the State Assembly, and it was the result of multilateral pressure from an ad hoc coalition of professional associations, NGOs, academics, and trade unions that delivered a rare defeat for the pro-Israel lobby pushing the bill. Copycat legislation, some of it patently unconstitutional, also failed in other states (Illinois, Maryland). A similar fate befell the Roskam-Lipinski bill in Congress (the Protect Academic Freedom Act), which would have barred federal funds from institutions that support BDS. Indeed, this wave of attempted legislation was either opposed or discouraged by organizations like the Jewish Anti-Defamation League, fearful of deepening the public perception that the pro-Israel lobby is powerful enough to manipulate US national policy.

The ASA resolution helped to open a door in the restraining wall that has held back the full expression of US public opinion about Israeli/Palestinian relations, but the crude effort to slam it shut, by efforts to outlaw any talk of boycotts, had the opposite effect. Many more people are now widening the door by passing through it. The wall is beginning to crumble, and it will be impossible to shore up or rebuild.

Of course, the backlash is not over. The tactics of intimidation and thuggery deployed by organized supporters of Israeli policy should remind us of the military violence at the heart of the occupation in Palestine. Indeed, that is the unspoken intention behind all the threats. Somewhere behind all the bullying and verbal posturing lies the metallic decree of armed force. But the permission to speak and act more freely in solidarity with the Palestinian cause comes more easily now. The effect has been described as "breaking the taboo," a strange locution, to be sure, but one that references the fear that envelops forbidden speech and irradiates those who want to distance themselves from it but cannot.[3] In the United States, at least, the mundane factor of money supply is never far from the surface. Politicians and university presidents know they will be cut off from donor support if they don't toe the pro-Israel line—it's often that simple, and everyone knows it.

In Israel, the backlash has the full force of state backing and has morphed into outright, and, in the case of some protests, violent censure of dissident views. In 2011, the Knesset passed legislation that effectively bans any public call for a boycott against the state of Israel or its West Bank settlements, making such action a punishable offense. This blatantly repressive bill was, in part, a response to the 2008 founding of Boycott from Within by prominent Jewish and Arab Israelis. More recently, the Committee of University Heads has created a task force to track and suppress academic support for BDS before it spreads from the liberal arts to the sciences. According to its chair, Zvi Ziegler, an emeritus professor at the Technion—Israel Institute of Technology, the institution most commonly associated with military-industrial research for the IDF—its goal is "to examine and map out the scope of the threat, gathering information on potential boycotts as well as coordinating with relevant parties and institutions in Israel and abroad to minimize the damage." Such information, in his view, "will help us thwart the initiative before it stews."[4] Stemming the BDS contagion was considered a priority after the European Commission announced new guidelines, in July 2013, that forbid funding, cooperation, research awards, or any similar relationship with any Israeli entity that has "direct or indirect links" to the occupied territories. Intense lobbying followed, aimed at producing an invitation for Israel to participate in the Horizon 2020 EU research program. While the agreement to do so was announced in February 2014, it may yet backfire.

Boycotts of Israeli academic institutions to promote Palestinian human rights date back to the April 2002 call "for a European Boycott of Research and Cultural Links with Israel," which was signed by around seven hundred Europe-based academics, ten of which were Israeli academics from various universities.[5] BDS, the most recent nonviolent call for solidarity, issuing from within Palestinian civil society and enjoying the support of all Palestinian trade unions, has profoundly altered the landscape in recent years. In Europe, Africa, and Latin America, responses to the BDS call now stretch all the way from grassroots groups to government-backed initiatives and national congresses of organized labor.

While it is only one of many initiatives that responded to the BDS call of the Palestinian Campaign for the Academic and Cultural Boycott of Israel (PACBI), the ASA resolution deserves a few additional comments here. Although the vote was widely condemned as a self-destructive act, the association actually increased membership in its wake, adding new programs and departments. Also lost in the furor was the significance of the boycott for the field of scholarship that sustains the ASA. The resolution marked a new departure for a field whose origins, in the

1940s, have often been described as an adjunct of state power. In the intervening decades, scholars struggled to liberate the ASA's institutional life from the State Department's orbit at the same time as they succeeded in digging the discipline out from under the heavy footprint of nationalism and US exceptionalism. In recent years, the most vibrant American studies scholarship has focused on the long shadow cast beyond US borders by Washington's exercise of influence in the service of capitalist profit.

Among other things, the boycott resolution reflects a growing scholarly consensus—that Israeli acquisition of, and settlement on, Palestinian land is a continuation of the wave of expansion that drove the colonial era and produced white settler states in the Americas, Africa, and Australia. The outcome of that expansion is still contested in the United States itself by populations who see the historical role of the US cavalry in "settling the West" being reprised today by the IDF in the West Bank. Far from an issue that lies outside the "legitimate" borders of the discipline, Washington's indispensable role in the Palestinian occupation lies close to the core of the new American studies. Criticism of these new scholarly directions by those who viewed the boycott as a further betrayal of the field's birthright is actually a closet recognition of the role that white America continues to play overseas in the last gasp of settler-colonialism.

THE LABOR FRONT

Of course, the resolutions passed by scholarly organizations were much more than expressions of academic analysis. They were also bold acts of solidarity from within a state that is as isolated from international opinion as Israel itself. Boycotts are tactics, not strategies, and while they can and often do have a long, tidal life (it's not easy to call them off), their vigor lies in their short-term impact. So far BDS has generated academic, cultural, and consumer boycotts. Expansion into other sectors, including trade and investment, will be critical. In Europe, Africa, and Latin America, this is already happening, and, in many cases, is the outcome of state action at the highest level.

These acts of censure include noteworthy contributions from organized labor. Dozens of individual unions and national congresses of unions (in Spain, Norway, Ireland, Scotland, France, Canada, United Kingdom, and Brazil) have endorsed BDS or severed relations with the Israeli labor federation Histradut for its backing of punitive wars and territorial expansionism. Dockworkers in Sweden, India, Greece, South Africa, Turkey, and California refused to off-load containers after the war on Gaza in 2008 and the Israeli naval assault on the Gaza Freedom Flotilla in

2010. Similar actions have sprung up in response to Operation Protective Edge—an Israeli ship was blockaded in August 2014 at the Port of Oakland in California. The US-based Labor for Palestine collected the signatures of hundreds of independent trade unionists for its letter of condemnation against Israeli militarism.[6]

These endorsements are formal gestures of solidarity, but they are seldom tied to recognition of how indigenous and overseas migrant labor is exploited in Israel and the occupied territories. Nor has this topic entered in any significant way into the debate about the rationale for BDS. Yet efficient access to indigenous labor is a key component of any colonial enterprise, and its profitable advancement is threatened by withdrawals of that labor. The mass stay-away by Palestinian workers that accompanied the First Intifada in 1987 brought whole sectors of the Israeli economy to a halt and interrupted an arrangement whereby the vast majority of "noncitizen Arab workers" were from Gaza and the West Bank. Most of that workforce has been replaced in the decades since then by overseas migrants.

By some estimates, close to a majority of the Palestinian labor force was migrant workers by the 1980s, and, at harvest time, an even greater number. Many were skilled, and some had college degrees. Israeli labor offices regulated the flow of labor, but informal "slave markets" developed for unregistered day laborers. Needless to say, the worst abuses occurred in this irregular economy, and Histradut was actively complicit in the exploitation of these migrants who had no rights whatsoever inside the Green Line. The harsh, discriminatory treatment of these workers, who were visibly employed in many sectors of Israeli society, planted the seeds for the mentality of Arab dehumanization that has flourished among the defenders of the occupation.

Israel's dependence on these Palestinian migrants was fully exposed during the First Intifada. In March 1993, the labor flows from the occupied territories were tightened, and, within a year, the mass importation of overseas migrants began, rising to more than two hundred thousand by the 2000s. Gazan workers were barred from entry in 2006, and the small number of West Bank residents (thirty-three thousand, by quota) who are still permitted in labor intensive workplaces—primarily in construction and agriculture—face highly restrictive conditions that limit their movements, rights, and labor conditions. The informal economy of day laborers still thrives, and these workers face arrest and worse if their employers opt to report them. Whether they hold permits or not, Palestinian workers who cross the Green Line encounter intensely precarious circumstances and endure chronic violations of international labor standards.

Even worse are the conditions of the hundreds of thousands of migrants imported from Thailand, China, the Philippines, and parts of Eastern Europe and

Africa. Burdened with massive recruitment debts, their passports are typically held by employers, and they are routinely cheated out of pay under circumstances that are designed for maximum exploitation.[7] Their very presence in Israel is an affront to the vision of the Jewish state upheld by the Zionist right, and so their abuse is magnified by racist discrimination. Official affirmations of the state's "Jewish character" have also driven the inhumane detention of African migrants from Eritrea and Sudan, who cross the border seeking asylum.

The administrative policy of replacing indigenous labor with imported migrants is a recurrent gesture of colonial history. In settler-colonialism, where the key motive is land acquisition and not the capture of natural or human resources, the means to that end is depopulation and evacuation of indigenous residents. For those who believe that Israel is set on claiming the whole of historic Palestine by reducing the Palestinian population from its current millions to a small native minority, the decision to remove the West Bank's Arabs from the labor market is part of an inexorable logic. Gaza presents a less tractable challenge, and that is why accusations of genocide are most forcibly directed against Israel's policy of isolation, deprivation, and collective punishment in that densely populated coastal strip.

Either way, the analogy with South African apartheid does not hold up so readily. Control over the use of indigenous labor was indispensable to the apartheid economy. In Israel, that has not been the case. The post-1994 preference for imported workers is officially justified because they are neither a "security" nor a "demographic" threat. But the shift away from dependence on Arab employment has given fresh impetus to those long bent on a Zionist land grab, and state power is increasingly in their hands.

As that vision takes hold, the distinction, preserved by many critics of the occupation, between boycotting settlement industries in the occupied territories and those inside Israel is a shaky one. According to a 2010 report by the Israeli human rights group B'Tselem, the jurisdiction and regional councils of the Jewish-only settlements controlled 42.7 percent of the West Bank, with much of the rest of the land under Israeli military control.[8] These settlements, which have expanded rapidly since 2010, are a direct and illegal product of Israeli state policy. In other words, they are colonies, not rogue outposts populated by rugged ex-urbanites or maverick entrepreneurs who buck the state's efforts to rein them in. The boundary between what lies inside and what falls outside Israel is constantly being shifted by the colonizing force, and, in the case of Palestine, the ability to expand with impunity depends directly on the power of institutions inside Israel: military, commercial, financial, and academic, in addition to other organizations that are arms of the state in all but name. The only counter-policy that makes sense is to boycott all Israeli institutions and companies. This was a marginal position until recently, but it has become more mainstream in the wake of the savagery inflicted on Gazans, and through recognition that the massacres commanded widespread support from institutional leaders, not to mention the Israeli population at large. If not now, when?

21

RASMEA ODEH, THE PALESTINIAN DIASPORA, AND BDS

NADINE NABER

In a historic vote, on December 4, a union of thirteen thousand teaching assistants and student workers at the University of California (United Auto Workers Local 2865) endorsed boycott, divestment, and sanctions (BDS) against Israel. As their campaign was developing, on November 4, feminist and queer UC student workers of Local 2865 called upon all union members to vote for BDS, stand against pink-washing,[1] and support Rasmea Odeh. Rasmea Odeh is a Chicago-based Palestinian American who was arrested on October 22, 2013, by Department of Homeland Security agents. The US government accuses Odeh of failing to answer a question truthfully on her naturalization application in 2004. The support Rasmea Odeh has received from various BDS groups—including the UC student workers, Students for Justice in Palestine (SJP), and the US Academic and Cultural Boycott of Israel (USACBI)—represents a growing trend in BDS activism in the United States, whereby activists are increasingly extending their solidarity with Palestinians in Palestine to diasporic Palestinian communities in the United States.

Many activists have said Rasmea Odeh embodies the Palestinian struggle against Israeli colonization, displacement, and racism. As Rasmea testified in court, she was born in Lifta, Palestine in 1947. Her family was displaced under the threat of Israeli invasion—the village fell under attack by Jewish militias, and they heard of massacres and rapes in nearby villages—before Lifta was completely depopulated in early 1948, three months prior to Israel's declaration of independence.[2] Her family lost everything they owned and were displaced to the West Bank, where they lived, first in a tent with nineteen people and then with four families squeezed into two small rooms in Ramallah, until Rasmea graduated from high school in 1967.

In 1969, when Israeli soldiers were occupying and invading the West Bank, and Israeli tanks attacked sections of their home, the family decided to join their father in Jericho so that, as she explains, her father told them, "If we die, we die together, and if we live, we live together." Rasmea's family walked for forty-eight hours to Jericho, "saw dead bodies burned" along the way, and thought they, too, would die. Rasmea's family was later swept up in the systematic Israeli practice of mass arrest, a gross violation of human rights whereby the only apparent criteria for arrest is being Palestinian. Five hundred Palestinians were picked up in the "random" sweep that included Rasmea Odeh and her family, including a sister, twenty-three at the time, who died in the process. In detention, in keeping with Israel's systematic practices of torture and sexual assault as a means of facilitating the colonization of Palestinian land, for forty-five days Rasmea Odeh was sexually assaulted and tortured into confessing to two bombings that had killed two people and injured many.

Odeh's 1969 conviction in Israel was determined by a court system that consistently abuses Palestinians' due process rights and convicts Palestinians at a rate of 99.74 percent.[3] The Israeli military justice system that is applied to occupied Palestinians, in fact, has itself been found to be in immense violation of international law—from the lack of protections against torture and rape while in custody to the simple fact that virtually no Palestinian walks away free from an Israeli trial. The Israeli state also unlawfully imprisoned and tortured Odeh's family and destroyed her family home soon after her arrest.[4] Rasmea revoked her confession shortly after she made it and she testified about the torture at the United Nations upon her release from prison in 1979.

Rasmea Odeh was displaced to Jordan and immigrated to the United States in the mid-1990s. She settled in Chicago, where she has remained active in the struggle for Palestinian liberation. Rasmea became the associate director of the Arab American Action Network (AAAN) and has been leading their Arab Women's Committee (AWC) since 2004.

The arrest of Rasmea Odeh by the Department of Justice (DOJ) can be placed within the context of escalating assaults (launched by Zionist movements and the US government) against the BDS movement and the Palestinian, Arab, and Muslim communities in retaliation for the growing successes of the BDS movement. These assaults also grow out of decades of government repression against Arab American and Palestine solidarity activism in the United States—from Operation Boulder in 1972, when the FBI spied on Arab Americans; to the "LA 8" case, in which seven Palestinians and one Kenyan national were targeted with deportation proceedings for twenty years, based on secret evidence from speech-protected activities[5]; to the ongoing, systematic targeting of Palestinian, Arab, and Muslim student activists, neighborhoods, and community-based institutions.[6]

Like Rasmea Odeh's, many of these cases have involved collaborations between the United States and Israel. Exemplifying this is the case of Muhammad Salah, initiated in Israel in 1993, when Salah was arrested while distributing money to disenfranchised occupied Palestinians. He was tortured and interrogated. He then returned to the United States, where he was labeled a specially designated terrorist "by executive order with no legal process, no limitation in time, and no process to challenge this."[7] In his high-profile 2007 trial, Israelis were feeding information to prosecutors based on Salah's confessions under torture.[8] Also consider the related 2008 conviction and indictment of Dr. Abdelhaleem Ashqar for obstruction of justice and criminal contempt when he refused to collaborate with federal grand juries' investigations' of Hamas and the Palestinian antioccupation movement. He was given the choice of informing or going to jail for criminal contempt. The US government asserted that Dr. Ashqar's refusal to testify before a grand jury required him to be sentenced as if he had aided and abetted terrorism.[9]

On November 4, 2014, the DOJ put Rasmea Odeh on trial for allegedly lying on her naturalization application ten years earlier, and failing to indicate that she had been previously imprisoned. On October 27, foreshadowing what was to come, a pretrial ruling enabled one of the major injustices of this case and the verdict itself. Judge Gershwin Drain ruled that Rasmea could testify, but she was instructed not to mention her experiences of torture at the hands of Israeli authorities. Before the trial even began, the setup was clear. Under the guise of immigration fraud, the prosecutor was granted the power to present Odeh as a Palestinian terrorist bomber—and, just as Israel had silenced her forty-five years ago, the United States would silence her once again by denying her a defense.

While Rasmea's torture experiences were barred from court, one hundred Israeli documents that had been used to convict Rasmea Odeh in 1969 became central to the prosecution. At the trial, reinforcing the logic of a culture of rape, Judge Drain repeatedly prevented Rasmea from discussing her sexual assault; diminished her experience using phrases like "torture, rape, and all that stuff"; and ensured that the perpetrators would remain protected. Moreover, he continued to allow the prosecutor to mention before the jury, more than fifty times throughout the trial, that Rasmea had been convicted of a bombing that had killed people.[10]

With her defense gutted, on November 10, 2014, Odeh was found guilty of "unlawful procurement of citizenship." Shortly after the verdict, Judge Drain decid-

ed Rasmea should not be released on bond because, as he stated, she had no sufficient ties to her community. The misogynist and heterosexist nature of the ruling
was clear in its insinuation that to have community a woman has to be married
with children. Belying this insult, every day, an average of thirty elderly women,
mothers, and coworkers traveled by bus from Chicago to Michigan overnight to
pack the courtroom in support of Rasmea that week, and most of Rasmea's defense
focused on her role as a beloved community leader, friend, and mentor.[11]

After the verdict, Rasmea spend one month in county jail, including three weeks
in solitary confinement, before she was released on bail. In March 2015, Rasmea
Odeh—survivor of displacement, of sexual torture in an Israeli prison, and now, of
the US prison-industrial complex and rape culture that prevented her from telling her
story in court—was sentenced to eighteen months in prison, followed by deportation.

PACKING THE COURTROOM

It was primarily diasporic Palestinians and Arabs who filled the courtroom and
joined the massive organizing and mobilizations to free Rasmea across the United
States. We have learned from history that the European and US empires legitimize
their violence by constructing the people they dominate as uncivilized savages and
muzzling their voices. Indeed, in this case, the DOJ ensured that Rasmea's supporters would be neither seen nor heard. A few weeks before the trial began and before
the jury was even selected, prosecutors filed a motion characterizing the defense
campaign as "hordes" and "mobs," "almost certainly criminal," and involved in
"jury tampering."[12] The motion asked Judge Drain for an "anonymous jury," to keep
the names of the jurors secret from the defense attorneys, and to put in place special
security measures to make it seem as if Rasmea were a threat.

Anonymous juries are not common. They are reserved for cases in which there
is some kind of potential threat to the jurors—typically mob cases in which there
is a history of witness coercion or tampering.

In continuity with the US/Israeli strategy of singling out, isolating, and crim-
inalizing individual Palestinians, the prosecutors motion specifically targeted Rasmea's colleague at the AAAN, Palestinian American Hatem Abudayyeh, stating
that he had "orchestrated a concerted effort to influence the criminal proceedings
against defendant, which has resulted, at each proceeding, in a large group outside
the Courthouse protesting and parading, carrying signs demanding dismissal of
charges and 'Justice for Rasmea' and displaying the Palestinian flag."[13]

Consolidating the imbalance of power, Judge Drain determined that the jury
would assemble in an off-site location and US marshals would transport them to

the courtroom in a bus with blackened windows. Under the guise of protecting the jurors, the judge basically blocked the jurors from witnessing Rasmea's humanity and what was happening outside the courtroom—the support of hundreds of people who cherished her, harmonizing in the street. Outside the courtroom, Detroiters affirmed that protesting outside courthouses is absolutely customary, and that the Detroit federal courthouse is especially known for protests—from the civil rights movement to struggles over gay marriage, the Detroit bankruptcy ruling, the recent verdict in Ferguson, and beyond. Detroiters were also discussing the irony wherein the US government was pumping massive funds into prosecuting this individual case while just around the corner, the city of Detroit was, without warning, shutting off the water of the majority-Black population.

As the trial began, US marshals lined up in the front row of the courtroom. Among those present were individuals from Israel—the family of one of the people killed in the bombing for which Rasmea had been imprisoned. Whether or not the United States invited them and paid their expenses, their presence was strategic. Judge Drain repeated that the case was not about her conviction in Israel or "politics." At the same time, however, he allowed the DOJ to construct their case upon a US and Israeli colonialist logic that centralizes the apparent suffering of the Israeli people at the hands of violent Palestinians—in this case, Israeli victims killed, allegedly, at the hands of Rasmea Odeh. He forbade Rasmea from telling her story of torture and forced conviction. The boundaries of acceptable speech in the courtroom (like the colonialist logic that legitimizes, justifies, and explains away Israeli settler-colonialism) obscured the unjust and unlawful structure of Israeli military courts and their convictions of Palestinians, concealed the imbalance of power between Israelis and Palestinians, and portrayed the victim as victimizer.

The court also refused to ask any questions in voir dire about Israel and Palestine to determine whether or not potential jurors could have opinions about Palestine and Israel that would interfere with their ability to be fair and impartial. With this tableau, the verdict was basically foreordained.[14]

Michael Deutsch, Rasmea's attorney, explains the government's case against Rasmea Odeh as the product of a "fishing expedition" and an example of the "selective use of the criminal law to target protected political work." The allegations of immigration fraud against Rasmea stemmed from the illegal investigation of twenty-three Chicago-based antiwar activists in 2010—an investigation targeting Palestine solidarity efforts and organizing in the Palestinian community. The FBI raided the homes of these activists. They received subpoenas to a grand jury in Chicago investigating material support for terrorism. Rasmea's colleagues, not Rasmea, were the focus of the investigation through which the United States garnered thousands of documents from the Israeli government, including Rasmea's forty-five-year-old record from Israel.

The case of the Holy Land Five set the precedent for allowing secret evidence from an anonymous Israeli intelligence officer[15] and since then, in several similar cases, the US government has allowed the use of Israeli expert witnesses to testify against Arab immigrants. These cases require us to think beyond nation-states here—to think about transnational imperial spaces and political formations not bound by the territories of nation-states—without erasing the material differences in access to safety and resources between Palestinians living under colonization and those of us living and working in the United States. Indeed, the US empire, founded upon settler-colonialism and the racialization of its victims, finds its perfect imperial ally in Israeli settler-colonialism, and this alliance connects back within the United States. Rasmea Odeh's case exposes just how interwoven the "domestic" US efforts to target diasporic Palestinian activists are with the Israeli colonization of Palestinian land. Given this, the United States cannot be understood as a secondary culprit or as a mere supporter of Zionism abroad but, in fact, as a principal spatial-temporal location of Zionism and Israeli colonization. BDS movements need to continue to grapple with the meaning of "solidarity with Palestinians" in relation to struggles over territory, colonial expansion, land, and sovereignty and the simultaneous intertwined struggles of de-territorialized, displaced, and diasporic Palestinians. We need to continue to account for Israeli settler-colonialism and the implications of US imperialism transnationally. We need to imagine solidarity with Palestinian liberation and think beyond the territories of nation-states.

ACCOUNTABILITY TO THE PALESTINIAN DIASPORA: PRESSURING ISRAEL AND THE UNITED STATES

BDS and SJPs are currently among the most central movements organizing for Palestinian liberation in the United States. And, as with any movement, their achievements bring to light new challenges. Perhaps foremost among them is that BDS movements are less connected to local Palestinian and Arab diasporic communities than the Palestine solidarity movements of previous eras. Of course, Palestinian and/or Arab diasporic communities are not monolithic enclaves, separated entirely from universities or the professional world. But some immigrant and refugee communities are indeed isolated from the BDS movement, SJPs, and US social movements more broadly, and the increasingly neoliberal university. How can BDS activism increase its relations *away* from the neoliberal university or the insistent lure of careers in the nonprofit-industrial complex, toward students' own communities, households, neighborhoods? What might community accountability look like between the BDS movement and displaced Palestinians living among us in the United States?[16]

Enter Rasmea Odeh's case. Since her arrest in October 2013, the campaign calling upon the DOJ to drop the charges against her included mobilizations across the United States: Boston, Oakland, Seattle, New York, Chicago, Michigan, Salt Lake City, and Fort Lauderdale are but a few of the cities where protests supporting Rasmea took place. Groups such as the US Palestinian Community Network and the Committee to Stop FBI Harassment coordinated the national movement, whereas SJP chapters, along with various Palestinian and Arab American organizations, carried the weight locally. While organizing for Rasmea, some SJP students in Chicago built new relations with organizers who were directly connected with Palestinian diaspora communities and the immigrant and refugee women with whom Rasmea works. As SJP organizer Nashiha Alam told me: "When we went to Detroit for the trial, it made us [SJP organizers] aware that Rasmea could be anyone's mother, sister, or daughter. She is connected to us and she brings the Palestinian community to the solidarity work. I can't say we were connected before Rasmea's case."[17]

If the goal of BDS is to put pressure on Israel, Rasmea's case reminds us of the urgency to broaden the ways we might accomplish this. For instance, how might we put pressure on Israel as well as the US government for allowing Israeli colonization to continue, repressing Palestine solidarity activism, and disproportionately targeting Palestinian, Arab, and Muslim scholars and activists? We can look to the BDS activists who have worked to hold the United States and Israel accountable simultaneously by challenging legislation against BDS, the intimidation of scholars supporting BDS, and attempts to criminalize BDS activists. In April 2014, the Illinois Coalition to Protect Academic Freedom and Free Speech challenged legislation introduced by senator Ira Silverstein in the Illinois State Senate to undermine academic boycotts as a form of protest. BDS activists might also increase our attention to the efforts of pro-Israel groups, such as the AMCHA Initiative and the Louis D. Brandeis Center for Human Rights Under Law, to lobby Congress and the Department of Education to penalize Middle East studies centers for presenting perspectives that do not toe the pro-Israeli party line. Their lobbying campaign seeks to stop the Department of Education from funding these centers through Title VI of the Higher Education Act or to require oversight of the departments to ensure perspectives sympathetic to the Israeli state.

The aftermath of the historic American Studies Association (ASA) endorsement of the academic boycott of Israel in December 2013 included death threats against ASA board members and threats of a lawsuit, as well as the firing of professor Steven Salaita, a leading advocate of the ASA boycott movement. It also exposed just how significant to sustaining Israeli colonization is the repression of Palestinian, Arab, and Muslim communities *and* Palestine solidarity activism in the United States. Indeed, the institutionalized targeting of Palestinians and Palestine activism are not simple coincidences or impacts of Israeli colonization. They are part and parcel of it. While the horrific action against professor Steven Salaita inspired more discussion on these connections, less attention continues to be paid to the many Arab scholars and activists in the United States whose careers are destroyed, who have little to no source of subsistence, and who lack the support base necessary to demand justice or tell their stories. BDS movements might turn more and more attention to the attacks on student activists, whereby the tactics of spying, intimidation, and witch hunts are used to equate BDS activism with anti-Semitism, a potentiality for violence, and criminality.

Dima Khalidi, director of Palestine Solidarity Legal Support (PSLS), an advocacy group protecting the constitutional rights of Palestinian rights activists across the United States, says the repression of Palestine activism is on the rise. In 2013, PSLS provided legal advice for 150 cases in which government bodies and private groups attempted to silence or criminalize constitutionally protected activism for Palestine. In September of 2014 alone, they addressed 35. In October, 2014, Khalidi told me:

> What is as troubling as these more prominent cases, and remains largely unseen, are the smaller cases that are being confidentially reported to PSLS. We're hearing repeatedly that students are being told they can't use the name SJP because it's too controversial; that they can't use the word "apartheid" when talking about Israel; schools are changing their policies in direct response to SJP activities, making it harder to hold events by charging security fees or requiring a list of RSVPs; student groups have had difficulty reserving spaces to hold events and getting funding; there have been instances of universities reporting to and asking for approval from Jewish Israel advocacy groups on campus about SJP event plans before the university approves them. Student groups and their advisors are being called in to explain what their events are about, and told they have to be civil, or that they can't have controversial or biased events—as if speaking up for Palestinian rights is somehow biased.

Supporting the mechanisms, such as PSLS, that exist to protect BDS activists from criminalization and targeting is one way to strengthen BDS in the United

States. It is also crucial to support the Palestinian, Arab American, and Muslim community organizations that are targeted alongside the growth of BDS—whether or not they are activists or involved in Palestinian liberation movements—as well as those standing in the line of fire, such as the activists with the Arab Resource and Organizing Center (AROC), the Arab American Action Network (AAAN), SJP, and the US Palestinian Community Network (USPCN).

Finally, the US police state and its structures of criminalization and militarism allow the alliance between the United States and Israel to continue to thrive. The Snowden leaks have already confirmed that US and Israeli cooperation enable Israeli military operations, including the Gaza massacre of 2014, and that the United States shares raw intelligence data with Israel. It is also now clear that Israeli-trained police forces occupied Missouri after the killing of Michael Brown, subjecting Ferguson to "a military-style crackdown by a squadron of local police departments dressed like combat soldiers."[18]

Building stronger ties with the many organizations working against police brutality, surveillance, and the criminalization of political activists (from Rasmea and the Holy Land Five to Ferguson and the DREAMers to anti-drone activists) in the United States will strengthen BDS and transnational movements against Zionism, US imperialism, and the US militarized police state, helping illuminate the meanings of freedom that we are fighting for—from Gaza to Ferguson and beyond.

[Ed. Note: For updates on Rasmea Odeh's case and to lend support, visit www.justice4rasmea.org]

22

WHY CHANGE IS HAPPENING AND WHY BDS IS KEY*

DAVID PALUMBO-LIU

It might seem counterintuitive to make the argument that Israel should no longer count on US support for its policies as assuredly it has in the past. After all, hasn't the Senate just passed not one but now two resolutions by unanimous consent declaring its backing of Israel's deadly attacks on and invasion of Gaza?

In the first, Resolution 498, the Senate

> reaffirms its support for Israel's right to defend its citizens and ensure the survival of the State of Israel; condemns the unprovoked rocket fire at Israel; calls on Hamas to immediately cease all rocket and other attacks against Israel; and calls on Palestinian Authority President Mahmoud Abbas to dissolve the unity governing arrangement with Hamas and condemn the attacks on Israel.[1]

The second—Resolution 526, passed again by unanimous consent on July 29, 2014—restates the Senate's support for Israel and adds a criticism of a United Nations report on the violence. Senate Majority Leader Harry Reid, D-Nev., said that the UN report "was 'disgusting' and failed to recognize that Israel is defending itself from attacks started by Hamas, a terrorist organization."[2]

Yet even with these unambiguous resolutions emanating from the Senate, we find more and more evidence that support for Israel from the US public is slipping. A recent report in the *Washington Post* noted that "A new Pew Research Center poll is the second in the past week to show a huge generational split on the current conflict in Gaza. While all age groups north of 30 years old clearly blame Hamas more than Israel for the current violence, young adults buck the trend in a big way. Among 18 to 29-year olds, 29 percent blame Israel more for the current wave of violence, while 21 percent blame Hamas."[3]

---

* This essay is in large part drawn from a piece published on August 1, 2014, in *Salon*: http://www.salon.com/2014/08/01/millennials_are_so_over_israel_a_new_generation_is_outraged_over_gaza_demands_change

Clearly there are a number of possible explanations for this; here are three that come to mind. First, Americans are used to having Israel and the issue of the Palestinians framed by two heretofore closely intertwined narratives: that of the Holocaust and that of the founding of the state of Israel. The terrible reality of the Holocaust, and the moral and ethical imperative that the world never let such a catastrophe occur again, has obscured the narrative of the gradual dispossession of the Palestinian people that began around the time of the First World War and ended with the expulsion of some seven hundred thousand Palestinians during the *Nakba* of 1948. The illegal occupation of the West Bank and Gaza after the 1967 war and the continued colonial projects of the settlements are also framed within a narrative of Holocaust prevention, not of colonization and apartheid.

The recent attacks on Jews in Europe have indeed brought the sense that a second Holocaust is on the horizon. A July 29, 2014, article in the *Jerusalem Post* is titled, "We Are Looking at the Beginnings of a Holocaust":

> Calling the rise in anti-Semitic incidents accompanying Israel's invasion of Gaza an "SOS situation," Sloutsker warned that if left unchecked, such behavior could lead to another European genocide. "Never before since the Holocaust, have we seen such a situation as today," he said, referring to the continent-wide demonstrations by pro-Palestinian activists, a number of which have degenerated into violence and many of which have featured racist rhetoric. "We are potentially looking at the beginning of another Holocaust now.[4]

As much as the world should strongly and unambiguously condemn such acts of anti-Semitism, to focus on a "second Holocaust" is to ignore the actual reason why anti-Semitism has today reared its ugly head again. It is not because of some essential, primordial racism against Jews. It is because of the actions of the state of Israel in staging a brutal, prolonged attack on the Palestinian people that is replete with violations of human rights and international law. That Hamas has also committed attacks on civilians does not erase the fact that Israel's violence violates basic international humanitarian laws regarding proportionality.

International support for Israel is ebbing because the Holocaust narrative can no longer offer an omnipotent shield against a critique of the second narrative, regarding the founding of the state of Israel. Israel is in fact risking losing the narrative war altogether, as more and more of the global public is asking questions that probe into that history, prompted by the evidence of Israel's current efforts to continue and expand Israeli power and land, efforts that are now increasingly regarded not as survival tactics but as violent colonial ones. In sum, there is now a widening band of light in between the heretofore seamless merger of the Holocaust and founding narratives, resulting in a weakening of the former in its capacity to act as an alibi for the latter. Again, this is especially important with regard to the United States, which has been the world's most generous supporter of Israel. More and more younger Americans, growing up well past the postwar era, find the Holocaust narrative to be less than absolutely and unquestionably a good reason to support the horrible killings in Gaza. And as they learn more, their support will wane further.

Second, the massive attack on Gaza and its obscene civilian death toll is now delivered to a global audience via a variety of media forms that far exceed the mainstream media. Contemporary forms of social media deliver images from Gaza and opinions on the invasion as it takes place. Notwithstanding Netanyahu's ghoulish assertion that Hamas was opportunistically using "telegenic" corpses to garner sympathy and political points[5] (and one cannot help but retort, "Who created those corpses in the first place?"), we are in a new era wherein "history" is immediately disseminated and debated globally by local testimonials, amateur photojournalists and video reporters, as well as a large number of non-mainstream news agencies. Younger people are open to these modes of narrative, curious to know more, and morally puzzled and deeply concerned, and they in turn become conveyers of opinion and witnessing, as seen in the Tumblr site, The World Stands With Palestine,[6] which documents the demonstrations taking place around the world by means of uploaded photos from the participants themselves.

Therefore the Holocaust narrative is being displaced by the overwhelming number of mutually referencing and mutually reconfirming images, stories, testimonials, critiques, from individuals to UN agencies such as the United Nations Relief and Works Agency, which has openly condemned Israel's bombing of one of its schools.[7] The Senate's criticism of the UN's findings on Gaza thus is immediately made questionable by stories like these and many others that create a cognitive dissonance in our minds between the claim of "equal violations" and the actual, not fabricated, figures that give quantitative weight to the visual images of disproportionate Palestinian death and destruction.

Finally, support for Israel is going to wane because unlike before, those who wish to criticize Israel today have already well-established and well-recognized modes of protest available to them. Most important of course is the boycott, divestment, and sanctions (BDS) movement, which was established in 2005. This call for solidarity from more than 170 Palestinian civil society organizations has been answered by more and more organizations and individuals worldwide. And new groups are springing up all the time. Many exist to express outrage and concern, others offer material support for relief and aid to the Palestinians, and, most important, still others urge specific targeted actions such as divestment. The most prominent among these might well be the Avaaz petition urging divestment from companies complicit with the Israel state; as of this writing it has gathered 1.6 million signatures. Its statement reads in part:

> Our governments have failed—while they have talked peace and passed UN resolutions, they and our companies have continued to aid, trade and invest in the violence. The only way to stop this hellish cycle of Israel confiscating Palestinian lands, daily collective punishment of innocent Palestinian families, Hamas firing rockets, and Israel bombing Gaza is to make the economic cost of this conflict too high to bear.[8]

The fact that more and more younger Americans are increasingly skeptical of supporting Israel's military efforts is encouraging in the long run. But we should not lose sight of the tremendous humanitarian crisis we are witnessing today. Change might be coming, but for now action is needed, and BDS is galvanizing those who wish to support Palestinians. It has proven to be a capacious, well-established beacon for young people, especially those active in the divestment movement.

On college campuses across the country the divestment component of BDS is a hugely attractive and powerful mechanism. Students have had huge successes, building patiently year after year, undeterred by initial defeats. Each "generation" has passed on its lessons in activism to the next class. Today, for example, six of nine campuses in the University of California system have passed a divestment resolution in their student governments: UC Berkeley, UC Irvine, UC San Diego, UC Santa Cruz, UC Riverside, and UCLA. Resolutions have also been passed at Arizona State University, the University of Michigan–Dearborn, the University of Massachusetts–Boston, Oberlin College, and at Loyola University. And in the United Kingdom divestment resolutions have been passed at the University of Exeter; by the Black Students' Campaign of the UK National Union of Students; by the University of Dundee, Scotland; the National University of Ireland; and Galway and King's College, London. Turning to graduate students, just recently UAW 2865, the student-worker union of the University of California, voted overwhelmingly to divest.[9] What we see then is that young people are increasingly rejecting the silence that has been mandated on campus, and are debating the issue of Israel/Palestine in passionate and committed ways that are being translated into action in solidarity with the call from Palestinian civil society. This, plus the emergence of the Open Hillel movement and the growing popularity of Students for Justice in Palestine (SJP), gives every indication that we are witnessing a sea change in the world's attitudes toward Palestine, at long last.

23

STEVEN SALAITA'S FIRING SHOWS WHERE ZIONISM MEETS NEOLIBERALISM ON US UNIVERSITY CAMPUSES

TITHI BHATTACHARYA AND BILL V. MULLEN

In 2014, the University of Illinois at Urbana–Champaign (UIUC) administration did two things of note: rejected the American Studies Association (ASA) vote to boycott Israeli universities, and fired Arab American boycott supporter Steven Salaita.

In February 2014, we asked in an essay, "Why Is the American Elite Scared of BDS?"[1]

In the case of UIUC, the answer is simple and clear: deep political and financial ties between university leadership and Israel.

But it's not just about Israel. Our university administrators are deeply embedded in a second project: that of corporate neoliberalism. In fact, the Salaita case clearly discloses how Zionism and neoliberalism can converge in the boardrooms of university presidents and trustees, and the perilous consequences for students and faculty.

Let us start with UIUC chancellor Phyllis Wise. Since 2009, Wise has served on the governing board of Nike Corporation.[2] Wise earns approximately $230,000 in annual salary and benefits for her service to Nike, on top of the more than $500,000 in salary she earns as UIUC chancellor.[3]

As it is a global company, it is no surprise that Nike sells shoes in Israel. It has stores in Tel Aviv, Jerusalem, Netanya, and eight other cities. Its Israeli websites promote "Nike Running Israel" and other slick athletic campaigns. One of Nike's suppliers is Delta Galil Industries, a manufacturer of textiles for undergarments. Delta Galil operates in the Barkan Industrial Zone, an illegal Israeli settlement in the West

Bank.[4] Delta Galil also has two shops operating in West Bank settlements: Ma'ale Adumim and Pisgat Ze'ev.

Companies including Victoria's Secret have been placed on official boycott lists by groups such as Who Profits for their excessive business dealings with Delta Galil. Nike is also named by several boycott sites as a company that receives supplies from the West Bank manufacturer.[5]

Phyllis Wise has said she opposed the ASA boycott resolution on grounds of "academic freedom"[6] and that Steven Salaita's political criticisms of Israel were not relevant to his firing.[7] Such sanctimonious sentiments would ring truer if Dr. Wise were not on the board of a company that directly profits from the Israeli occupation of Palestine. It is perhaps unreasonable for us to expect Chancellor Wise to act in the interests of scholarship when she is serving Nike, an arrangement that at its most polite could be called a "conflict of interest."

Now let's look at UIUC Board of Trustees president Christopher Kennedy, another vocal critic of Steven Salaita. In 2009, Kennedy was appointed to the UIUC Board of Trustees by Illinois governor Pat Quinn. Kennedy is on the Board of Trustees of Ariel Mutual Funds, part of the Chicago-based Ariel Investments. Ariel Investments' fortunes began to soar in 2010 when it added new stocks, including DeVry Inc., and Pfizer Inc.[8]

Both Pfizer and DeVry operate extensively in Israel.[9,10]

Chris Kennedy also has some interesting friends and business associates. Kennedy is the chairman of Joseph Kennedy Enterprises, Inc., an expansive financial entity named after his grandfather. One of the directors of Kennedy Enterprises is Roy J. Zuckerberg. When not acting as a director of Christopher Kennedy's company, Zuckerberg also serves as chairman of the Board of Governors of Ben Gurion University in the Negev.[11] In 2009, Zuckerberg received an honorary doctorate degree from Ben Gurion for his contributions as a "generous philanthropist, an enthusiastic Zionist, a concerned and influential member of the U.S. Jewish community."[12] The Negev (or Naqab) is, of course, a desert and semi-arid region from which since 1948 Israel has historically attempted to cleanse thousands of Palestinian Bedouins.[13] Israel has in fact long eyed the Negev for expanded Israeli settlements.

Roy Zuckerberg also helps us understand the close relationship between UIUC Board of Trustees members such as Kennedy and the governor of Illinois, Pat Quinn. It should be remembered that Governor Quinn is an ex-officio member of the UIUC Board of Trustees. Zuckerberg serves as honorary chairman of the Zuckerberg Institute for Water Research, which conducts research in water studies designed to improve the life of inhabitants of "drylands" like the Negev.[14]

In July 2011, Governor Pat Quinn went to Israel and signed two agreements[15]:

1. A "Sister Lakes" agreement to improve maintenance of water conditions in Lake Michigan and Israel's Lake Kinneret, which is a conduit for water to the Negev;

2. An agreement for student and faculty exchange between Zuckerberg's Ben Gurion University and the University of Illinois–Chicago.

It should also be noted that Governor Quinn's trip to Israel in 2011 was supported by the Jewish United Fund. On its own website, the National Jewish Democratic Council notes that Quinn is "an ardent supporter of Israel and has used his elected positions in Illinois to strengthen relations between Illinois and Israel."[16] The same website notes that prior to becoming governor, Quinn worked to make sure Illinois state bonds were invested in Israel. This is the same Governor Quinn who has appointed eight of the nine current members of the Board of Trustees of UIUC—people with the final say over Steven Salaita's job.

Should we be surprised then that the University of Illinois, whose public face is represented by figures with such a network of ties to Israel, virulently opposed the ASA boycott of Israeli universities? Or that figures such as Wise, Kennedy, and Quinn would approve the firing of Steven Salaita, a distinguished scholar, author of six books, and vocal critic of the Israeli occupation?

The answer is no. Indeed, in recent years, we have almost been forced to accept that the upper administration in US universities has very little to do with one aspect of the university—scholarship. But what should be of concern to people everywhere who care about such matters is that these individuals have enormous power over how scholarship is conducted, or who has the right to teach and learn.

Steven Salaita's disgraceful treatment by UIUC administrators is not just about their support for Israel. It is also a direct outcome of the increasing corporatization of higher education. When university policymakers consort with corporate profiteers, the direction of investments and profits will naturally shape university policy. In this case, the University of Illinois shows us how the neoliberal university allies itself with Zionism as a settler-colonial project. The illegal occupation of Palestine has helped savvy university presidents and trustees earn handsome dividends while using their positions to reject criticisms of Israel at the universities they head.

The solution is to "de-Zionize" our campuses. We need a movement to force our universities to divest from Israel. And we need a movement to force accountability and faculty governance from our top administrators. This is why, at this juncture in history, the boycott, divestment, sanctions (BDS) movement against Israel and faculty unionization should go hand in hand.

Imagine if there were already in place at UIUC a militant and unionized faculty. Better still, imagine if that faculty union had already voted for university divestment from Israel. Would Phyllis Wise, faced with this union, have been able to make her "executive decision" to fire Steven Salaita?

The Salaita case shows us the necessary next step in our struggle for him and for all of us. The Association of American University Professors (AAUP) has made a strong statement in defense of Steven Salaita.[17] The next step ought to be for AAUP and other teachers' unions in this country to follow in the footsteps of their sisters and brothers in Europe where Europe's largest teachers' union—Britain's National Union of Teachers (NUT)—voted for BDS.[18]

BDS activists have taught us not to cross the picket line against apartheid. It is time that similar picket lines appear against campus elites who claim to speak in our name.

24

RECOGNIZING PALESTINE, BDS, AND THE SURVIVAL OF ISRAEL

JOSEPH MASSAD

What is happening in European parliaments? In the span of six weeks at the end of 2014, the UK House of Commons and the Spanish, French, Portuguese, and Irish parliaments have all recognized Israel's eternal "right" to be a racist state via a much-touted recognition of an alleged Palestinian state within the West Bank and Gaza Strip, the areas of Palestine Israel occupied in 1967.

These moves followed the lead of Sweden's new center-left government, which decided shortly after coming to power to "recognize the State of Palestine" as part of the "two-state solution."[1] As there is no Palestinian state to recognize within the 1967 or any other borders, these political moves are engineered to undo the death of the two-state solution, the illusion of which had guaranteed Israel's survival as a Jewish racist state for decades. These parliamentary resolutions in fact aim to impose a de facto arrangement that prevents Israel's collapse and also prevents its replacement with a state that grants equal rights to all its citizens and is not based on colonial and racial privileges.

Unlike Israeli prime minister Benjamin Netanyahu,[2] who believes he can force the world to recognize, de jure, a greater racist Israel that annexes the territories occupied in 1967, the European parliaments are insisting that they will only guarantee Israel's survival as a racist state within Israel's 1948 borders and on whatever extra lands within the 1967 territories the Palestinian Authority (PA)—collaborating with Israel—agrees to concede in the form of "land swaps."

Denmark's parliament and the European Parliament itself are the latest bodies set to consider votes guaranteeing Israel's survival in its present form within the 1948 boundaries only. Even neutral Switzerland agreed, upon a request from the PA, to host a meeting of signatories of the Fourth Geneva Convention[4] to discuss the 1967 Israeli occupation only.[5] As expected, in addition to the Jewish settler-colony, the world's major settler-colonies—the United States, Canada, and Australia—are opposed to the meeting and will not attend.

These moves are unfolding as international support for the Palestinian-initiated boycott, divestment, and sanctions (BDS) movement[6] has begun an accelerated move into the mainstream in the United States and Western Europe. Academic associations calling for support for BDS include the Association for Asian American Studies (AAAS),[7] the Native American and Indigenous Studies Association (NAISA),[8] the American Studies Association (ASA),[9] and the American Anthropological Association (AAA),[10] which voted to defeat an anti-BDS resolution.[11]

An exception is MESA, the Middle East Studies Association,[12] whose members most recently voted to grant themselves the right to debate BDS, and in the process unwittingly granted the Zionists one full year to lobby and prepare to defeat a BDS resolution on which MESA members may be asked to vote next year.[13]

Even the Columbia University Center for Palestine Studies has reversed course. In April 2011, they insistently refused to host and sponsor a talk and book signing by Omar Barghouti,[14] a cofounder of the Palestinian Campaign for the Academic and Cultural Boycott of Israel (PACBI).[15] Instead, they hosted a speaker in April 2013 (in a closed, invitation-only event), who attacked Barghouti in an attempt to delegitimize PACBI. But in December 2014, they invited Barghouti to deliver a lecture.[16]

What do all these moves mean?

ISRAEL'S LIBERAL RACISTS EXPOSED

The context of these steps has to do with the recent conduct of the Netanyahu government, whose impatience is exposing Israel's liberal racist politicians—those who prefer a more patient approach to achieving the very same racist political goals as their conservative counterparts—to embarrassment. The situation has become so untenable that ardent American liberal Zionists, led by none other than Michael Walzer, emeritus professor at the Institute for Advanced Study in Princeton, have felt compelled to act. Walzer, notorious for justifying all of Israel's conquests as "just wars," and a group of like-minded figures calling themselves "Scholars for Israel and Palestine" recently called on the US government to impose a travel ban on right-wing Israeli politicians who support annexation of what remains of the West Bank.[17]

Whereas successive Israeli governments have shown an unyielding determination to strengthen Israel's right to be a racist state over all of historic Palestine, they have done so through the ruse of the "peace process," which they were committed to maintaining for decades to come without any resolution. This strategy has worked very well for the last two decades with hardly a peep from the PA, which owes its very existence to this unending "process." More recently, the political leadership of Hamas[18]—especially the branch in Qatar, where the group's leader, Khaled Meshal,[19] is based—has also been looking for the best way to join this project. But as the ongoing Netanyahu policies of visiting horrors on the Palestinian people persist across all of the territories Israel controls—policies that have exposed the "peace process" for the sham it always was, as well as Israel's claim to being "democratic" as a most fraudulent one—the international consensus that Israeli liberals have built over the decades to shield Israel's ugly reality from the world has been weakened, if not threatened with collapse altogether.

Israeli liberals realize that what Netanyahu is doing is threatening their entire project and the very survival of Israel as a racist Jewish state. It is in this context that European parliaments are rushing to rescue Israel's liberals by guaranteeing for them Israel's survival in its racist form through recognizing a nonexistent Palestinian state "within the 1967 borders."

It is also in this context that European governments in the last year or so have begun to speak of BDS as a possible weapon they could use to threaten the Netanyahu government if it continues in its refusal to "negotiate" with the Palestinians (the Europeans' use of the threat of BDS is limited to a threat of boycotting only the products of Israeli colonial settlements in the occupied territories); that is, to maintain the illusion of an ongoing "peace process." Herein lies the dilemma for those who support BDS.

BDS: A MEANS OR AN END IN ITSELF?

The Ramallah-based PACBI has always been clear that BDS is an instrument,[20] a means to be used to achieve strategic goals—namely, an end to Israel's occupation of Palestinian lands during and since 1967, an end to Israeli institutionalized racism inside the 1948 boundaries of Israel, and the right of return of the Palestinian refugees to their lands and homes.[21] In recent years, however, BDS has been transformed from a means to an end unto itself. Many of those in solidarity with the Palestinians have begun to articulate their positions as ones that support BDS as a goal rather than as a means.

The recent votes by academic organizations are a case in point. While three academic organizations that voted for BDS have declared their support for the end of the 1967 occupation, only two, NAISA and AAAS, explicitly opposed the racist policies of the state of Israel against its own Palestinian citizens. Only NAISA's resolution questioned Israeli racist laws and structures. The ASA, by contrast, cited only the occupation of the 1967 territories, while the Modern Language Association (MLA) merely censured Israel for denying Palestinian academics and students their academic freedom without condemning the occupation or Israeli state racism. MESA's resolution did not even mention any of the goals of BDS at all.

While these resolutions are a step in the right direction, and in many cases are the result of long and fierce battles waged by members deeply committed to all Palestinian rights, they mostly fail to articulate positions that accord with all the explicit goals of BDS. Indeed, not one of these organizations mentioned the third goal of BDS, namely, the right of the Palestinian refugees to return, which Israel continues to deny in defiance of UN resolutions and international law in order to safeguard a Jewish majority in the country.

As European politicians have recognized, BDS can now be used as a means to achieve ends decided by those who adopt it. Palestinians' monopoly on decision-making through PACBI and the Boycott National Committee (BNC)[22] and on determining the goals of BDS is not guaranteed. Different parties, declaring solidarity with the Palestinians, can and do dismiss PACBI altogether as only one of many international organizations that support BDS, arguing that each supporter of BDS can determine on its own whatever goals it deems fit. In short, the expanded support of BDS in the United States and Europe is not necessarily an expanded support for the goals of ending Israeli racism, Israel's occupation, and the Palestinian refugees' exile, rather simply support for the use of BDS as a means to achieve whatever the party using it determines as the sought-after goal.

As I have written[23] and explained since the signing of the 1993 Oslo accords,[24] all the "solutions" offered by Western and Arab governments and Israeli and PA liberals to end the so-called "Palestinian–Israeli conflict" are premised on guaranteeing Israel's survival as a racist Jewish state unscathed. All "solutions" that do not offer such a guarantee are dismissed a priori as impractical, unpragmatic, and even anti-Semitic. The recent attempts to co-opt BDS for that very same goal are in line with this commitment.

This explains the sudden downgrading of the threat of BDS from something that is untouchable by European and American officials and liberal academics and activists—who understood its ultimate goal as one that not only refuses to guarantee the survival of Israel as a racist state, but also aims specifically to dismantle all its racist structures—to something increasingly safe to adopt by most of them, as it now can be used to secure Israel's survival.

Palestinians and their supporters must be vigilant about this co-optation of BDS and must recognize that with the achievement of mainstreaming also come serious risks. Unless they reaffirm that support for BDS is support for the explicit goals that PACBI had initially set, this recent and apparent "transformation" in attitudes, which, in fact, is no transformation at all, will usher in a slippery slope—the end goal of which is, alas, too familiar for Palestinians to revisit yet again.

Due to the continued absence of an independent, representative, and unified Palestinian liberation movement capable of articulating a coherent strategy and leading the struggle for liberation, BDS will continue, contrary to PACBI's stated goals, to be utilized at best as a "threat" to Israel to end its 1967 occupation. This is nothing short of a smokescreen to perpetuate Israel's other forms of colonial control over historic Palestine and the Palestinians and to preserve its institutionalized and legal racism.

Rather than call on the international community to adopt BDS without an explicit commitment to its goals, Palestinians must insist that those in solidarity with them adopt BDS as a *strategy* and not as a *goal,* in order to bring about an end to Israel's racism and colonialism in all its forms, inside and outside the 1948 boundaries.

Otherwise, BDS can and will be used to strengthen the Jewish settler-colony and the Israeli liberal project that backs it.

Appendix

Materials in Support of Academic Boycott

Primary Source Materials
BDS Call for Academic Boycott
http://www.bdsmovement.net/activecamps/academic-boycott

Labor for Palestine
http://laborforpalestine.net/

Social Text: The US Academic and Cultural Boycott of Israel: Unsettling Exceptionalisms
http://www.usacbi.org/2012/07/social-text-the-us-academic-and-cultural-boycott
-of-israel-unsettling-exceptionalisms/

Targeting Israeli Apartheid: A Boycott, Divestment, and Sanctions Handbook
http://corporateoccupation.files.wordpress.com/2012/01/targeting-israeli-apart-
heid-jan-2012.pdf

USACBI Reports and Resources
http://www.usacbi.org/reports-and-resources/

Supporting Materials for Boycott Resolutions:
American Association of University Professors, *Journal of Academic Freedom* 4 (2013).
http://www.aaup.org/reports-publications/journal-academic-freedom/volume-4

Tithi Bhattacharya, "Israel's Fear of Boycott Rooted in Tactics of Historic Victories Against Colonialism," *Electronic Intifada*, December 2, 2014.
http://laborforpalestine.net/2014/12/02/israels-fear-of-boycott-rooted-in-tactics
-historic-victories-against-colonialism-electronic-intifada/

Institute for Middle East Understanding, "Israeli Violations of Palestinian Academic Freedom," February 6, 2014.
http://imeu.org/article/israeli-violations-of-palestinian-academic-freedom-access-to-education

Salim Vally, "The Campaign to Isolate Apartheid Israel: Lessons From South Africa," *Links: International Journal of Socialist Renewal* (April 2009).
http://links.org.au/node/979

SUPPORTING JOURNALS AND PUBLICATIONS:
Al-Shabaka, the Palestinian Policy Network
http://al-shabaka.org/

Electronic Intifada
http://electronicintifada.net/

Institute for Middle East Understanding
http://imeu.org/

Jadaliyya
http://www.jadaliyya.com/

Middle East Monitor
https://www.middleeastmonitor.com/

Middle East Research and Information Project (MERIP)
http://www.merip.org/

MIFTAH (The Palestinian Initiative for the Promotion of Global Dialogue and Democracy)
http://www.miftah.org/

Mondoweiss: The War of Ideas in the Middle East
http://mondoweiss.net/

Palestine Chronicle
http://www.palestinechronicle.com/

PROFESSIONAL ACADEMIC ORGANIZATIONS' BOYCOTT RESOLUTIONS:

ASA Council Resolution on Boycott of Israeli Academic Institutions
http://www.theasa.net/american_studies_association_resolution_on_academic_
boycott_of_israel

ASA Statement on Academic Boycott
http://www.theasa.net/what_does_the_academic_boycott_mean_for_the_asa/

Native American and Indigenous Studies Association
Declaration of Support for the Academic Boycott of Israeli Universities
http://www.naisa.org/declaration-of-support-for-the-boycott-of-israeli-academ-
ic-institutions.html

National Union of Teachers (UK) Resolution to Boycott Israeli Universities
http://www.bdsmovement.net/2014/europes-largest-teachers-union-endorses-isra-
el-boycott-call-12039

Peace and Justice Studies Association Boycott Resolution
http://www.peacejusticestudies.org/blog/pjsa/2014/11/peace-justice-studies-asso-
ciation-votes-endorse-boycott-divestment-sanctions-bds#resolution

RASMEA ODEH CASE:

Justice for Rasmea
www.justice4rasmea.org

STEVEN SALAITA CASE:

AAUP Statement on Case of Steven Salaita
http://www.aaup.org/media-release/statement-case-steven-salaita

Center for Constitutional Rights Statements and Documents
http://www.ccrjustice.org/ourcases/current-cases/professor-salaita-termina-
tion-speech-critical-israel

Reactions in the Academic World
http://mondoweiss.net/2014/08/top-legal-scholars-decry-chilling-effect-of-dehir-
ing-scholar-salaita.html

ORGANIZATIONS:

British Committee for the Universities of Palestine
http://www.bricup.org.uk/

International Solidarity Movement
http://palsolidarity.org/

Jewish Voice for Peace
http://jewishvoiceforpeace.org/

The Palestine Freedom Project
http://palestinefreedom.org/

Palestinian Campaign for the Academic and Cultural Boycott of Israel (PACBI)
http://www.pacbi.org/

Students for Justice in Palestine
http://sjpnational.org/

US Campaign for the Academic and Cultural Boycott of Israel (USACBI)
http://www.usacbi.org/

US Campaign to End the Israeli Occupation
http://www.endtheoccupation.org/

About the Contributors

Rabab Abdulhadi is an associate professor of ethnic studies/race and resistance studies and the Senior Scholar of the Arab and Muslim Ethnicities and Diasporas Initiative at the College of Ethnic Studies, San Francisco State University. Before joining SFSU, she served as the first director of the Center for Arab American Studies at the University of Michigan–Dearborn. She is the co-editor of *Arab and Arab American Feminisms: Gender, Violence and Belonging* (Syracuse University Press, 2011). Her work has appeared in *Gender and Society, Radical History Review, Peace Review, Journal of Women's History, Taiba: Women and Cultural Discourses, Cuadernos Metodologicos: Estudio de Casos, This Bridge We Call Home, New World Coming: The 1960s and the Shaping of Global Consciousness, Local Actions: Cultural Activism, Power and Public Life in America*, the *Guardian, Al-Fujr, Womanews, Palestine Focus, Voice of Palestinian Women*, and several Arabic-language publications, such as *Falasteen Al-Thahwra, Al-Hadaf*, and *Al-Hurriyah*.

Ali Abunimah is the author of *The Battle for Justice in Palestine* and *One Country: A Bold Proposal to End the Israeli Palestinian Impasse*, and cofounder and director of the widely acclaimed publication the *Electronic Intifada*. Based in the United States, he has written hundreds of articles and been an active part of the movement for justice in Palestine for twenty years. He is the recipient of a 2013 Lannan Cultural Freedom Fellowship.

Kristian Davis Bailey is a freelance journalist. He graduated from Stanford University in 2014 with a degree in Comparative Studies in Race and Ethnicity. As a student and recent graduate, Kristian participated in Stanford Students for Justice in Palestine, the steering committee of National Students for Justice in Palestine, and the Stanford Out of Occupied Palestine divestment campaign. In November 2014, he organized the first nationwide Palestinian Right to Education US Tour, in conjunction with the Right to Education Campaign at Birzeit University. His recent writing has focused on Black–Palestinian solidarity, with special attention to the Ferguson–Palestine connection and building relationships between youth organizers working on Black, brown, and Palestinian liberation.

Omar Barghouti is an independent Palestinian commentator and human rights activist. He is a founding member of the Palestinian Campaign for the Academic and Cultural Boycott of Israel (PACBI) and the Palestinian civil society boycott, divestment, and sanctions (BDS) campaign against Israel. He is the author of *BDS: The Global Struggle for Palestinian Rights* (Haymarket Books, 2011).

Tithi Bhattacharya is a professor of South Asian history at Purdue University, a longtime activist for Palestinian justice, and on the editorial board of the *International Socialist Review*.

Ashley Dawson is professor of English at the City University of New York's Graduate Center and at the College of Staten Island/CUNY. He is the author of *Capitalism and Extinction* (PM Press, forthcoming), *The Routledge Concise History of Twentieth-Century British Literature* (Routledge, 2013), and *Mongrel Nation: Diasporic Culture and the Making of Postcolonial Britain* (University of Michigan Press, 2007), and co-editor of three essay collections: *Democracy, the State, and the Struggle for Global Justice* (Routledge, 2009); *Dangerous Professors: Academic Freedom and the National Security Campus* (University of Michigan Press, 2009); and *Exceptional State: Contemporary U.S. Culture and the New Imperialism* (Duke University Press, 2007). He is former editor of *Social Text Online* and of the AAUP's *Journal of Academic Freedom*.

Vicente "Vince" Diaz is associate professor in American Indian studies at the University of Minnesota. He was associate professor of AI studies and anthropology at the University of Illinois at Urbana-Champaign from 2012 to 2015. Diaz teaches and researches in the area of critical indigenous theory, with specialties in anticolonial history and postcolonial historiography and native cultural studies in the Pacific Islands region. He is the author of *Repositioning the Missionary: Rewriting the Histories of Colonialism, Native Catholicism, and Indigeneity in Guam,* (University of Hawai'i Press, 2010) and many articles and essays that focus on indigenous critique in comparative and transnational veins. Diaz joined the faculty in American Indian studies at UIUC in 2012 after stints in Asian/Pacific Islander American Studies at the University of Michigan (2001–2012) and Pacific History and Micronesian Studies at the University of Guam (1991–2001).

Haidar Eid is associate professor of postcolonial and postmodern literature at Gaza's Al-Aqsa University. He has written widely on the Arab–Israeli conflict, including articles published at *Znet, Electronic Intifada, Palestine Chronicle,* and *Open Democracy.* He has published papers on cultural studies and literature in a number of journals, including *Nebula, Journal of American Studies* in Turkey, *Cultural Logic,* and the *Journal of Comparative Literature.*

Noura Erakat is a human rights attorney and activist. She is an assistant professor at George Mason University and a cofounder/editor of *Jadaliyya* e-zine. Most recently, she was a Freedman Teaching Fellow at Temple Law School and has taught international human rights law and the Middle East at Georgetown University since 2009. She served as legal counsel for a Congressional Subcommittee in the House of Representatives, chaired by congressman Dennis J. Kucinich. Noura's scholarly interests include humanitarian law, human rights law, refugee law, and national security law. Her scholarly publications include: "U.S. vs. ICRC-Customary International Humanitarian Law and Universal Jurisdiction" in the *Denver Journal of International Law & Policy,* "New Imminence in the Time of Obama: The Impact of Targeted Killings on the Law of Self-Defense" in the *Arizona Law Review,* and "Overlapping Refugee Legal Regimes: Closing the Protection Gap During Secondary Forced Displacement," in the *Oxford Journal of International Refugee Law.* Noura's media appearances include MSNBC, Fox News, PBS *NewsHour,* BBC World Service, NPR, *Democracy Now!,* and Al Jazeera. She has published in the *Nation,* the *New York Times,* the *Los Angeles Review of Books, Huffington Post, IntlLawGrrls, The Hill,* and *Foreign Policy,* among others. Noura is the coeditor of *Aborted State? The UN Initiative and New Palestinian Junctures,* an anthology related to the 2011 and 2012 Palestine bids for statehood at the UN.

Dianne Feeley and **David Finkel** are editors of *Against the Current,* a bimonthly socialist journal, where the interview with Rabab Abdulhadi first appeared. David Finkel is active in Palestine solidarity work and Dianne Feeley is active in Detroit Eviction Defense.

Sami Hermez received his PhD in anthropology from Princeton University. He has held positions as Visiting Professor in Contemporary International Issues at the University of Pittsburgh; Visiting Professor at Mount Holyoke College; postdoctoral fellow at the Centre for Lebanese Studies, University of Oxford; and Visiting Research Fellow at the Zentrum Moderner Orient and the Collaborative Research Center, Humboldt University, both in Berlin. He has also taught at the American University of Beirut.

Rima Najjar Kapitan is president of Kapitan Law Office. Her practice consists primarily of litigation on behalf of employees and advising of businesses on employment law matters. In recent years she has increasingly focused on academic cases, representing employees in appeals of tenure denials and employment litigation in free speech and discrimination cases. She has spoken on the topic of academic freedom at conferences of the American Association of University Professors, the Illinois AAUP, and California State University–Fresno. She also previously worked as managing partner of a seven-attorney law firm. Kapitan is a graduate of DePaul University College of Law and Indiana University's Individualized Major Program. She was admitted to practice by the State of Illinois Supreme Court in 2005, and is a member of the United States Court of Appeals for the Seventh Circuit and the United States District Court for the Northern, Central, and Southern Districts of Illinois.

David Lloyd, Distinguished Professor of English at the University of California–Riverside, has worked primarily on Irish culture and on postcolonial and cultural theory. He is the author of *Nationalism and Minor Literature* (University of California Press, 1987), *Anomalous States* (Duke University Press, 1993), and *Ireland After History* (1999); his most recent books in that field are *Irish Times: Temporalities of Irish Modernity* (Field Day Files, 2008) and *Irish Culture and Colonial Modernity: The Transformation of Oral Space* (Cambridge University Press, 2011). Having recently completed a book on Samuel Beckett and the visual arts, to be published by Field Day in Dublin, he is now turning back to focusing on poetry and beginning a book on poetry and violence that will include essays on W.B. Yeats, César Vallejo, Aimé Césaire, and Paul Celan. He has copublished several other books, including *The Nature and Context of Minority Discourse* (Oxford University Press, 1991), with Abdul JanMohamed; *Culture and the State*, coauthored with Paul Thomas (Routledge, 1997); *The Politics of Culture in the Shadow of Capital* (Duke University Press, 1997), with Lisa Lowe; and *The Black and Green Atlantic: Cross-Currents of the African and Irish Diasporas* (Palgrave MacMillan, 2009), edited with Peter D. O'Neill. He is also a poet and playwright: his *Arc & Sill: Poems 1979–2009* was published by Shearsman Books in the UK and New Writers' Press, Dublin, 2012, and his play, *The Press*, has had staged readings in Dublin, Los Angeles, Liverpool, and Manila, and premiered at Liverpool Hope University in 2010.

Sunaina Maira is professor of Asian American Studies at the University of California, Davis. She is the author of *Desis in the House: Indian American Youth Culture in New York City* (Temple University Press, 2002) and *Missing: Youth, Citizenship,* *and Empire After 9/11* (Duke University Press, 2009). She coedited *Contours of the Heart: South Asians Map North America* (Asian American Writers Workshop, 1998), which won the American Book Award in 1997, and *Youthscapes: The Popular, the National, and the Global* (University of Pennsylvania Press, 2004). Maira's recent publications include a a monograph based on ethnographic research, *Jil [Generation] Oslo: Palestinian Hip Hop, Youth Culture, and the Youth Movement* (Tadween, 2013), and a volume coedited with Piya Chatterjee, *The Imperial University: Academic Repression and Scholarly Dissent* (University of Minnesota Press, 2014). Her new book project is a study of South Asian, Arab, and Afghan American youth and political movements focused on civil and human rights and issues of sovereignty and surveillance in the War on Terror.

Joseph Massad teaches and writes about modern Arab politics and intellectual history. He has a particular interest in theories of identity and culture, including theories of nationalism, sexuality, race, and religion. He received his PhD from Columbia University in 1998. He is the author of *Desiring Arabs* (2007), which was awarded the Lionel Trilling Book Award; *The Persistence of the Palestinian Question: Essays on Zionism and the Palestinian Question* (2006); and *Colonial Effects: The Making of National Identity in Jordan* (2001). His book *Daymumat al-Mas'alah al-Filastiniyyah* was published by Dar Al-Adab in 2009, and *La persistance de la question palestinienne* was published by La Fabrique in 2009. The Arabic translation of *Desiring Arabs* was published in 2013 by Dar Al-Shuruq Press in Cairo under the title *Ishtiha' Al-'Arab.* His latest book is *Islam in Liberalism* (University of Chicago Press, 2015), and his latest articles are "Orientalism as Occidentalism," *History of the Present* (Spring 2015), "Love, Fear, and the Arab Spring," *Public Culture* (Winter 2014); "Olvidar el Semitismo," *Foro Internacional*, Mexico (July–September 2014); and "Forget Semitism!," in Elisabeth Weber, editor, *Living Together. Jacques Derrida's Communities of Peace and Violence*, (Fordham University Press, 2013).

Rima Najjar Merriman is a professor of English literature at Al-Quds University in the occupied West Bank. She is one of the contributing writers for *Al Jazeera English— Global News in a Changing World*, and a BDS activist on social media (www.facebook. com/rima.najjar.merriman), as described in her essay "Life in Abu Dis Continues Quietly" in *Life in Occupied Palestine: A Special Biography Issue* (Spring 2014).

Nerdeen Mohsen serves on the Steering Committee of the National Students for Justice in Palestine (SJP) and is a founding member of the New York City SJP. Past president of the College of Staten Island chapter, she is currently vice president of both the Hunter College and CSI chapters of SJP.

Bill V. Mullen is Professor of American Studies at Purdue University. He is a member of the Organizing Collective for USACBI (United States Campaign for the Academic and Cultural Boycott of Israel) and faculty advisor for Purdue Students for Justice in Palestine. In 2012 he was a member of a USACBI delegation to Palestine. He is the author of *Un-American: W. E. B. Du Bois and the Century of World Revolution* (Temple University Press, 2015), *Afro-Orientalism* (University of Minnesota Press, 2004), and *Popular Fronts: Chicago and African American Cultural Politics, 1935–1946* (University of Illinois Press, 1999). His writing on Palestine and academic boycott has appeared in *Electronic Intifada, Mondoweiss, Social Text*, and *International Socialist Review*. He lives in West Lafayette, Indiana.

Nadine Naber is a scholar-activist and an associate professor in the Department of Gender and Women's Studies and Asian American Studies at the University of Illinois–Chicago. She is author of *Arab America: Gender, Cultural Politics, and Activism* (NYU Press, 2012). She is coeditor of *Race and Arab Americans* (Syracuse University Press, 2008) and *Arab and Arab American Feminisms* (Syracuse University Press, 2010). Nadine is a board member of the Arab American Studies Association and the American Studies Association; an editorial board member of the Middle East Research and Information Project (MERIP); an advisory board member for the book series Expanding Frontiers: Interdisciplinary Approaches to Studies of Women, Gender (University of Nebraska Press) and an advisory board member for the book series Decolonizing Feminisms: Antiracist and Transnational Praxis (University of Washington Press). Nadine works closely with the Institute of Women's Studies at Birzeit University in Palestine as an International Fellow with the Open Society Foundation's Academic Fellowship Program (2013–2015). Nadine works with women of color, racial justice, and Palestine solidarity movements including the US Academic and Cultural Boycott of Israel (USACBI) and INCITE! Women, Gender Non-Conforming and Trans People of Color against Violence.

David Palumbo-Liu is the Louise Hewlett Nixon Professor at Stanford University and professor of Comparative Literature. His most recent books are *The Deliverance of Others: Reading Literature in a Global Age* and a coedited volume, *Immanuel Wallerstein and the Problem of the World: System, Scale, Culture*. He writes for the *Nation, Salon, Huffington Post, Truthout,* and *Al Jazeera*. He is also a contributing editor for the *Los Angeles Review of Books*.

Ilan Pappé obtained his BA degree from the Hebrew University in Jerusalem in 1979 and the D Phil from the University of Oxford in 1984. He founded and directed the Academic Institute for Peace in Givat Haviva, Israel, between 1992 and 2000 and was the chair of the Emil Tuma Institute for Palestine Studies in Haifa between 2000 and 2006. Professor Pappé was a senior lecturer in the Department of Middle Eastern History and the Department of Political Science at Haifa University, Israel, between 1984 and 2006. He was appointed as chair of the Department of History of the Cornwall Campus from 2007 to 2009 and became a fellow of the Institute of Arab and Islamic Studies (IAIS) in 2010. His research focuses on the modern Middle East and, in particular, on the history of Israel and Palestine. He has also written on multiculturalism, critical discourse analysis, and on power and knowledge in general. He is the author of *The Ethnic Cleansing of Palestine* (One World Publications, 2007) and other books.

Andrew Ross is a social activist and professor of social and cultural analysis at NYU. A contributor to the *Guardian*, the *New York Times*, the *Nation*, and *Al Jazeera*, he is the author of many books, including *Creditocracy and the Case for Debt Refusal* (OR Books, 2014), *Bird On Fire: Lessons from the World's Least Sustainable City* (Oxford University Press, 2013), *Nice Work if You Can Get It: Life and Labor in Precarious Times* (NYU Press, 2009), *Fast Boat to China—Lessons from Shanghai* (Vintage, 2007), *No-Collar: The Humane Workplace and its Hidden Costs* (Basic Books, 2002), and *The Celebration Chronicles: Life, Liberty, and the Pursuit of Property Value in Disney's New Town* (Ballantine Books, 2011). His most recent book is *The Gulf: High Culture/Hard Labor*, available from OR Books.

Steven Salaita currently serves as the Edward Said Chair of American Studies at the American University of Beirut. His latest book is *Uncivil Rites: Palestine and the Limits of Academic Freedom.*

Malini Johar Schueller is professor of English at the University of Florida, where she teaches courses on US empire and race studies, postcolonial theory, and Asian American studies. She is the author of *The Politics of Voice: Liberalism and Social Criticism from Franklin to Kingston* (SUNY Press, 1992), *U.S. Orientalisms: Race, Nation, and Gender in Literature, 1790–1890* (University of Michigan Press, 1998), and *Locating Race: Global Sites of Post-Colonial Citizenship* (SUNY Press,2009). She has coedited three essay collections, *Messy Beginnings: Postcoloniality and Early American Studies* (with Edward Watts, Rutgers University Press, 2003), *Exceptional*

State: Contemporary U.S. Culture and the New Imperialism (with Ashley Dawson, Duke University Press, 2007), and *Dangerous Professors: Academic Freedom and the National Security Campus* (with Ashley Dawson, University of Michigan Press, 2009). She has recently made a documentary, *In His Own Home*, about racist police militarization.

Sarah Schulman is the author of seventeen books, most recently *Israel/Palestine and the Queer International* (Duke University Press, 2012) and the forthcoming *Conflict Is Not Abuse: Overstating Harm, Community Responsibility and the Duty of Repair*. She is Distinguished Professor of the Humanities at the City University of New York, College of Staten Island.

Joan W. Scott received her PhD in history from the University of Wisconsin, Madison. She has taught at the University of Illinois–Chicago; Northwestern University; the University of North Carolina, Chapel Hill; and Brown University, where she was the founding director of the Pembroke Center for Teaching and Research on Women. She was professor in the School of Social Science at the Institute for Advanced Study from 1985 to 2014. She is now Professor Emerita there. She is the author of *Only Paradoxes to Offer: French Feminists and the Rights of Man* (Harvard University Press, 1996); *Parité: Sexual Equality and the Crisis of French Universalism* (University of Chicago Press, 2005); and *The Politics of the Veil* (Princeton University Press, 2007). She has also prepared a collection of her essays that deals with the uses of psychoanalysis, particularly fantasy, for historical interpretation, *The Fantasy of Feminist History* (Duke University Press, 2011). She is the author of "The New Thought Police," an analysis of the use of "civility" to silence critical speech on campus (*Nation*, May 2, 2015). Scott is a founding editor of *History of the Present*, a journal of critical history.

Magid Shihade is a faculty member at Birzeit University, Birzeit, Palestine.

Mayssoun Sukarieh received her PhD from the University of California–Berkeley in 2009. Since then she has lectured in anthropology and development studies in universities around the Arab region (American University of Beirut, American University of Cairo) and the United States (Columbia and Brown Universities). Her research interests focus on youth, education, development, and social movements in the Arab region, with a particular interest in studying the political, economic, cultural, and social structures and processes that tie the region in complex and contradictory ways to the larger global political economy. Her first book, *Youth Rising?*

The Politics of Youth in the Global Economy (coauthored with Stuart Tannock) was published in 2015 by Routledge's Critical Youth Studies series. Her articles have appeared in *PoLAR*, *Sociology*, and the *Journal of Youth Studies*.

Lisa Taraki is a sociologist at Birzeit University in Palestine. In addition to her academic work on Palestinian society, politics, and social history, she has been an activist in the struggle for the right to education in Palestine since the late 1970s. She is one of the founders of the Palestinian Campaign for the Academic and Cultural Boycott of Israel (PACBI), established in Ramallah in 2004.

Salim Vally is associate professor in the faculty of education at the University of Johannesburg and director of the Centre for Education Rights and Transformation and visiting professor at the Nelson Mandela Metropolitan University. He is a longtime Palestine solidarity activist and member of the Palestine Solidarity Campaign (South Africa). He serves on the boards of various local and global professional, academic, and nongovernmental organizations, and is active in various social movements and solidarity organizations. He is also a regular commentator in the mass print and electronic media.

NOTES

FOREWORD

1. Avinoam Baral, "The Real Winner in Israel's Election: BDS," *Haaretz*, March 20, 2015.
2. Abraham Greenhouse, "Why Did Israel Intervene for Convicted US Felon Adam Milstein?" *Electronic Intifada*, December 15, 2014, http://electronicintifada.net/content/why-did-israel-intervene-convicted-us-felon-adam-milstein/14117.
3. Baral, "The Real Winner in Israel's Election."
4. Ibid.
5. The David Project, *A Burning Campus? Rethinking Israel Advocacy at America's Universities and Colleges* (Boston, MA: The David Project, 2012). www.davidproject.org/wp-content/uploads/2012524-ABurningCampus-RethinkingIsraelAdvocacyAmericasUniversitiesColleges.pdf.

INTRODUCTION

1. Archbishop Desmond Tutu, "Apartheid in the Holy Land," *Guardian*, April 28, 2002. http://www.theguardian.com/world/2002/apr/29/comment.
2. Ibid.
3. Peter Beaumont, "Israel Risks Becoming An Apartheid State If Peace Talks Fail, Says John Kerry," *Guardian*, April 28, 2014. http://www.theguardian.com/world/2014/apr/28/israel-apartheid-state-peace-talks-john-kerry
4. Peter Beaumont, "John Kerry Apologizes for Apartheid Remark," *Guardian*, April 29, 2014. http://www.theguardian.com/world/2014/apr/29/john-kerry-apologises-israel-apartheid-remarks.
5. For a more extensive discussion of Israel as an apartheid state, see Ben White, *Israeli Apartheid: A Beginner's Guide* (New York: Pluto Press, 2014).
6. United Nations, "International Convention on the Suppression and Punishment of the Crime of Apartheid," November 30, 1973. http://legal.un.org/avl/ha/cspca/cspca.html.
7. United Nations, International Criminal Court, "Rome Statute of the International Criminal Court," July 17, 1998. http://www.icc-cpi.int/nr/rdonlyres/ea9aeff7-5752-4f84-be94-0a655e-b30e16/0/rome_statute_english.pdf.
8. Omar Barghouti, *BDS: The Global Struggle for Palestinian Rights* (Chicago: Haymarket Books, 2011), 63.
9. Ibid.
10. This account of South African apartheid is drawn from the South African Human Sciences Research Council (HSRC) report, *Occupation, Colonialism, Apartheid?: A Re-Assessment of Israel's Conduct in the Occupied Palestinian Territories Under International Law* (Cape Town: HSRC, May 2009), 4-6.
11. Ibid, 21.
12. Ibid.
13. Eyal Weizman, *Hollow Land: Israel's Architecture of Occupation* (New York: Verso, 2007), 80.
14. Ibid., 81.

15. HSRC, 21.

16. United Nations General Assembly, "Report of the Special Rapporteur on Independence of Judges and Lawyers," June 18, 2010. http://unispal.un.org/UNISPAL.NSF/0/57D-00BE6597450FF8525774D0064F621.

17. HSRC, 22.

18. Ilan Pappé, *The Ethnic Cleansing of Palestine* (Oxford: One World, 2007).

19. Oren Yiftachel, "'Ethnocracy': the Politics of Judaizing Israel/Palestine," *Constellations: International Journal of Critical and Democratic Theory* 6, no. 3 (1999): 364–390.

20. Ali Abunimah, *The Battle for Justice in Palestine* (Chicago: Haymarket Books, 2014), 56.

21. Ben White, *Israeli Apartheid*: A Beginner's Guide (London: Pluto Press, 2009), 21.

22. Ibid., 36.

23. Ibid.

24. Yiftachel, "Ethnocracy."

25. David Remnick, "The One-State Reality," *New Yorker*, November 17, 2014, www.newyorker.com/magazine/2014/11/17/one-state-reality.

26. Abunimah, *The Battle for Justice in Palestine*, 48–53.

27. Ibid., 54.

28. Palestinian Campaign for the Academic and Cultural Boycott of Israel: http://pacbi.org/etemplate.php?id=869.

29. Ibid.

30. United States Campaign for the Academic and Cultural Boycott of Israel (USACBI) Mission Statement: www.usacbi.org/mission-statement/.

31. "Historic Landslide BDS Vote by Grad Student Union at University of California," Labor for Palestine, December 10, 2014, http://laborforpalestine.net/2014/12/10/historic-landslide-bds-vote-by-grad-student-union-at-university-of-california/.

32. Chomsky, for example, has been a consistent critic of BDS strategy. See Noam Chomsky, "On Israel-Palestine and BDS," *Nation*, July 2, 2014. www.thenation.com/article/180492/israel-palestine-and-bds. See also "Responses to Noam Chomsky on Israel-Palestine and BDS," Nation, July 10, 2014, www.thenation.com/article/180590/responses-noam-chomsky-israel-palestine-and-bds.

33. See Wael Elasady, "Chomsky and the BDS Struggle" in *Socialist Worker*, July 15, 2014, http://socialistworker.org/2014/07/15/chomsky-and-the-bds-struggle.

34. Ibid.

35. "Past Is Present: Settler Colonialism in Palestine," *Settler Colonial Studies* (June 2012), http://antipodefoundation.org/2012/06/08/intervention-past-is-present-settler-colonialism-in-palestine/.

36. In addition to these sources an excellent book about teaching Palestinian life under Occupation and resistance is Marcy Jane Knopf-Newman's *The Politics of Teaching Palestine to Americans: Addressing Pedagogical Strategies* (New York: Palgrave MacMillan, 2013).

37. See "AAAS Academic Boycott Resolution" at http://aaastudies.org/content/index.php/about-aaas/resolutions.

38. See "Council Resolution on Boycott of Israeli Academic Institutions" at www.theasa.net/american_studies_association_resolution_on_academic_boycott_of_israel.

39. Ibid.

40. See Nora Barrows-Friedman *In Our Power: U.S. Students Organize for Justice in Palestine* (Charlottesville: Just World Books, 2014).

41. See Edward Saakashvili and Isabel Knight, "Following Swat Hillel's Lead, Vassar Becomes Second Open Hillel Chapter," *Daily Swarthmore*, February 20, 2014. http://daily.swarthmore.edu

/2014/02/20/following-swat-hillels-lead-vassar-chapter-becomes-second-open-hillel/.

42. See the excellent resource site "Pinkwatching Israel" for activists seeking to support BDS: http://www.pinkwatchingisrael.com/.

43. See Ali Abunimah, *The Battle For Justice in Palestine* (Chicago: Haymarket Books, 2014), especially chapter 6, "The War on Campus."

44. AMCHA, for example, has an entire web page dedicated to trying to delegitimize BDS: http://www.amchainitiative.org/1842-2/.

45. See Piya Chatterjee and Sunaina Maira, editors, *The Imperial University: Academic Repression and Scholarly Dissent* (Minneapolis: University of Minnesota Press, 2014).

46. See Nora Barrows-Friedman, "California's 'Pepper-Spray Chancellor' Stays Silent over Racist Abuse of Arab and Muslim Students," *Electronic Intifada*, February 2, 2015. http://electronicintifada.net/blogs/nora-barrows-friedman/californias-pepper-spray-chancellor-stays-silent-over-racist-abuse-arab.

47. The response of university presidents also motivated some stirring political rejoinders and defenses of academic boycott, like this one from William James Martin in *Veterans News Now* on March 21, 2014, www.veteransnewsnow.com/2014/03/21/reply-to-university-presidents-who-condemned-asa-boycott/.

48. American Association of University Professors, *Journal of Academic Freedom* 4 (2013), www.aaup.org/reports-publications/journal-academic-freedom/volume-4-2013/editors-introduction-volume-4.

CHAPTER 1

1. Joel Greenberg, "Yehoshafat Harkabi, Israeli Spy and Adviser, Is Dead at 72," *New York Times,* August 27, 1994, www.nytimes.com/1994/08/27/obituaries/yehoshafat-harkabi-israeli-spy-and-adviser-is-dead-at-72.html.

2. Avi Shlaim, "Obituary: Professor Yehoshafat Harkabi," *Independent*, September 14, 1994, www.independent.co.uk/news/people/obituary-professor-yehoshafat-harkabi-1448686.html.

3. Institute for National Security Studies, "Shlomo Gazit," www.inss.org.il/index.aspx?id=4300&researcherid=5006. See also http://www.quazoo.com/q/Shlomo%20Gazit.

4. Gil Eyal, "Dangerous Liaisons Between Military Intelligence and Middle Eastern Studies in Israel," *Theory and Society* 31(2002): 653.

5. Lesley Pearl, "Ex-West Bank `Mayor' in Berkeley Visit, Says Jews Must Study Arab Culture," November 24, 1995, www.jweekly.com/article/full/2038/ex-west-bank-mayor-in-berkeley-visit-says-jews-must-study-arab-culture/.

6. Institute for National Security Studies, "Mission." www.inss.org.il/about.php?cat=55&in=0 (accessed July 2010; that text, with the same URL, has been replaced by a more benign description; accessed December 2014).

7. SOAS Palestine Society, "Urgent Briefing Paper: Tel Aviv University—a Leading Israeli Military Research Centre," February 2009, www.electronicintifada.net/downloads/pdf/090708-soas-palestine-society.pdf.

8. Uri Yakobi Keller, *The Economy of the Occupation: Academic Boycott of Israel*, (Alternative Information Center, October 2009). http://alternativenews.org/archive/images/stories/downloads/Economy_of_the_occupation_23-24.pdf?phpMyAdmin=Ig1cpb2q2HtKHF2OcmHXPP7EbG9.

9. SOAS Palestine Society.

10. "The NSSC," National Security Studies Center, http://nssc.haifa.ac.il/profile.htm (accessed July 2010; this text has now been rewritten in less obvious language. See http://nssc.haifa.ac.il/index.php/en/2012-07-18-06-55-57/2012-07-18-06-56-49, accessed December 2014).

11. Tel Aviv University, *Tel Aviv University Review: In Defense of the Nation* (Tel Aviv: Development

and Public Affairs Division, Winter 2008–2009). http://english.tau.ac.il/sites/default/files/media _server/TAU%20Review%202008-09.pdf.

12. Deganit Paikowsky and Isaac Ben Israel, "Science and Technology for National Development: the Case of Israel's Space Program," *Acta Astronautica* 64, 9–10 (November–December 2009).

13. Josef Federman, "Military Units Provide Training Ground for Israeli Tech Leaders," *USA Today*, February 4, 2004, www.usatoday.com/tech/world/2004-02-04-israeli-military-tech_x.htm; Christopher Rhoads, "How an Elite Military School Feeds Israel's Tech Industry," *Wall Street Journal*, July 6, 2007. http://online.wsj.com/public/article/SB118368825920758806.html; Also see http://www.israel21c.org/technology/the-idf-incubator-for-israels-future-ceos/ and http://www.idf.il/1283-13885-en/Dover.aspx.

14. "Welcome to the Military Medicine Track," (in Hebrew), the Hebrew University Faculty of Medicine, March 6, 2013. https://medicine.ekmd.huji.ac.il/He/Education/tzameret/Pages /default_he.aspx#3. See also "Largest-Ever Class of Military Track Med Students to Begin Studies," the Hebrew University of Jerusalem, October 10, 2013; http://support.huji.ac.il/HeaderMenu /news-events/press/elite_military_medicine/ ; American Friends of the Hebrew University, "The Elite Military Medicine Track at the Hebrew University of Jerusalem," https://www.afhu.org /the-elite-military-medicine-track-at-the-hebrew-university-of-jerusalem/medicine/; http://www .hadassah-med.com/hadassah-schools/military-medicine.

15. "Letter from Physicians to World Medical Association," www.bricup.org.uk/documents/medical/ BlacharWMA.pdf; and www.pacbi.org/etemplate.php?id=464&key=health.

16. "Haifa University 'Proud to Be Academic Home of (Israeli) Security Forces,'" *Alternative Information Center*, June 15, 2010, http://wordpress.haifa.ac.il/?p=2642 (Hebrew); also at http://www .pacbi.org/etemplate.php?id=1274; see also "M.A. in Security Studies in Israel in English," http:// www.en.universities-colleges.org.il/Terrorism-and-Homeland/.

17. "Elbit Systems," *Who Profits*, http://whoprofits.org/company/elbit-systems.

18. Ibid.; emphasis added.

19. Palestinian BDS National Committee, "Elbit Systems Loses Key Brazil Deal over Palestine Protests," *BDS Movement*, December 3, 2014. www.bdsmovement.net/2014/elbit-systems-loses-key -brazil-deal-12878.

20. "The Technion," New Yorkers Against the Cornell–Technion Partership, http://nyact.net/links /about-the-technion/.

21. Ali Abunimah, "Warrior Students: How Israeli Universities Are Supporting War Crimes in Gaza," *Electronic Intifada*, August 18, 2014, http://electronicintifada.net/blogs/ali-abunimah/ warrior-students-how-israeli-universities-are-supporting-war-crimes-gaza.

22. "The Academy Council's Statement Regarding Access Restrictions Imposed on Palestinian Students and Scientist," Israel Academy of Sciences and Humanities, November 5, 2006, www.academy .ac.il/english/asp/news/news_in.asp?news_id=47; also see "A Statement Regarding Access Restrictions Imposed on Palestinian Students and Scientists," Gisha Legal Center for Freedom of Movement, October 25, 2006, http://gisha.org/legal/482; and Committee on Human Rights, October 31, 2006, www7.nationalacademies.org/humanrights/CHR_044044.htm.

23. Israeli Academics, "Academic Freedom for Whom?" 2008, http://academic-access.weebly.com/.

24. BRICUP Newsletter, no. 7, August 2007, www.bricup.org.uk/documents/archive/BRICUPNewsletter7.pdf.

CHAPTER 2

1. "Gaza Calling: All Out on Saturday 9 Day of Rage," *BDS Movement*, August 6, 2014, www .bdsmovement.net/2014/gaza-calling-all-out-on-saturday-9-august-day-of-rage-12423.

2.   In the *Jerusalem Post* interview, Soffer set out a vision of Gaza's future ("It's the demography, stupid," May 21, 2004—the original interview is not online but a 2007 follow up which recounts his 2004 statements can be found at www.jpost.com/Features/I-didnt-suggest-we-kill-Palestinians).

3.   "Ronnie Kasril's Speech at Israeli Apartheid Week 2009," BDS Movement, March 20, 2009, www.bdsmovement.net/2009/ronnie-kasrils-speech-at-israeli-apartheid-week-2009-347.

4.   Steve Biko, *I Write What I Like* (Portsmouth, NH: Heinemann, 1987), 66.

5.   John Pilger, "Holocaust Denied: The Lying Silence of Those Who Know," *New Statesman*, January 8, 2009, www.newstatesman.com/middle-east/2009/01/pilger-israel-gaza-palestine.

6.   My own university, Al-Aqsa, has lost twelve staff members and forty students in the latest Israeli onslaught on Gaza.

CHAPTER 3

1.   Noga Kadman, *Acting the Landlord: Israel's Policy in Area C, the West Bank* (B'Tselem Publications, June 2013), www.btselem.org/publications/summaries/201306_acting_the_landlord.

2.   Haidar Eid, "The Oslo Accords: A Critique," *Al Jazeera*, September 13, 2013, www.aljazeera.com /indepth/opinion/2013/09/201391282358965793.html.

3.   Palestinian BDS National Committee, "The Amazing Things We Achieved Together in 2014," *BDS Movement*, December 27, 2014, www.bdsmovement.net/2014/round-up-13017#sthash .jdm4j4jl.dpuf.

4.   David Palumbo-Liu, "Return of the Blacklist? Cowardice and Censorship at the University of Illinois: Job Offer to World-Renowned Scholar Reportedly Revoked under Pressure, Likely over Gaza Opinions on Twitter," *Salon*, August 7, 2014, www.salon.com/2014/08/07/return_of_the _blacklist_cowardice_and_censorship_at_the_university_of_illinois/.

5.   "Statement by Jewish Studies Professors in North America Regarding the AMCHA Initiative," *The Jewish Daily Forward*, October 1, 2014, http://forward.com/articles/206629/statement-by -jewish-studies-professors-in-north-am/.

6.   Institute for National Security Studies, "The Case Against Academic Boycotts of Israel,", book release, December 22, 2014, www.inss.org.il/index.aspx?id=4480&eventid=8334.

7.   Those who challenge the dominant discourse often do so at great personal and professional cost. It is therefore no wonder that so many groups are careful how they launch a challenge to a sacrosanct issue, especially in the United States. Jewish Voice for Peace, as an example, only gradually introduced language into its campaigns that reflects its evolving advocacy of BDS as a strategy and BDS goals. In its first fundraising drive this year, the BDS movement itself used soft and ambiguous language in its appeals to describe BDS goals, formulations such as "end Israeli impunity and Palestinian dispossession" and prevent Israel from "continuing with its occupation and dispossession of Palestinian lands."

8.   American Studies Association, "Council Resolution on Boycott of Israeli Academic Institutions," December 4, 2013, www.theasa.net/american_studies_association_resolution_on_academic_boycott _of_israel.

9.   Omar Barghouti makes a distinction between self-determination for Jewish settlers (unacceptable) and integrating former colonizers after justice and reparations for Palestinians have taken place. Watch "Omar Barghouti on 'ethical decolonization' and moving beyond Zionist racism," *Electronic Intifada*, September 29, 2013, http://electronicintifada.net/blogs/benjamin-doherty/ watch-omar-barghouti-ethical-decolonization-and-moving-beyond-zionist-racism.

10.   "Palestinian Civil Society Call for BDS," *BDS Movement*, July 9, 2005, www.bdsmovement.net/call.

11.   Khaled Abu Toameh, "*Mabrouk* to Abbas on Tenth Year of His Four-Year Term," Gatestone Institute International Policy Council, January 24, 2014, http://www.gatestoneinstitute.org/4141

/abbas-term-of-office.

12. Osamah Khalil, "'Who Are You?': The PLO and the Limits of Representation," March 18, 2013, *Al-Shabaka*, http://al-shabaka.org/node/585.

13. Ali Abunimah, "How Palestinian Authority's UN 'Statehood' Bid Endangers Palestinian Rights," *Electronic Intifada*, August 8, 2011, http://electronicintifada.net/blogs/ali-abunimah/how-palestinian-authoritys-un-statehood-bid-endangers-palestinian-rights.

14. "BNC Reiterates its Position on 'September,'" BDS Movement, August 8, 2011, www.bdsmovement.net/2011/bnc-reiterates-its-position-on-september-7794.

15. Edward Said, "What Price Oslo?" *CounterPunch*, March 23–25, 2002, www.counterpunch.org/2002/03/23/what-price-oslo/.

16. Osamah Khalil, "Oslo's Roots: Kissinger, the PLO, and the Peace Process," *Al-Shabaka*, September 4, 2013, http://al-shabaka.org/policy-brief/negotiations/oslos-roots-kissinger-plo-and-peace-process?page=show.

17. Tariq Dana, "The Palestinian Capitalists That Have Gone Too Far," *Al-Shabaka*, January 14, 2014, http://al-shabaka.org/policy-brief/economic-issues/palestinian-capitalists-have-gone-too-far.

18. "Geneva Convention Calls on Israel to Obey International Law," Anadolu Agency, December 17, 2014, www.aa.com.tr/en/s/437033--geneva-convention-calls-on-israel-to-obey-international-law.

19. Gideon Levy, "Israel Does Not Want Peace," *Haaretz*, July 4, 2014, www.haaretz.com/news/diplomacy-defense/israel-peace-conference/1.601112.

20. Khaled Elgindy, "Programmed for Failure," Brookings Institute, April 11, 2014, www.brookings.edu/research/opinions/2014/04/11-israel-palestine-negotiations-elgindy.

21. Omar Barghouti, "Academic Panel Stirs Controversy," *WBEZ Worldview* podcast segment, January 9, 2014, https://soundcloud.com/wbez-worldview/academic-panel-stirs.

22. Marwan Barghouti is a senior figure within Fateh and is serving five life sentences for alleged involvement in attacks on Israeli targets. He was arrested in 2002 and sentenced two years later.

23. Palestinian Information Center, "Abu Marzouk Calls for Revealing Amendments on UN Draft Resolution," December 27, 2014, http://english.palinfo.com/site/pages/details.aspx?itemid=69320.

24. "Jailed Fatah leader criticizes UN resolution on Palestine," *Ma'an News*, December 24, 2014, http://maannews.net/eng/ViewDetails.aspx?ID=749072.

25. This is exactly the opposite of what happened in Ireland (although a referendum was involved there). When negotiations that ultimately led to the Good Friday Agreement started, one of the options excluded in advance was "a Protestant state for a Protestant people" in the North of Ireland (and, equally, a Catholic state for a Catholic people in the Republic). "The Irish Peace Process worked because all sides stopped armed actions, agreed to negotiations, implemented full demilitarisation, and embraced conflict resolution. This approach is urgently required in the Middle East. It applies equally to Palestinian and Israeli military organisations." Declan Kearney, "Irish Peace Process Template Applies to Gaza/Israel," *Anphoblacht*, July 24, 2014, www.anphoblacht.com/contents/24230.

26. Ali Abunimah, "Why I Want Obama to Veto Abbas' UN Resolution on Palestine," *Electronic Intifada*, December 18, 2014, http://electronicintifada.net/blogs/ali-abunimah/why-i-want-obama-veto-abbas-un-resolution-palestine.

27. "Barghouti Criticizes UN Draft Resolution on Palestinian Statehood," *Al Akhbar* (English), December 23, 2014, english.al-akhbar.com/node/22996.

28. Daoud Kuttab, "France Waters Down Arab Draft Resolution on Palestine," *Al-Monitor*, December 23, 2014, http://www.al-monitor.com/pulse/originals/2014/12/palestine-resolution-security-council-french-arab.html#ixzz3NgIDkYav.

29. Tikva Honig-Parnass, like many others, makes the connection between the political stance of

the United States/European Union in the matter of two states and that of apartheid South Africa: "In Apartheid South Africa the erection of the Bantustans aimed (among other things) to serve as a façade of independent states which would convince the international public opinion to accept the 'new' state of South Africa which presumably ended the Apartheid rule. The present decision to recognize a Palestinian Bantustan state aims to play a similar role. That is, to create a deceptive appearance of a two-state solution to what is called the Palestinian-Israeli 'conflict,' while ignoring the fact that the Palestinian Bantustan is already part and parcel of the one singular colonial Apartheid regime in Palestine." In the comment sections of Joseph Massad, "Recognizing Palestine, BDS, and the survival of Israel," *Electronic Intifada*, December 16, 2014, http://electronicintifada.net/content/recognizing-palestine-bds-and-survival-israel/14123.

30. Joseph Massad, "Recognizing Palestine, BDS, and the survival of Israel," *Electronic Intifada*, December 16, 2014, http://electronicintifada.net/content/recognizing-palestine-bds-and-survival-israel/14123.

31. "Academic Boycotts," Editorial, *Jerusalem Post*, December 21, 2014, www.jpost.com/landedpages/printarticle.aspx?id=385338.

32. Philip Weiss, "Chris Hedges Is Blackballed by Penn after Likening ISIS to Israel," *Mondoweiss*, December 26, 2014, http://mondoweiss.net/2014/12/blacklisted-likening-israel#sthash.yLT9E6ye.dpuf.

33. Anna Goldenberg, "Beleaguered Theater J Slammed Over 'Blatantly Political Firing' of Ari Roth," *Jewish Daily Forward*, December 25, 2014, http://forward.com/articles/211575/beleaguered-theater-j-slammed-over-blatantly-polit/.

34. Ali Abunimah, *The Battle for Justice in Palestine* (Chicago: Haymarket Books, 2014).

35. Philip Weiss, "Lieberman Unveils Racist Peace Plan: Pay Palestinians to Leave Israel," *Mondoweiss*, November 28, 2014, http://mondoweiss.net/2014/11/lieberman-unveils-palestinians#sthash.yfzISRle.dpuf.

36. Randa Farah, "Palestinian Dead End Highlights the Right of Return," *Al-Shabaka*, May 6, 2014, http://al-shabaka.org/node/764. Palestinian Dead End Highlights the Right of Return http://al-shabaka.org/node/764.

37. Maureen Clare Murphy, "Israel Violates Gaza Ceasefire Nearly Every Day," *Electronic Intifada*, December 22, 2014, electronicintifada.net/blogs/maureen-clare-murphy/israel-violates-gaza-ceasefire-nearly-every-day.

38. "Egypt Closes Rafah Border until Further Notice," *Middle East Monitor*, December 24, 2014, www.middleeastmonitor.com/news/africa/15986-egypt-closes-rafah-border-until-further-notice.

39. David A. Kirshbaum, "Israeli Apartheid: A Basic Legal Perspective," Israel Law Resource Center, February 2007, http://www.israellawresourcecenter.org/israellaws/essays/israellawsessay.htm.

40. "114 Administrative Detention Orders Issued in December Targeting Palestinian Human Rights Defenders and Activists," Samidoun: Palestinian Prisoner Solidarity Network, December 28, 2014, http://samidoun.ca/2014/12/114-administrative-detention-orders-issued-in-december-targeting-palestinian-human-rights-defenders-and-activists/.

41. B'Tselem, "Palestinians Killed by Israeli Security Forces in the West Bank, after Operation Cast Lead 2014," www.btselem.org/hebrew/statistics/fatalities/after-cast-lead/by-date-of-event/westbank/palestinians-killed-by-israeli-security-forces.

42. "Palestinian Refugees from Syria in Lebanon," *Anera Report* 4 (April 2013), www.anera.org/wp-content/uploads/2013/04/PalestinianRefugeesFromSyriainLebanon.pdf.

43. Ramzy Baroud, "Five Reasons Why 2014 Was a Game Changer for the People of Palestine," Stop the War Coalition, December 25, 2014, http://stopwar.org.uk/news/five-reasons-why-2014-was-a-game-changer-for-the-people-of-palestine.

44. Abunimah, *Battle for Justice in Palestine*.

45.   Omar Barghouti, *Boycott, Divestment, Sanctions: The Global Struggle for Palestinian Rights* (Chicago: Haymarket Books, 2011), 62

CHAPTER 4—SELECTED REFERENCES

Adalah: The Legal Center for Arab Minority Rights in Israel (www.adalah.org).

Mossawa Center (September 2014). *The New Wave of Israeli Discriminatory Laws.* http://mossawa.org/my_Documents/pic002/183_The_New_Wave_of_Israel%27s_Discriminatory_ Laws___Report_FINAL_2014.pdf (Accessed on December 23, 2014).

Palestinian Campaign for the Academic and Cultural Boycott of Israel (www.pacbi.org).

Right to Enter (www.righttoenter.ps).

Right to Education Campaign (right2edu.birzeit.edu).

Sa'di Ahmad, *Thorough Surveillance: The Genesis of Israeli Policies of Population Management, Surveillance and Political Control Towards the Palestinian Minority* (Manchester, UK: University of Manchester Press, 2013).

US Campaign for the Academic and Cultural Boycott of Israel (www.usacbi.org).

CHAPTER 5

1.   Shabtai Shavit, "Former Mossad Chief: For the First Time, I Fear for the Future of Zionism," *Haaretz*, November 24, 2014, www.haaretz.com/opinion/.premium-1.628038.

2.   Ibid.

3.   Harriet Sherwood, "Ehud Barak Formally Approves West Bank University of Ariel," *Guardian*, December 26, 2012, www.guardian.co.uk/world/2012/dec/26/ehud-barak-approves-ariel-university.

4.   Gidi Weitz, "Former PM Barak: Netanyahu Leading Israel to Disaster," Haaretz, January 8, 2015, www.haaretz.com/news/diplomacy-defense/.premium-1.635978.

5.   Ben White, "Behind Brand Israel: Israel's Recent Propaganda Efforts," *Electronic Intifada*, February 23, 2010, http://electronicintifada.net/content/behind-brand-israel-israels-recent-propaganda -efforts/8694.

6.   Jonathan Freedland, "When the Israel Boycott Goes Mainstream," *Jewish Chronicle Online*, June 7, 2013, www.thejc.com/comment-and-debate/columnists/108363/when-israel-boycott-goes -mainstream.

7.   Birzeit University Institute of Law, *Advocating for Palestinian Rights in Conformity with International Law Guidelines* (Jerusalem: Civic Coalition for Palestinian Rights in Jerusalem, 2014), http://lawcenter.birzeit.edu/iol/en/project/outputfile/6/986afcc6c9.pdf.

8.   Boycott from Within, http://boycottisrael.info/.

9.   Omar Barghouti, "Palestine's SA Moment," *City Press*, July 8, 2014, www.citypress.co.za/columnists/palestines-sa-moment/.

10.   "Negative Views of Russia on the Rise: Global Poll," *BBC World Service*, press release, June 3, 2014, www.globescan.com/images/images/pressreleases/bbc2014_country_ratings/2014_country _rating_poll_bbc_globescan.pdf.

11.   Patrick Martin, "Netanyahu Views Trade Boycott as Strategic Threat to Israel," *Globe and Mail*, February 4, 2014, http://www.theglobeandmail.com/news/world/netanyahu-views-trade-boycott -as-strategic-threat-to-israel/article16701792/.

12.   Among world leaders condemning Israel's atrocities in Gaza in the summer of 2014 as a "massacre" were Brazil's president and France's foreign minister. See Associated Press, "Brazilian President Dima Rousseff Calls Israel's Conflict with Hamas 'a Massacre,'" *Fox News*, July 28, 2014, http:// www.foxnews.com/world/2014/07/28/brazilian-president-dilma-rousseff-calls-israel-conflict

-with-hamas-massacre/; see also "Gaza Conflict: France Condemns Israel 'Massacre,'" *BBC News*, August 4, 2014, http://www.bbc.com/news/world-europe-28637577.

13. Isabel Kershner, "Israel Claims Nearly 1,000 Acres of West Bank Land Near Bethlehem," *New York Times*, August 31, 2014, http://www.nytimes.com/2014/09/01/world/middleeast/israel-claims -nearly-1000-acres-of-west-bank-land-near-bethlehem.html?_r=0.

14. "Timeline," *BDS Movement*, www.bdsmovement.net/timeline.

15. Palestinian BDS National Committee, "Palestinian Civil Society Calls for Boycott, Divestment, and Sanctions against Israel Until It Complies with International Law and Universal Principles of Human Rights," *BDS Movement*, July 9, 2005, www.bdsmovement.net/call.

16. Bureau of Democracy, Human Rights, and Labor, US Department of State, *2010 Human Rights Report: Israel and the Occupied Territories*, April 8, 2011, www.state.gov/g/drl/rls/hrrpt/2010/nea /154463.htm.

17. United Nations, Resolutions Adopted on the Reports of the Third Committee, "International Convention on the Suppression and Punishment of the Crime of Apartheid," 2185th Plenary Meeting, November 30, 1973, www.un.org/ga/search/view_doc.asp?symbol=A/res/3068(XXVIII) .

18. Palestinian Liberation Organization Affairs Department, "Palestinian Refugees," Updated May 2011, www.nad-plo.org/userfiles/file/FAQ/Refugees_FAQ_Fact%20Sheet_May2011.pdf

19. Barak Ravid, "Swell of Boycotts Driving Israel into International Isolation," *Haaretz*, December 12, 2013, www.haaretz.com/news/diplomacy-defense/.premium-1.563242.

20. "As the Gaza Crisis Deepens, Boycotts Raise the Price of Israel's Impunity," *World Observer Online*, August 23, 2014, http://worldobserveronline.com/2014/08/23/gaza-crisis-deepens-boycotts -can-raise-price-israels-impunity/.

21. The White House, Office of the Press Secretary, "Remarks as Prepared by White House Coordinator for the Middle East, North Africa, and the Gulf Region Philip Gordon at the Ha'aretz Israel Conference for Peace," July 8, 2014, www.whitehouse.gov/the-press-office/2014/07/08/ remarks-prepared-white-house-coordinator-middle-east-north-africa-and-gu.

22. John Prescott, "Israel's Bombardment of Gaza Is a War Crime—and It Must End," *Mirror*, July 26, 2014, www.mirror.co.uk/news/world-news/john-prescott-israels-bombardment-gaza-3918413.

23. Dominique de Villepin, "Lever la voix face au massacre perpétré à Gaza," *Le Figaro*, August 1, 2014, www.lefigaro.fr/vox/monde/2014/07/31/31002-20140731ARTFIG00381-dominique-de -villepin-lever-la-voix-face-au-massacre-perpetre-a-gaza.php.

24. Raphael Ahren, "Senior German Politician Wants to Stop Arms Exports to Israel," *Times of Israel*, September 7, 2014, www.timesofisrael.com/senior-german-politician-wants-to-stop-arms-exports -to-israel/.

25. Barak Ravid, "El Salvador Becomes Fifth Latin American Country to Recall Israel Envoy," *Haaretz*, July 29, 2014, http://www.haaretz.com/news/diplomacy-defense/1.607915.

26. Ibid.

27. "Apello internazionale Primo firmatario Presidente della Bolivia Evo Morales," *Nuestra America*, undated, www.nuestra-america.it/index.php/it/espanol/bolivia/item/998-appello-internazionale -primo-firmatario-presidente-della-bolivia-evo-morales.

28. Raphael Ahren, "Israel's Founding a 'Crime against Humanity,' Says South Africa's ANC," *Times of Israel*, September 14, 2014, www.timesofisrael.com/israels-founding-a-crime-against-humanity -says-south-africas-anc/.

29. Organization of Islamic Cooperation, August 12, 2014, www.oic-oci.org/oicv2/subweb/fm /ext/2014/ar/docs/OIC-PAL-02-2014-EXCOM-12AUG-FC-Ar.pdf.

30. *Middle East Monitor*, "Kuwait Boycotts International Corporations Working with Israel in the Occupied Territories," October 22, 2014, https://www.middleeastmonitor.com/news/middle-east

/14798-kuwait-boycotts-international-companies-working-with-israel-in-the-occupied-territories.

31. Vivien Sansour, "Palestinian Farmers Lose Land for Failed Economic Zones," *Al Jazeera*, August 17, 2014, www.aljazeera.com/indepth/opinion/2014/08/palestinian-farmers-lose-land -f-201481173618790947.html.

32. Yael Marom and Jessica Devaney, "Bringing the Boycott Back Home: Palestinian Stores Drop Israeli Goods," *+972 Magazine*, September 3, 2014, http://972mag.com/bringing-the-boycott -back-home-palestinian-stores-drop-israeli-goods/96278/.

33. Ahmad Melhem, "Sales of Israeli Goods Down 50% Due to Boycott," *US News and World Report*, August 22, 2014, www.usnews.com/news/articles/2014/08/22/sales-of-israeli-goods-in-west -bank-down-50-due-to-boycott.

34. C. J. R. Dugard, "The Future of International Law: A Human Rights Perspective," valedictory address, Universiteit Leiden, Netherlands, April 20, 2007. https://openaccess.leidenuniv.nl/bit- stream/handle/1887/12401/afscheidsrede_dugard.pdf?sequence=1.

35. Visit http://endtheoccupation.org/.

36. "Israel-Palestine: This Is How It Ends," *Avaaz*, petition, https://secure.avaaz.org/en/israel_palestine _this_is_how_it_ends_loc/.

37. "USACBI Congratulates and Thanks the Critical Ethnic Studies Association and the African Literature Association for Endorsing the Academic Boycott of Israel," US Campaign for the Academic and Cultural Boycott of Israel, July 22, 2014, www.usacbi.org/2014/07/usacbi -congratulates-and-thanks-the-critical-ethnic-studies-association-and-the-african-literature -association-for-endorsing-the-academic-boycott-of-israel/.

38. Nathaniel Popper, "Israel Aims to Improve Its Public Image," *Jewish Daily Forward*, October 14, 2005, http://forward.com/articles/2070/israel-aims-to-improve-its-public-image/.

39. Visit www.pacbi.org.

40. "Israeli Universities Deeply Involved in Gaza Massacre: Academic Boycott Now!" Palestinian Campaign for the Academic and Cultural Boycott of Israel, August 3, 2014, www.pacbi.org /etemplate.php?id=2522.

41. Raja Zaatry and Muhammad Khalaileh, *Via Dolorosa: 14 Obstacles to the Access of the Arab-Pales- tinian Society to Higher Education in Israel and 10 Recommendations for Their Removal* (Nazareth: Hirak—Center for the Advancement of Higher Education in Arab Society, June 2013), http:// pacbi.org/pics/Accessability%20Report%20-%20Eng%20%281%29.pdf.

42. The Academic Watch, *Annual Summary Report 2011/2012* (Arab Culture Association, November 2012), http://alrasedproject.files.wordpress.com/2013/02/alrased1_eng.pdf.

43. Palestinian Campaign for the Academic and Cultural Boycott of Israel, "Campaign to Boycott the Oral History Conference at Hebrew University of Jerusalem," December 1, 2013, http:// pacbi.org/etemplate.php?id=2293.

44. Ali Abunimah, "Israeli Universities Lend Support to Gaza Massacre," *Electronic Intifada*, July 25, 2014, http://electronicintifada.net/blogs/ali-abunimah/israeli-universities-lend-support-gaza -massacre.

45. "BIU to Provide Scholarships for Called-Up Soliders," *Arutz Sheva—Israel National News*, July 30, 2014, www.israelnationalnews.com/News/Flash.aspx/300185#.U9nyo_mSyS8.

46. Harriet Sherwood, "Israeli Polls Show Overwhelming Support for Gaza Campaign," *Guardian*, July 31, 2014, www.theguardian.com/world/2014/jul/31/israeli-polls-support-gaza-campaign-media.

47. New Yorkers against the Cornell–Technion Partership, "The Technion," http://nyact.net/links /about-the-technion/.

48. Institute for Middle East Understanding, "The Dahiyu Doctrine and Israel's Use of Dispro- portionate Force," December 7, 2012, http://imeu.org/article/the-dahiya-doctrine-and-israels

-use-of-disproportionate-force.

49. SOAS Palestine Society, "Tel Aviv University—A Leading Israeli Military Research Centre," brief-
     ing paper, February 2009, http://pacbi.org/pics/file/SOAS-Palestine-Society-Paper-TAU-Military
     -Complicity-Feb-2009.pdf.

50. PACBI, August 3, 2014, www.pacbi.org/etemplate.php?id=2522.

51. "UN Rights Chief: Israel Defying International Law in Gaza, Must Be Held Accountable,"
     Haaretz, July 31, 2014, www.haaretz.com/news/diplomacy-defense/1.608237.

52. UN News Service, "UN Mission Finds Evidence of War Crimes by Both Sides in Gaza Con-
     flict," *UN News Centre*, September 15, 2009, www.un.org/apps/news/story.asp?NewsID=32057#
     .U9yr5fmSzTp.

53. Amos Harel, "The Philosopher Who Gave the IDF Moral Justification in Gaza," *Haaretz*, February 6,
     2009, www.haaretz.com/print-edition/news/the-philosopher-who-gave-the-idf-moral-justification
     -in-gaza-1.269527.

54. SOAS Palestine Society, op cit.

55. Ibid.

56. "Israeli Universities," PACBI, op. cit.

57. Gianluca Mezzofiore, "Israeli Professor: Rape Hamas Militants' Mothers and Sisters to Deter Ter-
     rorist Attacks," *International Business Times*, July 22, 2014, www.ibtimes.co.uk/israeli-professor
     -rape-hamas-militiants-mothers-sisters-deter-terrorist-attacks-1457836.

58. Abunimah, "Israeli Universities Lend Support to Gaza Massacre," http://electronicintifada.net/
     blogs/ali-abunimah/israeli-universities-lend-support-gaza-massacre.

59. United Nations, Office of the High Commissioner on Human Rights, "Declaration on Human
     Rights Education and Training," 2011, www.ohchr.org/EN/Issues/Education/Training/Compila-
     tion/Pages/UnitedNationsDeclarationHumanRightsEducationandTraining(2011).aspx.

60. "PACBI Guidelines for the International Academic Boycott of Israel," July 31, 2014, *BDS Move-
     ment*, www.pacbi.org/etemplate.php?id=1108.

61. "Scholasticide," Schott's Vocab blog, *New York Times*, January 14, 2009, http://schott.blogs.ny-
     times.com/2009/01/14/scholasticide/?_r=0.

62. "Researcher: Israel Destroyed Palestinian Books," *YNet News*, January 28, 2010, www.ynetnews.com
     /articles/0,7340,L-3841252,00.html.

63. Palestine and Arabic Studies Program, Birzeit University, "History of Birzeit University," http://
     sites.birzeit.edu/pas/content/history-birzeit-university.

64. "Israelis Kill 3 in Occupied Lands," *Lawrence Journal-World* (KS), December 30, 1988, http://
     news.google.com/newspapers?nid=2199&dat=19881230&id=kUIyAAAAIBAJ&sjid=HeY-
     FAAAAIBAJ&pg=3400,6780177.

65. Riham Barghouti, "The Struggle for an Equal Right to Academic Freedom," *US Campaign for
     the Academic and Cultural Boycott of Israel*, June 2011, http://www.usacbi.org/2011/06/barghouti
     -struggle-equal-right/.

66. Akram Habeeb, "Why Would Israel Bomb a University?" *Electronic Intifada*, December 29, 2008,
     http://electronicintifada.net/content/why-would-israel-bomb-university/7887.

67. Judith Butler, "Academic Freedom and the ASA's Boycott of Israel: A Response to Michelle
     Goldberg," *Nation*, December 8, 2013, www.thenation.com/article/177512/academic-freedom
     -and-asas-boycott-israel-response-michelle-goldberg.

68. Human Rights Watch, *Second Class: Discrimination against Palestinian Arab Children in Israel's
     Schools* (Human Rights Watch, September 2001), www.hrw.org/reports/2001/israel2.

69. Omar Barghouti, "A Tipping Point?" *Inside Higher Ed*, January 3, 2014, www.insidehighered.com
     /views/2014/01/03/essay-growth-support-boycott-israeli-universities.

70. Omar Barghouti, "Boycott, Academic Freedom, and the Moral Responsibility to Uphold Human Rights," *Journal of Academic Freedom* 4 (2013), www.aaup.org/sites/default/files/files/JAF/2013%20JAF/Barghouti.pdf.

71. United Nations, Office of the High Commissioner for Human Rights, "Vienna Declaration and Programme of Action," adopted by the World Conference on Human Rights, June 25, 1993, www.ohchr.org/Documents/ProfessionalInterest/vienna.pdf.

72. Naomi Klein, "Enough. It's Time for a Boycott," *Guardian*, January 9, 2009, www.theguardian.com/commentisfree/2009/jan/10/naomi-klein-boycott-israel.

73. "Hendrik Mattheus (Henk) van Randwijk," Dodenakkers.nl, www.dodenakkers.nl/beroemd/algemeen/29-randwijk.html.

CHAPTER 6

1. Uri Yacobi Keller, "Academic Boycott of Israel and the Complicity of Israeli Academic Institutions in Occupation of Palestinian Territories," *The Economy of the Occupation: Socioeconomic Bulletin* 23 (October 2009), http://usacbi.files.wordpress.com/2009/11/economy_of_the_occupation_23-24.pdf.

2. See "International Law and Israel," Israel Law Resource Center, www.israellawresourcecenter.org/internationallaw/studyguides/sgil3i.htm.

3. See Ameera Ahmad and Ed Vulliamy, "In Gaza, the Schools Are Dying Too," *Guardian*, January 10, 2009, www.guardian.co.uk/world/2009/jan/10/gaza-schools; see also Riham Barghouti, "The Struggle for an Equal Right to Academic Freedom," archived at www.usacbi.org/2011/06/barghouti-struggle-equal-right/. These articles use the term "scholasticide" as an appropriate descriptor for what Palestinians daily confront.

4. "The AAUP Opposes Academic Boycotts," *Academe: Bulletin of the AAUP* 91, no. 4 (Jul/Aug2005), 57, www.aaup.org//AAUP/pubsres/academe/2006/SO/Boycott/onAcademicBoycotts.htm.

5. "On Academic Boycotts," *Academe: Bulletin of the AAUP* (September–October 2006):39-42, http://www.aaup.org/file/On-Academic-Boycotts_0.pdf.

6. Mohamed Abed, "In Defense of Academic Boycotts: A Response to Martha Nussbaum," *Dissent* 54, no. 4 (Fall 2007), available at http://usacbi.org/defending-boycotts/; Marcy Jane Knopf-Newman, "The Fallacy of Academic Freedom and the Academic Boycott of Israel," *CR: The New Centennial Review* 8, no. 2 (2008), 87–110; Judith Butler, "Israel/Palestine and the Paradoxes of Academic Freedom," *Radical Philosophy* 135 (January/February 2006), 10; Omar Barghouti and Lisa Taraki, "Academic Freedom in Context," *Al-Ahram Weekly*, no. 747 (June 2005), 16–22. http://weekly.ahram.org.eg/2005/747/op13.htm.

7. Butler, p. 16.

8. Giorgio Agamben, *State of Exception*, trans. Kevin Attell (Chicago: University of Chicago Press, 2005), 2.

9. "On Academic Boycotts," 40.

10. Jonathan Cook, "Israel Creates First Army-Owned University," *ZNet*, January 25, 2010. https://zcomm.org/znetarticle/israel-creates-first-army-owned-university-by-jonathan-cook/.

11. American Association of University Professors, "2008 Annual Meeting Resolutions," www.aaup.org/AAUP/about/anmtgs/2008resolutions.htm.

12. "Cary Nelson and Kenneth Stern Pen Open Letter on Anti-Semitism on Campus," American Association of University Professors, April 10, 2011, http://www.aaup.org/news/cary-nelson-and-kenneth-stern-pen-open-letter-campus-antisemitism.

13. "Telling the Truth in Difficult Times" *Academe: Bulletin of the AAUP* 93, no. 4 (July/August 2007), www.aaup.org/AAUP/pubsres/academe/2007/JA/AM/am.htm.

14.   "On Academic Boycotts," 42.

15.   Howard Zinn, "Academic Freedom: Collaboration and Resistance: The Twenty-Third T. B. Davie Memorial Lecture Delivered in the University of Cape Town on July 23, 1982," (University of Cape Town, 1982), 6.

CHAPTER 7

1.   Derek Gregory, *The Colonial Present* (New York: Wiley-Blackwell, 2004).

2.   For example, Howard Bliss, president of the Syrian Protestant College, remarked in 1919 that the natives "lack balance; they are easily discouraged; they lack political fairness, they do not easily recognize the limitations of their own rights," in Hisham Shirabi, *Neopatriarchy: A Theory of Distorted Change in Arab Society.* (Oxford: Oxford University Press, 1992), 78.

3.   See "American Universities in the Middle East: Agents of Change in the Arab World," Council on Foreign Relations, video, March 29, 2007, www.cfr.org/education/american-universities-middle -east-agents-change-arab-world/p12981.

4.   Ibid.

5.   See PACBI, "Israel's Exceptionalism: Normalizing the Abnormal," October 31, 2011, http://pacbi .org/etemplate.php?id=1749.

6.   Ibid.

7.   For the original petition by the AUB community see "#BDS: 'Not in Our Name': AUB Faculty, Staff, and Students Object to Honoring James Wolfensohn," *Youth against Normalization*, June 7, 2011, http://youthanormalization.blogspot.com/2011/06/bds-not-in-our-name-aub-faculty-staff .html?spref=tw.

8.   For details about the incident see Yazan al-Saadi, "Beirut Honors Friend of Israel, Again," *Al-Akhbar*, June 21, 2012, http://english.al-akhbar.com/content/beirut-honors-friend-israel-again.

9.   For a breakdown of Israeli academic institutional ties to the Israeli military see "The Case for Academic Boycott against Israel," *Alternative Information Center*, August 2007, http://palestinejournal .net/gaza/alternative-infromation-center_The_Case_for_Academic_Boycott_against_Israel.pdf.

10.   AUB provost, internal communication to the AUB community, March 10, 2010.

11.   See "On Academic Boycotts," *Academe: Bulletin of the AAUP* (September–October 2006), www. aaup.org/file/On-Academic-Boycotts_0.pdf, as well as articles by Barghouti, Mullen, and Malini and Lloyd in this volume.

12.   Judith Butler, "Israel/Palestine and the Paradoxes of Academic Freedom," *Radical Philosophy* 135 (January/February 2006): 8-17, www.egs.edu/faculty/judith-butler/articles/israel-palestine-paradoxes -of-academic-freedom/.

13.   See Council on Foreign Relations, "American Universities in the Middle East."

14.   For Dorman's commencement speech see Maha al Azar and Firas Talhouk, "Dorman to the Graduating Class of 2011: 'You Will Have a Voice in Shaping Tomorrow's Societies," American University of Beirut, June 27, 2011, www.aub.edu.lb/news/Pages/commencement-2011.aspx.

15.   See "Lebanese Boycott Law 1955" (in Arabic), Boycott Monitor, June 1, 2011, http://boycottmonitor .com/index.php?option=com_content&view=article&id=2&Itemid=8.

16.   Peter Dorman, internal communication to the AUB community, June 10, 2011.

17.   "Message from the President on James Wolfensohn," American University of Beirut, June 10, 2011, www.aub.edu.lb/news/Pages/wolfensohn.aspx.

18.   For details of AUB and CIA relations see Richard Harris Smith, *OSS: The Secret History of America's First Central Intelligence Agency* (Guilford, CT: Lyons Press, 2005).

19.   "Thank You, Mr. President, Al-Akhbar Will Remain at the Frontline!" *Al-Akhbar Arabic*, July 5, 2012, www.al-akhbar.com/node/97003.

20. Peter Dorman, "Message on Honorary Degrees Addressed to AUB Community," July 3, 2012.
21. "Thank You, Mr. President," *Al-Akhbar Arabic.*
22. See "AUB Joins Other Academic Institutions in Agreement to Foster US-Style Education Abroad," American University of Beirut, May 27, 2008, www.aub.edu.lb/news/Pages/83960.aspx.
23. See Usama Makdisi, *Artillery of Heaven: American Missionaries and the Failed Conversion of the Middle East* (Ithaca, NY: Cornell University Press, 2009).
24. See Butrus al-Bustani, *The Story of As'ad Shidyak* (Hamra Publishing House: Beirut, 1992), 213.
25. See Constantine Zurayk, "The University and Society," *International Association of Universities Newsletter* 6.1 (2000).
26. See Betty S. Anderson, "Liberal Education and the American University of Beirut," Middle East Institute, July 2010 (reposted February 23, 2012), www.mei.edu/content/liberal-education-and-american-university-beirut-aub.
27. Ibid.

CHAPTER 8

1. For example, Reut Institute, "Eroding Israel's Legitimacy in the International Arena," January 28, 2010, http://reut-institute.org/Publication.aspx?PublicationId=3766.
2. Amjad Barham, "Address to the UCU Congress by Amjad Barham, president of PFUUPE," Palestinian Campaign for the Academic and Cultural Boycott of Israel, posted June 2, 2009, http://pacbi.org/pacbi140812/?p=1026.
3. See USACBI, "Reports and Resources," www.usacbi.org/reports-and-resources/.
4. This and subsequent first-person quotes are from direct interviews by the author.

CHAPTER 9

1. Dara Lind, "Why There Wasn't Accountability for the Police in Ferguson," *Vox*, August 14, 2014, www.vox.com/2014/8/14/6002291/ferguson-police-st-louis-county-in-charge-jay-nixon-tear-gas-officer-fired.
2. *Rand Daily Mail*, November 23, 1961.
3. "On Academic Boycotts," *Academe: Bulletin of the AAUP* (September–October 2006):39-42, www.aaup.org/file/On-Academic-Boycotts_0.pdf.
4. Ibid.
5. Sasha Polakow-Suransky, *The Unspoken Alliance: Israel's Secret Relationship with Apartheid South Africa* (Johannesburg: Jacana Media, 2010), 119.
6. Bertram Lubner, a director of Plate Glass Holdings and the vice chairperson of Ben Gurion's board of governors.
7. University of Johannesburg, "UJ Sets Conditions for Link with Israeli University," www.uj.ac.za/EN/Newsroom/News/Pages/UJsetsconditionsforlinkwithIsraeliuniversity.aspx. See also the UJ Petition Committee, "The UJ-BGU Report," CharlotteKates.org, March 15, 2011, www.charlottekates.org/usacbi/wp/wp-content/uploads/2011/03/the-uj-bgu-report-15-march-20111.pdf.
8. Kerzner originally established his hotel and casino empire in South Africa's Bantustans and enjoyed close relations with collaborators such as Bophuthatswana's Mangope as well as successive Israeli leaders.
9. University of Johannesburg, "UJ Senate Votes on Ben Gurion Partnership," www.uj.ac.za/EN/Newsroom/News/Pages/UJSenatevotesonBenGurionpartnership.aspx.
10. See LifeSource at www.lifesource.ps; Palestinian Hydrology Group at www.phg.org; Palestinian Environmental NGO Network at www.pengon.org.

11. Amnesty International, *Thirsting for Justice: Palestinian Access to Water Restricted*, Demand Dignity Campaign Digest, Index MDE 15/028/2009, October 29, 2007, www.amnesty.org/en/documents/MDE15/028/2009/en/.

12. Ben Hartman, "University of Johannesburg Votes to Sever Ties with BGU," *Jerusalem Post*, March 24, 2011, www.jpost.com/International/University-of-Johannesburg-votes-to-sever-ties-with-BGU.

CHAPTER 10

1. For more information see: Institute for Middle East Understanding, "The Nakba, 65 Years of Dispossession and Apartheid," May 8, 2013, http://imeu.net/news/article0023923.shtml.

2. "Al-Kurd Family Home Take-Over (Sheikh Jarrah)," YouTube video, 2:10, posted by "dfedwing," December 1, 2009, www.youtube.com/watch?v=wlQf41CJjjc.

3. American Studies Association, "Reflections on the Annual Meeting, San Juan, Puerto Rico, November, 2012," March 15, 2013, www.theasa.net/from_the_editors/item/asa_members_vote_to_endorse_academic_boycott/.

4. "Demolition and Eviction of Bedouin Citizens of Israel in the Naqab (Negev)—The Prawer Plan," *Adalah*, www.adalah.org/en/content/view/7589.

5. For more information, go to www.bdsmovement.net.

6. "Open Letter to Trinity College President and Dean," *Jadaliyya*, January 2014, www.jadaliyya.com/pages/index/15772/open-letter-to-trinity-college-president-and-dean.

7. "Netanyahu's AIPAC Speech: The Full Transcript," *Haaretz*, March 4, 2014, www.haaretz.com/news/diplomacy-defense/1.577920.

8. http://civiccoalition-jerusalem.org/system/files/eviction_restitution_in_jerusaleme.pdf.

9. Ibid.

10. Ibid.

11. Meron Benvenisti, *West Bank Data Project: A Survey of Israel's Policies* (Washington, DC: American Enterprise Institute, 1984).

12. http://civiccoalition-jerusalem.org/system/files/eviction_restitution_in_jerusaleme.pdf.

13. Bill Van Esveld, *Separate and Unequal: Israel's Discriminatory Treatment of Palestinians in the Occupied Palestinian Territories* (New York: Human Rights Watch, 2010), www.hrw.org/sites/default/files/reports/iopt1210webwcover_0.pdf.

14. "Revocation of Residency in East Jerusalem," *B'Tselem*, updated August 18, 2013, http://www.btselem.org/jerusalem/revocation_of_residency.

15. "Statistics on Revocation of Residency in East Jerusalem," *B'Tselem*, updated August 7, 2013, www.btselem.org/jerusalem/revocation_statistics.

16. Ibid.

17. "Revocation of Residency in East Jerusalem," August 18, 2013.

18. Jerusalem Municipality, "Local Outline Plan Jerusalem 2000—Report No. 4: The Proposed Plan and the Main Planning Policies," August 2004, http://pcc-jer.org/arabic/Publication/jerusalem_master_plan/engchapt/Intro.pdf.

19. Van Esveld, "Separate and Unequal."

20. Ibid.

21. Ibid.

22. Ibid.

23. Dror Etkes and Lara Friedman, "Settlers vs Palestinians: Double Standards and Illegal Construction," *Settlements in Focus* 2, no. 4 (2006), http://archive.peacenow.org/entries/archive2292#more.

24. "Discrimination in Planning, Building, and Land Expropriation," *B'Tselem,* January 1, 2011, www.btselem.org/jerusalem/discriminating_policy.

25. UN Conference on Trade and Development, *The Palestinian Economy in East Jerusalem: Enduring Annexation, Isolation and Disintegration* (New York and Geneva: UNCTAD, 2013), http://unispal .un.org/pdfs/UNCTADGDSAPP20121.pdf.

26. David Hughes, Nathan Derejko, Alaa Mahajna, *Dispossession and Eviction in Jerusalem: The Cases and Stories of Sheikh Jarrah* (Jerusalem: Civic Coalition for Defending Palestinian Rights in Jerusalem, December 2009), http://adalah.org/newsletter/eng/feb10/docs/Sheikh_Jarrah_Report-Final.pdf.

27. Ibid.

28. Ibid.

29. United Nations, Security Council Resolution 476 (1980), June 30, 1980, http://unispal.un.org/ UNISPAL.NSF/0/6DE6DA8A650B4C3B852560DF00663826.

30. Hughes, Derejko, and Mahajna, "Dispossession and Eviction in Jerusalem."

31. Ibid.

32. United Nations, Security Council Resolution 476.

33. Khaled Elgindy, "Original Sin: How the Oslo Accords Enabled Original Settlement Growth," *Muftah,* August 2, 2010, http://muftah.org/original-sin-how-the-oslo-accords-enabled-continued -settlement-growth-by-khaled-elgindy/.

34. Colum Lynch, "U.S. Vetoes Security Council Resolution Denouncing Israeli Settlements," *Washington Post,* February 18, 2011, www.washingtonpost.com/wp-dyn/content/article/2011/02/18 /AR2011021805442.html.

35. Aaron David Miller, "Israel's Lawyer," *Washington Post,* May 23, 2005, www.washingtonpost.com /wp-dyn/content/article/2005/05/22/AR2005052200883.html.

36. Ethan Bronner, "As Biden Visits Israel Unveils Plans for New Settlements," *The New York Times,* March 9, 2010, www.nytimes.com/2010/03/10/world/middleeast/10biden.html?_r=0.

37. Jennifer Rubin, "Contentions RE: A New Low," *Commentary,* March 13, 2010, www.commen-tarymagazine.com/2010/03/13/re-a-new-low/.

38. "Pence: America Stands with Israel," YouTube video, 1:16, March 23, 2010, www.youtube.com /watch?v=bkvmdFV5izE.

39. International Court of Justice, "Legal Consequences of the Construction of a Wall in the Occupied Palestinian Territory," press release, July 9, 2004, www.icj-cij.org/docket/index.php ?pr=71&code=mwp&p1=3&p2=4&p3=6.

40. Silvia Boarini, "Apartheid Wall: 10 Years of Existence," *Al Haq,* June 12, 2012, www.alhaq.org /10yrs/openions-expert-org/expert-opinion/651-apartheid-wall-10-years-of-existence.

41. "Legal Consequences of the Construction of a Wall in the Occupied Palestinian Territory."

42. Gerhard Peters and John Wooley, "George W. Bush: Press Gaggle by Scott McClellan, July 9, 2004," *The American Presidency Project,* www.presidency.ucsb.edu/ws/?pid=66024.

43. "Palestinian Civil Society Call for BDS," *BDS Movement,* July 9, 2005, www.bdsmovement.net/call.

44. Barak Ravid, "Denmark's Largest Bank Blacklists Israel Hapoalim over Settlement Construction," *Haaretz,* February 1, 2014, www.haaretz.com/news/diplomacy-defense/1.571849.

45. Ravid, *Haaretz,* February 1, 2014.

46. Joseph Dana, "South African University to End Relationship with Ben Gurion University," *+972,* March 23, 2011, 972mag.com/south-african-university-to-divest-from-ben-gurion-univeristy/ 12447/. See also chapter 9 of this volume.

47. Naomi Klein, "Israel: Boycott, Divest, Sanction," *Naomi Klein* (blog), January 8, 2009, www. naomiklein.org/articles/2009/01/israel-boycott-divest-sanction.

48. Adam Horowitz, "Costello Cancels Israel Concerts: Sometimes It's 'Impossible to Simply Look the

Other Way,'" *Mondoweiss*, May 17, 2010, http://mondoweiss.net/2010/05/elvis-costello-cancels -israel-concerts-sometimes-its-impossible-to-simply-look-the-other-way.html.

49.   Hillary Rose and Steven Rose, "Stephen Hawking's Boycott Hits Israel Where It Hurts: Sci-' ence," *Guardian*, May 13, 2013, www.theguardian.com/science/political-science/2013/may/13 /stephen-hawking-boycott-israel-science.

50.   "Filmmaker Ken Loach Joins the Cultural Boycott of Israel," *Electronic Intifada*, August 24, 2006, http://electronicintifada.net/content/filmmaker-ken-loach-joins-cultural-boycott-israel/622.

51.   Elizabeth Redden, "A First for the Israel Boycott?," *Inside Higher Ed*, April 24, 2013, www.in-sidehighered.com/news/2013/04/24/asian-american-studies-association-endorses-boycott-israe-li-universities.

52.   "Native American Studies Group Joins Israel Boycott," *Inside Higher Ed*, December 18, 2013, www.insidehighered.com/quicktakes/2013/12/18/native-american-studies-group-joins-israel -boycott.

53.   American Studies Association, "Reflections on the Annual Meeting, San Juan, Puerto Rico, No-vember, 2012," March 15, 2013, www.theasa.net/from_the_editors/item/asa_members_vote_to _endorse_academic_boycott/.

54.   For more examples see *BDS Movement*, www.bdsmovement.net/category/news.

55.   Peter Beinart, "The Real Problem with the American Studies Associations' Boycott of Israel," *Dai-ly Beast*, December 17, 2013, www.thedailybeast.com/articles/2013/12/17/the-american-studies -association-is-really-boycotting-israel-s-existence.html.

56.   Ibid.

57.   Absentees' Property Law, Israel: Law No. 5710-1950, March 14, 1950, http://unispal.un.org /UNISPAL.NSF/0/E0B719E95E3B494885256F9A005AB90A.

58.   Rebecca Manski, "Blueprint Negev," *Mondoweiss*, November 9, 2010, http://mondoweiss.net /2010/11/blueprint-negev.

59. Cary Nelson, "Why the ASA Boycott Is Both Disingenuous and Futile," *Al Jazeera America*, Decem-ber 23, 2013, http://america.aljazeera.com/opinions/2013/12/asa-boycott-israelhighereducation .html.

60.   Phan Ngyuen, "Cary Nelson, the AAUP, and the Privilege of Bestowing Academic Freedom," *Mon-doweiss*, January 17, 2014, http://mondoweiss.net/2014/01/privilege-bestowing-academic.html.

61.   Hannah Arendt, *Imperialism: Part Two of the Origins of Totalitarianism* (New York: Harcourt Brace Jovanovich, 1968), 176.

CHAPTER 11

1.   Ilan Pappé, "Zionism as Colonialism: A Comparative View of Diluted Colonialism in Asia and Africa," *South Atlantic Quarterly* 107, no. 4 (2008): 611–33.

2.   See Gabriel Piterberg, *The Returns of Zionism: Myths, Politics and Scholarship in Israel* (New York: Verso, 2009).

3.   Ilan Pappé, "Ingathering," *London Review of Books*, April 20, 2006, 15.

CHAPTER 12

1.   "On Academic Boycotts," *Academe: Bulletin of the AAUP* (September–October 2006):39-42, www.aaup.org/file/On-Academic-Boycotts_0.pdf

2.   David Remmick, "The One-State Reality," *New Yorker*, November 17, 2014. http://archives .newyorker.com/?iid=106231&startpage=page0000008#folio=006.

CHAPTER 13

1. Rabab Abdulhadi, "Living under Occupation," *Against the Current*(July/Aug 2012), https://solidarity-us.org/pdfs/ATC%20159--Rabab.pdf.
2. "About AMCHA," AMCHA Initiative, www.amchainitiative.org/about/.
3. AMCHA Initiative, "8 Groups to CA Controller: Audit SFSU-Funded Terrorist Meetings," press release, www.amchainitiative.org/sfsu-defends-taxpayer-funded-pro-terror-trips-by-professors.
4. Sheldon Adelson is the casino mogul who claimed to be spending $100 million in 2012 supporting Mitt Romney and who forced New Jersey Governor Christie to apologize for calling the West Bank "occupied territories."
5. For information on the Reut Institute's efforts at suppressing critical dissent in Israel, see, for example, "Breaking: Israeli Knesset Plenum Votes to Investigate Human Rights Groups," http://muzzlewatch.com/category/reut-institute/.
6. "Allegations of Improper Faculty Travel Investigated; No Merit Found," *SF State News*, June 24, 2014, http://news.sfsu.edu/news/allegations-improper-faculty-travel-investigated-no-merit-found.
7. "Enough Is Enough," Facebook search, https://www.facebook.com/search/str/enough is enough Abdulhadi/keywords_top, accessed May 12, 2015; Kenneth Monteiro, e-mail communication to Rabab Abdulhadi, November 20, 2013.
8. See https://diva.sfsu.edu/browse/collections/collection-5.
9. Selma James and Sara Kershnar, "A New War on Speech," *Jacobin*, April 24, 2014, www.jacobinmag.com/2014/04/a-new-war-on-speech/.
10. Sherry Gorelick, "Right-Wing Group's New Vendetta: Demonizing California Professor Critical of Israel," *Mondoweiss*, May 15, 2014, http://mondoweiss.net/2014/05/demonizing-california-professor.html.
11. International Jewish Anti-Zionist Network, "Jewish Community Letter in Support of Prof. Rabab Abdulhadi," July 1, 2014, http://ijsn.net/campus/jewish-community-letter-in-support-of-prof-rabab-abdulhadi/.
12. See Patrick Strickland, "Israeli Forces Rearrest Hunger Striker Samer Issawi," *Electronic Intifada*, http://electronicintifada.net/blogs/patrick-strickland/israeli-forces-rearrest-hunger-striker-samer-issawi.
13. The decision to divest was based on these companies' involvement in the brutal practices of the Israeli occupation.
14. "Bodies of Missing Settlers Found in West Bank," *Al Jazeera*, June 30, 2014, www.aljazeera.com/news/middleeast/2014/06/report-israel-finds-three-bodies-hebron-2014630162857704850.html.
15. An-Najah National University is located in Nablus, Palestine.
16. See Tammi Rossman Benjamin, "Identity Politics, the Pursuit of Social Justice, and the Rise of Campus Antisemitism: A Case Study," in *Resurgent Antisemitism: A Global Perspective*, ed. Alvin H. Rosenfeld (Bloomington, IN: Indiana University Press, 2013), www.amchainitiative.org/wp-content/uploads/2013/08/Chapter-18-manuscript.pdf.
17. Joanne Barker blogged at Tequila Sovereign but has since taken down her blog.
18. In demanding that we develop a proposal for an MOU that was already signed by their counterparts at An-Najah National University in Palestine, SFSU was probably seeking to shield itself from future Zionist attacks that would threaten the funding the university receives from Zionist donors. Thus the university would achieve collaboration in an area of the world in which it had no connections whatsoever and at the same time demonstrate that the collaboration emerged out of faculty interest and that it was thoroughly vetted by the bureaucratic channels.
19. Actually Palestinian student activism on campus has been subjected to concerted Zionist efforts throughout the 1980s, 1990s, and 2000s and especially post-9/11/2001. But the specific target-

ing has escalated with the emergence of AMED in 2007 and the mounting of the Palestinian cultural mural honoring the late Palestinian professor Edward Said in the same year. This is primarily because the creation of AMED and the mounting of the mural are threatening to the Zionist movement on an institutional level, and are much harder to eliminate than driving one faculty member out of the university.

CHAPTER 14

1. For more on BDS, see "Tags, BDS," *Electronic Intifada*, http://electronicintifada.net/tags/bds.
2. For more on USACBI, see "Endorse Our Call to Boycott," US Campaign for the Academic and Cultural Boycott of Israel, http://www.usacbi.org/about/.
3. For more on SJP, see "Tags, Students for Justice in Palestine," *Electronic Intifada*, http://electronicintifada.net/tags/students-justice-palestine.
4. Mike Coogan,"US States Should Act Against Israel's Denial of Entry to Americans," *Electronic Intifada*, April 30, 2014, http://electronicintifada.net/content/us-states-should-act-against-israels-denial-entry-americans/13356.

CHAPTER 16

1. Ali Abunimah, "Israel Lobby Launches Fierce Counterattack against American Studies Association," *Electronic Intifada*, December 22, 2013, http://electronicintifada.net/blogs/ali-abunimah/israel-lobby-launches-fierce-counterattack-against-american-studies-association.
2. Cary Nelson, "The Problem with Judith Butler: The Philosophy of the Movement to Boycott Israel," in *The Case Against Academic Boycotts of Israel*, ed. Cary Nelson and Gabriel Brahm (Chicago: MLA Members for Scholars' Rights, 2015).
3. Ibid., emphasis added.
4. Ibid.
5. See, for example, Protect Academic Freedom Act, United States House of Representatives, H.R. 4009, February 6, 2014.
6. William A. Jacobson, "University Statements Rejecting Academic Boycott of Israel," *Legal Insurrection*, December 22, 2013, http://legalinsurrection.com/2013/12/indiana-wash-u-st-louis-gwu-northwestern-cornell-reject-academic-boycott-of-israel/.
7. Katherine Flynn, "Shackling the Scholar: Israel's Administrative Detention of Palestinian Students," *Mondoweiss*, May 28, 2013, http://mondoweiss.net/2013/05/administrative-detention-palestinian.
8. Ruth Eglash, "Israel Withholds Tax Revenue from Palestinian Authority as Dispute Escalates," *Washington Post*, January 3, 2015, www.washingtonpost.com/world/middle_east/israel-withholds-tax-revenues-from-palestinian-authority-as-dispute-escalates/2015/01/03/3718e5c4-9378-11e4-a66f-0ca5037a597d_story.html.
9. Cary Nelson, "Defining Academic Freedom," *Inside Higher Ed*, December 21, 2010. www.insidehighered.com/views/2010/12/21/nelson_on_academic_freedom.
10. "PACBI Guidelines for the International Academic Boycott of Israel," Palestinian Campaign for the Academic and Cultural Boycott of Israel, revised July 2014, http://www.pacbi.org/etemplate.php?id=1108.
11. Martha Nussbaum, "Against Academic Boycotts," in Nelson and Brahm, *Case against Academic Boycotts of Israel*; "PACBI Guidelines for the International Academic Boycott of Israel."
12. Stanley Fish, *Versions of Academic Freedom* (Chicago: University of Chicago Press, 2014), Kindle edition.

13. Ibid.

14. Ibid.

15. Cornelius v. NAACP Legal Defense and Educational Fund, Inc., 473 U.S. 788, 799–800 (1985): "Even protected speech is not equally permissible in all places and at all times."

16. State of New York, Bill S6438-2013, "An Act Prohibiting the Use of State Aid by Colleges and Universities for Certain Academic Institutions," January 23, 2014.

17. AAUP, Brief of Amici Curiae in Support of Plaintiffs in SAME et al., v. Donald Rumsfeld, Civil Action No. 3:03CV01867, 13 (emphasis in original); citing Boy Scouts of America v. Dale, 530 U.S. 640, 655 (2000).

18. Rima Kapitan, "Academic Freedom Encompasses the Right to Boycott," *Journal of Academic Freedom* 4 (2013).

19. "On Academic Boycotts," *Academe: Bulletin of the AAUP* (September–October 2006): 40, http://www.aaup.org/file/On-Academic-Boycotts_0.pdf.

20. "Cincinnati State Faculty Strike," AAUP Updates, American Association of University Professors, September 29, 2011, www.aaup.org/news/cincinnati-state-faculty-strike.

21. Bryan G. Pfeifer, "Faculty Strike at Detroit-Area University, Protesting Cuts Amid Surplus," *Labor Notes*, September 8, 2009, www.labornotes.org/node/2414.

22. Audrey Williams June, "Faculty Strike Shuts Down Michigan's Oakland U," *The Chronicle of Higher Education*, September 3, 2009, http://chronicle.com/article/Faculty-Strike-Shuts-Down/48286/.

23. "The AAUP Stands with the Chicago Teachers Union," AAUP Updates, American Association of University Professors, September 7, 2012, www.aaup.org/news/aaup-stands-chicago-teachers-union.

24. Ibid.

25. "On Academic Boycotts," 42.

26. Judith Butler, "Academic Freedom and the ASA's Boycott of Israel: A Response to Michelle Goldberg," *Nation*, December 8, 2013, www.thenation.com/article/177512/academic-freedom-and-asas-boycott-israel-response-michelle-goldberg.

27. Donna Euben, Ann Springer and David Rabban, Robert Post, "Brief for Amicus Curiae the American Association of University Professors in Support of Respondents," Rumsfeld v. Forum for Academic and Institutional Rights (September 21, 2005); citing Regents of Univ. of Mich. v. Ewing, 474 U.S. 214, 226 & n.12 (1985).

28. AAUP Committee A on Academic Freedom & Tenure, "An Open Letter from the AAUP to the Yale Community," American Association of University Professors, www.aaup.org/news/2012/open-letter-aaup-yale-community.

29. Ibid.

CHAPTER 17

1. This essay is a synthesis of two articles I've written—one about education under occupation following my 2013 trip to Palestine, and another about R2E students' encounters with St. Louis activists in November 2014: Kristian Davis Bailey, "Challenging Bullets, Not Boycotts: Education Under Occupation in Palestine," *Truthout*, May 14, 2014, http://www.truth-out.org/news/item/23684-challenging-bullets-not-boycotts-education-under-occupation-in-palestine; and Kristian Davis Bailey, "Building Unity, Wrecking Walls: Palestinians Come to Ferguson," *Ebony.com*, November 14, 2014, www.ebony.com/news-views/building-unity-wrecking-walls-palestinians-come-to-ferguson-032.

2. Ma'an News Agency, "Israeli Forces Clash with al-Quds University Students," September 8, 2013,

www.maannews.com/Content.aspx?id=627920.

3.   WAFA News Agency, "Al-Quds University Shuts Down Campus Following Israeli Raid," October 22, 2013, http://english.wafa.ps/index.php?action-detail?id=23455.

4.   Ma'an News Agency, "Israeli Forces Raid Abu Dis and Attack al-Quds University, Injuring 40," November 17, 2013, www.maannews.com/Content.aspx?id=648111.

5.   Ariel Kaminer, "Assembly Withdraws Bill to Limit Anti-Israel Boycotts," *New York Times*, February 4, 2014, www.nytimes.com/2014/02/05/nyregion/assembly-withdraws-bill-to-limit -anti-israel-boycotts.html?_r=2; Rebecca Shimoni Stoil, "Illinois Congressmen Submit Anti-Boycott Bill," *Times of Israel*, February 7, 2014, www.timesofisrael.com/illinois-congressmen-submit -anti-boycott-bill/; *Baltimore Sun*, "A Chilling Effect," editorial, March 10, 2014, http://articles .baltimoresun.com/2014-03-10/news/bs-ed-israel-boycotts," *Washington Free Beacon*, February 6, 2014, http://freebeacon.com/national-security/house-bill-would-cut-funding-to-backers-of-israeli -boycotts/.

6.   Association of American Universities, "AAU Statement on Boycott of Israeli Universities," press release, December 20, 2013, www.aau.edu/WorkArea/DownloadAsset.aspx?id=14859.

7.   "Tags, Closure of Education Institutions," Right to Education Campaign, Birzeit University, http://right2edu.birzeit.edu.closure-of-eductation-institutions/.

8.   Birzeit University, *Annual Report 2011–2012* (Birzeit, Palestine: Birzeit University Public Relations Office, 2012), http://birzeit.edu/sites/default/files/annual_report/en/annual_report_2011 _2012_en.pdf.

9.   World Bank, "Palestinians Access to Area C Key to Economic Recovery and Sustainable Growth," press release, October 8, 2013, www.worldbank.org/en/news/press-release/2013/10/07/palestinians -access-area-c-economic-recovery-sustainable-growth.

10. State of Palestine, Palestinian Central Bureau of Statistics, "The Labour Force Survey Results First Quarter (January-March)," May 16, 2013, www.pcbs.gov.ps/site/512/default.aspx?tabID =512&lang=en&ItemID=790&mid=3172&wversion=Staging.

11. Joel Greenberg, "Israel to Release Withheld Tax Funds to Palestinians," *Washington Post*, November 30, 2011, www.washingtonpost.com/world/middle_east/israel-to-release-held-tax-funds-to -palestinians/2011/11/30/gIQAqPDdCO_story.html.

12. "Student Strike at Birzeit University Continues," *Alternative News*, July 23, 2013, http://www. alternativenews.org/english/index.php/features/updates/7023-student-strike-birzeit-university -continues.

13. Khalid Amaryeh, "Cash Crunch Cripples Palestinian Colleges," *Al Jazeera*, October 28, 2013, www.aljazeera.com/indepth/features/2013/10/cash-crunch-cripples-palestinian-colleges -20131026112250999517.html?utm=from_old_mobile.

14. Right to Enter, "Academia Undermined: Israeli Restrictions on Foreign National Academics in Palestinian Higher Education Institutions," May 2013, www.righttoenter.ps/wp-content/up-loads/2013/11/EducationReportAcademiaUnderminedMay2013.pdf.

15. Tovah Lazaroff, "Deputy Foreign Minister: Jordan Valley Must Be under Israeli Sovereignty," *Jerusalem Post*, January 2, 2014, www.jpost.com/Diplomacy-and-Politics/Likud-hawks-warn -Netanyahu-against-suicidal-concessions-to-Palestinians-336852.

16. Noga Kadman, *Acting the Landlord: Israel's Policy in Area C, the West Bank* (Jerusalem: B'Tselem, July 2013), www.btselem.org/publications/summaries/201306_acting_the_landlord.

17. "Bedouins Around Ma'ale Adumiim," *B'Tselem*, November 16, 2013, updated May 18, 2014, www.btselem.org/area_c/maale_adumim_bedouins; J. K. D'Amours, "From a Life in the Open Spaces to Shacks and Sardine Tins," *Jews for Justice for Palestinians*, May 1, 2013, http://jfjfp. com/?p=42767.

18. See Lajee Center, www.lajee.org/.

19. According to Nablus residents, the Israeli military utilized this space to operate tanks against Old Askar and New Askar during the Second Intifada. This created an effective "no man's land" and cut off any access to school students might have had during the fighting.

20. Naseej, Nablus Association for Social & Community Development, Facebook page, www.facebook.com/Naseej.Nablus/info#!/Naseej.Nablus/info?tab=page_info.

21. See Youth Against Settlements, www.youthagainstsettlements.org/.

22. Lisa Goldstein, "Israel's Most Liberal City Introduces Racially Segregated Kindergartens," *Daily Beast*, August 23, 2013, www.thedailybeast.com/articles/2013/08/23/the-banality-of-racism-in-israel-s-most-liberal-city.html#.

23. Noam Sheizaf, "Day 2 of African Asylum Seeker Protest:What Do They Want?" *+972*, January 6, 2014, http://972mag.com/day-2-of-african-asylum-seeker-protest-what-do-they-want/85092/.

24. Amira Hass, "High Court Rejects Gaza Students' Petition to Study in West Bank," *Haaretz*, September 27, 2012, www.haaretz.com/news/national/high-court-rejects-gaza-students-petition-to-study-in-west-bank-1.466867#!.

25. Ibid.

26. Mohammed Suliman, "Gaza Students Prepare for Finals without Electricity," *Al-Monitor*, June 21, 2013, www.al-monitor.com/pulse/originals/2013/06/gaza-finals-exams-electricity-cuts.html.

27. "Mind-Blowing: Four Months after Conflict, Gaza Mental Health in Crisis," UN Relief and Works Agency for Palestine Refugees in the Near East, March 11, 2013, www.unrwa.org/newsroom/features/mind-blowing-four-months-after-conflict-gaza-mental-health-crisis.

28. Amnesty International, "Syria: Squeezing the Life out of Yarmouk: War Crimes against Besieged Civilians," March 10, 2014, www.amnesty.org/en/documents/MDE24/008/2014/en/.

29. Allison Deger, "Six Palestinians Killed in 24 Hours by Israeli Forces," *Mondoweiss*, March 11, 2014, http://mondoweiss.net/2014/03/palestinians-israeli-forces.

30. Assata Shakur, "To My People," It's About Time BPP Legacy and Alumni, www.itsabouttimebpp.com/women_bpp/TO_MY_PEOPLE_By_ASSATA_SHAKUR.html.

CHAPTER 19

1. Albert Einstein, Hannah Arendt, Sidney Hook, et al, "New Palestine Party: Visit of Menachem Begin and Aims of Political Movement Discussed," *New York Times*, letter to the editor, December 4, 1948. archive.org/details/AlbertEinsteinLetterToTheNewYorkTimes.December41948.

2. See PACBI, "Israel's Exceptionalism: Normalizing the Abnormal," October 31, 2011, http://pacbi.org/etemplate.php?id=1749.

3. Ibid.

4. "On BDS Bashers and Their Search for Fig Leaves," Palestinian Campaign for the Academic and Cultural Boycott of Israel, June 29, 2011, http://www.pacbi.org/etemplate.php?id=1645.

5. "Israel's Exceptionalism," October 31, 2011.

6. Ibid.

7. Ibid.

CHAPTER 20

1. Richard Falk and Howard Friel, *Israel-Palestine on Record: How the* New York Times *Misreports Conflict in the Middle East* (New York: Verso, 2007).

2. Alex Kane, "Bill Targeting Academic Groups that Boycott Israel Halted in New York Assembly, " Mondoweiss, February 4, 2014, http://mondoweiss.net/2014/02/targeting-academic-assembly.

3. The first significant step in taboo-breaking was the publication of John J. Mearsheimer and Stephen M. Walt, "The Israel Lobby," *London Review of Books* 28, no. 6 (March 23, 2006):3-12.

4. Lidar Gravé-Lazi, "Israeli University Heads Establish Forum to Counter Academic Boycotts," Jerusalem Post, August 7, 2014.

5. Paul Duffill and Gabriella Skoff, "Growing Jewish Support for Boycott and the Changing Landscape of the BDS Debate," Mondoweiss, June 17, 2014, http://mondoweiss.net/2014/06/boycott-changing-landscape#sthash.GDTGqaJq.dpuf.

6. "Growing Support for Labor for Palestine Statement," Labor for Palestine, http://laborforpalestine .net/2014/08/05/growing-support-for-labor-for-palestine-statement-stop-the-war-on-gaza-no -arms-for-apartheid-israel-boycott-divestment-and-sanctions/.

7. Michael Ellman and Smain Laacher, *Migrant Labor in Israel: A Contemporary Form of Slavery* (Copenhagen/Paris: International Federation for Human Rights and the Euro-Mediterranean Human Rights Network, 2003).

8. Dan Izenberg and Gil Hoffman, "Settlements Control 42% of West Bank," *Jerusalem Post*, June 7, 2010, www.jpost.com/International/Settlements-control-42-percent-of-West-Bank.

CHAPTER 21

1. "Pinkwashing" refers to a deliberate strategy to distract from the crimes committed against Palestinians by promoting an image of Israel as progressive and modern on the topic of LGBT rights.

2. Jacob Pace, "Ethnic Cleansing 101: The Case of Lifta Village," *Electronic Intifada*, March 2, 2005, http://electronicintifada.net/content/ethnic-cleansing-101-case-lifta-village/5493.

3. Noam Sheizaf, "Conviction Rate for Palestinians in Israel's Military Courts: 99.74%," +*972mag*, http://972mag.com/conviction-rate-for-palestinians-in-israels-military-courts-99-74-percent /28579/.

4. Nadine Naber, "Justice for Rasmea Odeh," Middle East Research and Information Program, June 19, 2014, www.merip.org/justice-rasmea-odeh.

5. Interview with Michel Shehadeh by Joan Mandell, 'Is This Case for Real?" *Middle East Report* 202 (Winter 1996): 42; Michel Shehadeh, "A Never-Ending Saga: The Case of The Los Angeles Eight," *Washington Report on Middle East Affairs* (April–May 1997):33; Jeanne A. Butterfield, "Do Immigrants Have First Amendment Rights? Revisiting the Los Angeles Eight Case," *Middle East Report* 212 (Autumn 1999): 4–6.

6. Ali Abunimah, "Climate of Fear Silencing Palestinian, Muslim Students at University of California, Rights Groups Warn," *Electronic Intifada*, December 4, 2012, http://electronicintifada. net/blogs/ali-abunimah/climate-fear-silencing-palestinian-muslim-students-university-california-rights; Center for Constitutional Rights, "In Appeal of 'Irvine 11' Convictions, CCR, JVP Submit Amicus Brief Highlighting Prospect of Discriminatory Prosecution against Muslim Students Who Spoke Out for Palestinian Human Rights," Palestinian Solidarity Legal Support, October 10, 2013, http://palestinelegalsupport.org/2013/10/10/in-appeal-of-irvine -11-convictions-ccr-jvp-submit-amicus-brief-highlighting-prospect-of-discriminatory-prosecution-against-muslim-students-who-spoke-out-for-palestinian-human-right/.

7. Ali Abunimah, "Victory: Palestinian-American Muhammad Salah removed from US 'Terrorist List,' after Law Suit Challenge," *Electronic Intifada*, November 6, 2012, http://electronicintifada .net/blogs/ali-abunimah/victory-palestinian-american-muhammad-salah-removed-us-terrorist -list-after.

8. See Ahmed Rehab, "The Muhammad Salah Bottomline," February 1, 2007, *Electronic Intifada*, http://electronicintifada.net/content/muhammad-salah-bottomline/6732.
    See also Michael Deutsch and Erica Thompson, "Secrets and Lies: The Persecution of Muham-

mad Salah," *Journey of Palestine Studies* 38, no. 1 (Autumn 2008).

9.   Nadine Naber, "Organizing after the Rasmea Odeh Verdict," *Jacobin*, January 14, 2015, https://www.jacobinmag.com/2015/01/rasmea-odeh-verdict-organizing/.

10. Ibid.

11. See Michael Deutsch, "The Grand Jury and the Persecution of Dr. Abdelhaleem Ashqar," *Electronic Intifada*, January 13, 2008, http://electronicintifada.net/content/grand-jury-and-persecution-dr-abdelhaleem-ashqar/7296.

12. Ali Abunimah, "US Says Rallies outside Rasmea Odeh Hearings May Be 'Criminal,'" *Electronic Intifada*, October 6, 2014, http://electronicintifada.net/blogs/ali-abunimah/us-says-rallies-outside-rasmea-odeh-hearings-may-be-criminal; see also United States District Court, Eastern District of Michigan, Southern Division, "Motion of the United States to Empanel an Anonymous Jury and to Take Other Measures Necessary to Ensure an Untainted Jury," October 3, 2014, uspcn.ipower.com/wp/wp/wp-content/uploads/2014/10/government-filing-on-jury-tampering-10-3-14.pdf.

13. Charlotte Silver, "Dozens Travel to Detroit to Support Rasmea Odeh as Trial Begins," *Electronic Intifada*, November 5, 2014, http://electronicintifada.net/blogs/charlotte-silver/dozens-travel-detroit-support-rasmea-odeh-trial-begins.

14. US Palestinian Community Network, "All Out for Detroit: Rasmea's Pre-Trial Hearing," October 18, 2014, press release, http://uspcn.org/2014/10/18/october-21-all-out-for-detroit-rasmeas-pre-trial-hearing/.

15. Allison Deger, "Holy Land Five Appeal Could Set Precedent on Using 'Secret Evidence' in US Courts," *Mondoweiss*, October 28, 2012, http://mondoweiss.net/2012/10/holy-land-five-appeal-could-set-precedent-on-using-secret-evidence-in-u-s-courts.

16. Nadine Naber, "Organizing after the Rasmea Odeh Verdict."

17. Ibid.

18. Rania Khalek, "Israeli-Trained Police 'Occupy' Missouri after Killing of Black Youth," *Electronic Intifada*, September 15, 2014, http://electronicintifada.net/blogs/rania-khalek/israel-trained-police-occupy-missouri-after-killing-black-youth.

CHAPTER 22

1.   S. Res. 498 (13th): A Resolution Expressing the Sense of the Senate Regarding US Support for the State of Israel as It Defends Itself from Rocket Attacks by the Hamas Terrorist Organization, agreed to July 17, 2014, www.govtrack.us/congress/bills/113/sres498.

2.   Ramsey Cox, "Senate Passes Resolution Supporting Israel," *The Hill*, July 29, 2014, http://thehill.com/blogs/floor-action/senate/213746-senate-passes-resolution-supporting-israel.

3.   Aaron Blake, "Young Americans Take a Dim View of Israel's Actions," *Washington Post*, July 29, 2014, www.washingtonpost.com/blogs/the-fix/wp/2014/07/29/young-americans-take-a-dim-view-of-israels-actions/?Post+generic=?tid=sm_twitter_washingtonpost; Pew Research Center, "Hamas Seen as More to Blame Than Israel for Current Violence," July 28, 2014.

4.   Sam Sokol, "We Are Looking at the Beginnings of a Holocaust," *Jerusalem Post*, July 28, 2014, www.jpost.com/Jewish-World/Jewish-News/We-are-looking-at-the-beginnings-of-a-Holocaust-369165.

5.   Sarah Kenzdior, "The Telegenically Dead: Why Israel and Its Supporters Fear Gaza's Dead," *Al Jazeera*, August 14, 2014, www.aljazeera.com/indepth/opinion/2014/08/telegenically-dead-201481182312870982.html.

6.   The World Stands with Palestine, http://theworldstandswithpalestine.tumblr.com/. rwa.org/newsroom/official-statements/unrwa-strongly-condemns-israeli-shelling-its-school-gaza-serious#.U9j4_QWqqZ8.facebook.

7.   "What Is BDS?" *BDS Movement*, www.bdsmovement.net/.

8. "Israel-Palestine: This is How It Ends," *Avaaz*, https://secure.avaaz.org/en/israel_palestine_this_is _how_it_ends_loc/?slideshow.

9. "Statements," *BDS Movement*, www.bdsmovement.net/activecamps/stu.

CHAPTER 23

1. Tithi Bhattacharya and Bill V. Mullen, "Why Is the American Elite Scared of BDS?" *Mondoweiss*, February 7, 2014, http://mondoweiss.net/2014/02/american-elite-scared.

2. Christine Des Garennes, "Wise Expects to Stay on Nike Board," *News-Gazette* (Champaign), September 17, 2012, www.news-gazette.com/news/local/2012-09-17/wise-expects-stay-nike-board .html.

3. Ibid.

4. "Delta Galil Industries," *Who Profits from the Occupation*, www.whoprofits.org/company/delta -galil-industries.

5. Bay Area Campaign to End Israeli Apartheid, "Top Ten Brands to Boycott," November 17, 2009, www.baceia.org/2009/11/top-ten-brands-to-boycott/.

6. "Illinois Opposes Boycott of Israeli Academic Institutions," University of Illinois, December 27, 2013, http://illinois.edu/lb/article/1303/80478.

7. David Palumbo-Liu, "Is Criticizing Israel Worse Than Murder in Illinois?" *Electronic Intifada*, August 25, 2014, http://electronicintifada.net/content/criticizing-israel-worse-murder-university -illinois/13801.

8. Lynne Marek, ""Ariel Investments Logs Best Year Ever, Reversing Painful Losing Streak," *Crain's*, May 15, 2010, www.chicagobusiness.com/article/20100515/ISSUE01/100033389/ariel-investments -logs-best-year-ever-reversing-painful-losing-streak.

9. Ibid.

10. Pfizer Inc., "CliniWorks Forms a Strategic Alliance with Pfizer to Develop a Population Health Management Platform with Advanced Analytics and Patient Care Capabilities," press release, July 7, 2014, www.pfizer.com/news/press-release/press-release-detail/cliniworks_forms_a_strategic_alliance _with_pfizer_to_develop_a_population_health_management_platform_with_advanced_analytics _and_patient_care_capabilities.

11. Samson Capital Advisors, "Roy J. Zuckerberg, Non-Executive Chairman of the Advisory Board," www.samsonca.com/roy-j-zuckerberg/.

12. American Associates of Ben-Gurion University of the Negev, "BGU Confers Honorary Doctoral Degree on Philanthropist Roy J. Zuckerberg," June 25, 2009, http://aabgu.org/bgu-confers-honorary-doctoral-degree-on-philanthropist-roy-j-zuckerberg/.

13. Juan Cole, "Israel to Ethnically Cleanse 70,000 Palestinians in Massive Negev Land Grab," *Informed Comment*, December 1, 2013, www.juancole.com/2013/12/israeli-cleansing-palestinian.html.

14. Samson Capital Advisors, "Roy J. Zuckerberg."

15. Lauren Chooljian, "Governonr Quinn on Week-Long Trip to Israel," *WBEZ*, July 19, 2011, www. wbez.org/story/governor-quinn-week-long-trip-israel-89378.

16. National Jewish Democratic Council, "Governor Pat Quinn: A Good Friend to the Jewish Community of Illinois," http://c0491782.cdn.cloudfiles.rackspacecloud.com/QuinnFactSheetFINAL.pdf.

17. American Association of University Professors, "Statement on the Case of Steven Salaita," press release, August 7, 2014, www.aaup.org/media-release/statement-case-steven-salaita.

18. "Europe's Largest Teachers' Union Endorses Israel Boycott Call," *BDS Movement*, April 28, 2014, www.bdsmovement.net/2014/europes-largest-teachers-union-endorses-israel-boycott-call-12039.

Chapter 24

1.   Ali Abunimah, "By Recognizing 'State of Palestine,' Sweden Could Harm Palestinians," *Electronic Intifada*, October 6, 2014, http://electronicintifada.net/blogs/ali-abunimah/recognizing-state-palestine-sweden-could-harm-palestinians.

2.   "Tags: Benjamin Netanyahu," *Electronic Intifada*, http://electronicintifada.net/tags/benjamin-netanyahu.

3.   "Tags: Palestinian Authority," *Electronic Intifada*, http://electronicintifada.net/tags/palestinian-authority.

4.   "Tags: Fourth Geneva Convention," *Electronic Intifada*, http://electronicintifada.net/tags/fourth-geneva-convention.

5.   Agence-France Presse, "Swiss to Host Conference on Occupied Palestinian Territories," *Yahoo! News*, December 11, 2014, http://news.yahoo.com/swiss-host-conference-occupied-palestinian-territories-225643042.html.

6.   "Tags: BDS Movement," *Electronic Intifada*, http://electronicintifada.net/tags/bds.

7.   "Tags: Association for Asian American Studies," *Electronic Intifada*, http://electronicintifada.net/tags/association-asian-american-studies-aaas.

8.   "Tags: Native American and Indigenous Studies Association," *Electronic Intifada*, http://electronicintifada.net/tags/native-american-and-indigenous-studies-association-naisa.

9.   "Tags: American Studies Association," *Electronic Intifada*, http://electronicintifada.net/tags/american-studies-association.

10. "Tags:AmericanAnthropologicalAssociation,"*ElectronicIntifada*,http://electronicintifada.net/tags/american-anthropological-association-aaa.

11. Ali Abunimah, "Effort to Block Israel Boycott Backfires at Anthropology Association," *Electronic Intifada*, December 9, 2014, http://electronicintifada.net/blogs/ali-abunimah/effort-block-israel-boycott-backfires-anthropology-association.

12. "Tags: Middle East Studies Association," *Electronic Intifada*, http://electronicintifada.net/tags/middle-east-studies-association.

13. Sarah Irving, America's Middle East Scholars Finally Discuss 'Boycott Israel' Call," *Electronic Intifada*, December 12, 2014, http://electronicintifada.net/blogs/sarah-irving/americas-middle-east-scholars-finally-discuss-boycott-israel-call.

14. "Tags: Omar Barghouti," *Electronic Intifada*, http://electronicintifada.net/tags/omar-barghouti.

15. "Tags: PABCI," *Electronic Intifada*, http://electronicintifada.net/tags/pacbi.

16. Omar Barghouti, "Palestine's South Africa Moment? The Boycott, Divestment, and Sanctions Movement," lecture, Columbia University, December 2, 2014, http://www.columbia.edu/cu/palestine/programs/pastevents.html.

17. Philip Weiss, "Liberal Zionists Hope to Strip Naftali Bennett of Freedom to Travel in Hope of Saving Two-State Solution," *Mondoweiss*, December 12, 2014, http://mondoweiss.net/2014/12/liberal-zionists-solution.

18. "Tags: Hamas," *Electronic Intifada*, http://electronicintifada.net/tags/hamas.

19. "Tags: Khaled Meshal," *Electronic Intifada*, http://electronicintifada.net/tags/khaled-meshal.

20. Palestinian Campaign for the Academic and Cultural Boycott of Israel, "Call for the Academic and Cultural Boycott of Israel," July 6, 2004, http://pacbi.org/etemplate.php?id=869.

21. "Tags: Right of Return," *Electronic Intifada*, http://electronicintifada.net/tags/right-return.

22. "Tags: BNC," *Electronic Intifada*, http://electronicintifada.net/tags/bnc.

23. Joseph Massad, "Israel's Right to be Racist," *Al-Ahram Weekly*, no. 836 (March 15–21, 2007), http://weekly.ahram.org.eg/2007/836/op1.htm.

24. "Tags: Oslo Accords," Electronic Intifada, http://electronicintifada.net/tags/oslo-accords.

INDEX

Printed in the USA
CPSIA information can be obtained
at www.ICGtesting.com
JSHW011032040524
62359JS00004B/4